Ideas for English 101

Teaching Writing in College

Edited by Richard Ohmann
and W. B. Coley

National Council of Teachers of English
1111 Kenyon Road, Urbana, Illinois 61801

The articles in this collection appeared originally in various issues, from March 1967 to January 1975, of *College English,* an official journal of the National Council of Teachers of English edited by Richard Ohmann, Wesleyan University.

NCTE Editorial Board: Charles R. Cooper, Evelyn M. Copeland, Bernice E. Cullinan, Richard Lloyd-Jones, Frank Zidonis, Robert F. Hogan, *ex officio,* Paul O'Dea, *ex officio*

Cover by Bob Bingenheimer

Graphics selected by Joseph W. Reed, Jr.

Library of Congress Catalog Card Number 75-21357

NCTE Stock Number 22450   ISBN 0-8141-2245-0

CONTENTS

Drawings by Arthur B. Frost, from Lewis Carroll's *Rhyme?*
and Reason? (New York: Macmillan & Co., 1888)

Preface

Not long after freshman English was invented, it began to draw the wrath of critics, reformers, and abolitionists in large numbers. It's a course nobody loves. But it endures.

Chronicling "The Tradition of Complaint" which has attached itself to this course, Leonard Greenbaum concluded,

> Unfortunately, there is no contest. Freshman English flourishes; its opponents die, retire, languish in exile. 1974 will mark its 100th anniversary. (COLLEGE ENGLISH, Nov. 1969, p. 187)

Greenbaum was more or less right. At about the time he wrote this, freshman English was in temporary retreat. Some colleges were dropping it; others were making it optional or requiring it for only a quarter or a semester. And most freshman English staffs were experimenting in some way with the form and content of the course. Greenbaum wrote in the middle of an extraordinarily vigorous period of educational criticism and change. Since freshman English formed the base of the requirement system, naturally enough it was caught up in the movement for educational freedom.

But this movement, which began about 1964, had pretty well run its course by 1974, and it left freshman English to celebrate its centenary a bit shaken but recuperating. In economic hard times, college students are less eager to break idols and more concerned to learn the skills which may (or may not) find them good jobs. Hard-pressed administrations and legislatures enforce this change in mood by demanding "accountability." Political reaction joins in thinning out the heady atmosphere of experiment. And from the pundits there is always the charge of a decline in literacy. With the slogan "back to basics" in their ears, teachers of freshman English may well feel now that their only option is to dust off the old handbooks and get cracking on punctuation and usage.

It would be easy to forget, in times like the present, how much was usefully thought and said about freshman English during the past decade. That would be a pity. We hope instead that the lively and serious debates about this course will be kept alive, and even carried forward. We hope that teachers will not lose track of the many ingenious ideas for teaching composition which came out of this period. So, in this book, we are preserving a selection of both the keenest theoretical discussions and the most useful technical plans which appeared in COLLEGE ENGLISH from 1966 to 1975, the period of our editorship.

We intend the book for those who are teaching composition now and for those about to begin. We want it to be a help, too, for freshman English staffs and committees planning or revising the course. At such times, it is good to look beyond the boundaries of the home campus, and also to avoid the historical foreshortening which often narrows thought about freshman English. In sum, as the venerable (if not venerated) course begins its second hundred years, we hope it will continue to learn from its first hundred.

Richard Ohmann, Editor
W. B. Coley, Associate Editor
COLLEGE ENGLISH
Wesleyan University
Middletown, Connecticut

Part I. What Should Freshman English Be? Methods and Controversies

Toward Competence and
Creativity in an Open Class

THERE'S LOTS OF OPTIMISTIC TALK these days about opening up the college classroom. The disparaging commentaries are also coming in. Not only from teachers committed to classical rhetoric and traditional grammar. Disillusioned innovators are publicizing their failures.

In *The New York Times*, July 22, 1971 (p. 33, col. 3), we hear of a man who bestowed upon his class the Rhetoric of Freedom. He read an excerpt from Jerry Farber's "The Student As Nigger" on the first day and delivered a sermon for the damned on the last day. The enslaved had not written up to the expectations of their liberator. In *College English*, December, 1971 (p. 293), we find a gloomy postmortem: "In a student-directed course it is the blind leading the blind."

At the end of the second year of a pilot study in an open approach to Rhetoric at the University of Iowa, we still face many problems, we still have many unanswered questions. We know we have not found the easy way out of the frustration and boredom generations of freshmen have known in English 101, Communication Skills and Rhetoric. We know an open class is not achieved by

Lou Kelly directs the Writing Lab and the Open-Class Project and teaches freshman rhetoric and a course for college teachers at the University of Iowa. The concept of learning and teaching presented here is extended in From Dialogue to Discourse, *a text for teacher and students who wish to become an open class.*

casually deciding to try something new you've heard about. You can't walk in the first day, announce you're making no assignments and setting no requirements, then sit down and wait for something exciting and impressive to happen. The teachers who try, then denounce, the open class as another romantic educational myth may not be assuming their rightful share of responsibility for what doesn't happen. Maybe they invite their students *not* to learn. Maybe it's teachers —not students—who fail. Because they plunge into their little experiments with no self-examination, no clear notion of what a teacher must give when he asks students to create something to replace the old ways he has discarded.

Twenty-one Iowa teachers know the agonizing it takes, alone and together, to achieve what we believe in. But we all agree with our new Writing Supervisor, Cleo Martin: in the open class the low days are lower and the high days are higher. And, we still believe we're into a better way of learning.

My own convictions evolved from an experience where I was trapped—between departmental "standards" and all my despairing, sometimes hostile, students. For them the old ways of teaching composition meant failure. The freshmen were getting D's and F's on every theme they wrote for Rhetoric. Most of the sophomores had already flunked the departmental theme exam after completing one or two semesters of Rhetoric; the others were failing their first literature course because they were writing failing papers. The upperclassmen were failing a course because they had encountered a professor who not only required but graded papers. And the graduate students were living with the threat of failure as they struggled with their dissertations. For all these students, learning to write meant getting through a teacher's drudging assignments so they could turn out a finished product that would pass somebody's inspection. They rarely, if ever, thought of writing as human communication. For them, it was just a phony game, played for the chips called grades.

Working with these students changed my concept of myself as teacher, changed my concept of teaching composition. To put a little joy and a lot of reality into *my* teaching, into *their* learning—into *our* hours together gradually became the goals of the Writing Lab at Iowa. And the voices I heard there, year after year, convinced me that the student's own language and the experiences —external and internal—that he wishes to share make the best content for composition. Or to say it another way: the content of composition is the writer— as he reveals his *self*, thoughtfully and feelingly, in his own language, with his own voice. And while he's doing that for someone who responds to and questions what he says, he'll learn to analyze, limit, organize, and support whatever he writes.

Our open-class project began and continues with teachers, experienced and inexperienced, who are somewhat or highly disillusioned with textbook-oriented, assignment-centered, teacher-dominated classes. We want to turn the sterile academic classroom into a place where everybody will *enjoy* sharing his knowledge and skills and opinions with other human beings. We want the class to become a *community of learners*. We want students to become responsible for their own learning. We want them to see writing as human behavior. Like talking. Talking to say whatever they are concerned about—whatever they think is worth saying.

And we believe people learn to write better by *talking*—in class and on paper —using the linguistic skills and the rhetorical strategies they have been learning and using, learning *by* using, all their lives. Young children not only learn to talk by living in a family of talkers. They learn to use words in meaningful contexts, they learn to accomplish things with words, by using what they have already learned in personal encounters with their families—wih the group and with the individuals in the group. These experiences prepare them to cope, with varying degrees of success, with the people and the situations they encounter in the world they discover beyond the family. On playground and street, in the homes of playmates, and at planned and unplanned gatherings of friends and strangers, they relate and interact with others in various ways, but in almost every instance they also use words to convey what they are thinking and feeling. And each experience helps them develop more competence in using language to connect with others.

That is learning through living. And I think learning to write at all educational levels should be an extension of that living-learning process. For it is the kind of learning that becomes a significant addition to the continuum of experience that is a person, that is a life. It is the kind of learning we value most. Because it changes us, our attitudes and our behaviors, in some significant way. And that change has a lasting effect upon us.

The open class at Iowa attempts to help students experience that kind of learning. It is not an exercise in empty idealism, but a natural, practical way for people to develop more competence in sending and receiving messages, oral and written. The help the teacher offers and the feedback students give each other are always part of someone's effort to convey what he wants to convey to the class that is his audience.

We are trying to make Rhetoric an extension of the learner and what he has already learned, what he has already experienced, instead of an extension of the teacher and his superior and special knowledge and experience. There are no lectures, handbooks, or class discussions "to cover" rhetorical principles or linguistic theories; no workbooks or programmed texts or learning systems "to clean up" the grammar, the misspelling, and the punctuation errors; no required readers "to supply" models for analysis and emulation or to generate ideas for significant papers; no prescribed assignments "to produce" a required number of specified kinds of papers.

Instead of all or any of that, we ask each student to share his own knowledge and skills, his own ideas and opinions, his own feelings—whatever he wants to share with teacher and classmates. And that throws us into the endless debate over what the content of the course should be. A debate I do not expect to win. Not in my lifetime. Given the elitist humanism of professors of English and Rhetoric, any approach that makes the students' ideas more important than the teacher's, anyone who claims the resources the student brings with him are more important to his learning than the superior resources the teacher can provide, is bound to be labeled lowbrow. If

not anti-intellectual. Because, they say, students have no ideas; students can't think; class discussions die in trivia and boredom when teacher does not feed in some structure, when teacher and text do not feed in some "college level" subject matter for discussion.

But we believe the knowledge our students bring with them, though it may not be as extensive or as academic as ours, is equally valid. Though they may not understand and cannot analyze all their experience, it is just as full of implications as ours is. So we stifle every impulse to fill the hour with our ideas when their talk—in class or on paper—seems simplistic or meaningless to us. Instead, we ask ourselves if they trust us and each other enough to share what they really think. And in discussions and papers that may sound superficial, in chatter that could become boring, we listen for insights into what each person's particular experience means to him; we search for ways to help him see the implications he seems to be missing. If we are intent on *learning our students* instead of teaching them, if we want to know what's going on inside their heads instead of wanting to fill their heads with what we know, we never tune them out. Someone's frequent or occasional comment and all the nonverbal signals everyone is always sending out become tiny pieces of a human jigsaw puzzle. And day after day, we try to fit it all together. So we can *see and respond* to the whole person. So we can *hear and respond* to the ideas he is trying to express. So we can help him express his ideas more fluently, more clearly, and more forcefully. So we can help him extend his language, his ideas, and his *self*.

Instead of giving assignments to be graded by a teacher, we attempt to engage each person in a meaningful dialogue by asking him to talk on paper—in his own everyday language, about anything he wants to talk about. The students begin cautiously, of course. No matter what we say, they still hear The Voice of Authority. They still feel The Threat of The Superior Intellect. They still see The Stranger who professes to know what The Educated need to know. And they hope they can psyche us out early, so they'll know how hard they must work to ace the course or merely get by.

But if we can convince them that we're listening for the sound of their voices instead of looking for errors or evaluating their ideas as we read what they write, if we can give them non-threatening feedback instead of normative grades, they will gradually begin to believe that we are receiving and trying to understand the messages they are sending us. And they will begin to see us as a person who wants to know what they think and feel. Then the vast distance between student and teacher, though it may never be breached, is diminished. Dialogues that begin with skepticism—with student testing teacher, wondering if the whole approach is a gimmick, yet wanting to trust and be trusted—move along with refreshing candor. And they are soon talking freely about self and others, about the world they live in and the people they live with. Then we hear their keen awareness or their dull indifference, their egotism and confidence or their self-doubt and uncertainty, their passive acceptance or their constant questioning of the values they grew up on. We see some of the inner conflict, we feel some of the alienation and despair—whatever it is that fills the heads and hearts of our students. Each is trying to analyze and understand his own prob-lems, trying to search out the answers to his own questions, trying to express the complexities of his own heart.

It takes a lot of psychic strength to respond to that kind of writing. The teacher's comments can no longer be dominated by corrections, or by suggestions for turning an F paper into a C paper or a C paper into an A paper. Instead, we, too, must ask questions. Questions to help each person find his own unique answers. Questions to move all our students toward writing that is a special way of defining, discovering, and knowing self—and others. But that does not mean you must turn your office into a confessional booth or try to become a swivel chair therapist. Hearing and responding to others is, I hope, natural human behavior which, I hope, we all engage in whenever we encounter another human being.

But hearing and responding every class day to forty or sixty—*a hundred?*—individual human beings is obviously impossible. At least for most of us. When we read of teachers who say they do it, when we listen to them tell how they do it, most of us feel like the young teacher who spoke quite despairingly at the evaluation session of a recent national convention. She had come with the hope of hearing, of finding something that would make her a better teacher. She was returning home with the feeling that all she had heard about successful teaching depended not upon anything she could learn and utilize in her classroom, but upon the personal attributes of one teacher. Though I admire and congratulate the great among us, their expertise, their genius, need not diminish the rest of us. For a teacher's greatness lies not in what he teaches but in what his students learn.

They arrive unresponsive. Anticipating our required course with unloving words and equally expressive groans. But they are our only *indispensable* resource. We must let them, and help them, bring the realities of their own lives into the classroom. We must let them, and help them, respond to each other.

Because I have spent most of my teaching life working in one-to-one conferences with students, I believe any attempt to achieve an open class must begin with a personal dialogue (talking on paper) between the teacher and each person in the class. It is, I think, the best way to let them know that we accept them as persons of worth, whose ideas and feelings are worth expressing, whose imperfections do not diminish them or their ideas. Our response to each person can give the initial sense of freedom and fulfillment that is so important, perhaps essential, to achieving competence and creativity in writing or speaking.

But every writer and every speaker needs an audience beyond the teacher, needs many responses to whatever he has to say on paper and in class. Everybody needs to be seen and heard by the group he is a member of, needs to feel that he is an identifiable and worthwhile member of that group. And that, I fear, shall never happen for all our students unless we abandon the old ways of class discussion.

Going from neat, straight rows-of-students with the teacher-at-center-front to teacher-sitting-with-students in a circle of chairs or around a ring of tables is an improvement *only* if all the people sitting in those chairs are really talking and listening to each other. While trying to face that challenge at Iowa, we are asking some questions that suggest some of the fundamental changes the open class hopes to achieve:

How many persons (or what proportion) participate, frequently and extensively, in my class discussions?

How many participate only when I directly invite them to?

How many do not participate at all?

How many really get involved?

Do I talk more than anybody else? more than everybody else?

Do I *direct* the discussion? Do I ask the questions and make the responses that take the class in the direction *I* want it to go? to the conclusion *I* want it to reach?

Do my students address most of their comments to me?

Do they raise their hands because it's just a habit or because I intimidate them?

Can my students talk freely when I am the discussion leader?

We believe teachers must learn to sit down and shut up. So students can get to know each other. So they can share what they know with each other. So they can learn from the feedback they give each other.

We keep no pedagogical secrets from our students because in the open class the pedagogical process is not the exclusive responsibility of the teacher. The distinctions between teaching and learning that are clear to everyone in the traditional classroom are not so clear, in fact, they gradually disappear as a class develops its own direction, its own structure and content. For the teacher also learns and each learner also teaches.

We never lose our teacher-identity, we never become "just another student," but we see ourselves, and our students perceive us, as a participating member of the group, not the voice of authority that controls the group. Like all other members of the group, we give of our ideas, our knowledge, our competence. We give of self. By responding. To each person and to the group. But we never forget that in the open class the power lies in listening.

What we say and do on a particular day develops not from our past teaching experience but from whatever is happening in class on that day. Instead of following the sequence of assignments that worked *last* year, we respond to the experiences—external and internal—that students talk about, in class and on paper, day by day, *this* year. We respond by sharing a bit of our experience that seems relevant or by asking questions that will help each person better understand his own ideas and the ideas of others, questions that will help each person express his ideas more clearly and more forcefully. But we are always trying *not* to dominate everything that happens.

Very few students are prepared for that kind of learning. They arrive expecting to learn only from the teacher, sure that everything that is said in a classroom is a performance for the teacher, to be praised or criticized by the teacher. To most of them, class discussion means showing off what they know so they will get a good grade. The ones who have learned to do that talk a lot. The ones who haven't don't. Because they don't want to be compared with their glib and confident classmates. Because they are afraid of sounding stupid. When they try to put what's going on inside them onto paper, we hear the fears of the quiet ones and we get a glimpse behind the masks the easy talkers wear.

> When I was sitting in class I could not express my feelings clearly. I just wasn't at ease. I felt trapped in a cage, afraid to respond to anything around.

> How can I write honestly about myself when I don't know who I am? I would like to know more why's. If something goes wrong, does that mean I shouldn't have done it or was it because I sinned the day before?

> I'm really bothered with having to write things down and letting someone else read them or show them to the class. I feel that what I have written isn't good enough. I'm afraid if I say something wrong I will be laughed at. I don't want to be laughed at so I try to act like someone else and not be myself.

> I like to see and hear what other people have to say before I show myself to them. I like to know where another person stands so that I might act in a way that would keep me up and even with that person. This I find is sometimes very hard to do.

> My first time away from home. Watching my parents turn their backs and walk away. Watching security and guidance and love walk away. *God* am I lonely.

> When Bill, Murphy and Melvin were talking about being black, I felt so ignorant. I had prepared a little speech but I just couldn't say anything. I feel so insignificant when I hear people talking about important world issues.

> Even though no one knows you're on academic probation, you feel as though everyone is staring at you and thinking "boy are you stupid" and this makes me afraid to talk because then someone would know for sure that I am dumb and on probation.

> You can never really know a person. A person can put on all kinds of fronts for you. You can dig a person for a lengthy time and still never know him. A person puts forth what he wants to put forth in any manner he chooses and at any time.

To help students come to know each

other, to help them come to trust each other, we begin by learning names and faces. Then for a day or two we visit together in groups of three to five persons. The teacher moves from group to group. Mostly listening but sometimes responding. Perhaps mentioning something someone in the group has said in his first writing. During the first few days I try to chat a moment with each person in the class. To express my delight in something he has written. To express my concern about some troubling thought he has shared with me. Or to ask why he hasn't written.

Moving the class from social chatter to more academic matters can be quite natural if, after the first or second day, the groups for conversation become "task" groups. For several days the tasks can be anything to ease the uneasiness, anything to fill the strained silence with people talking to each other. But it's important, no later than the second week, to talk about the concept of an open class. They need to understand the kind of learning we want them to experience; we need to understand their attitudes toward the approach. So we talk about their previous learning experiences and any misconceptions they seem to have about the open class we are asking them to help us create. And we talk about tentative goals and expectations.

From the beginning each person must try to understand the responsibilities that come with the freedom that comes with the open class. Though we make no *required* assignments for the whole class, no one is free to do nothing, on one is free *not* to learn, no one is free *not* to respond to classmates and teacher. If the dialogues do not develop, if there is no ongoing interchange of ideas, the class is not open. Instead it is a collection of closed mouths, closed ears, closed minds, and closed hearts.

But if we believe our students possess the youthful virtue Erik Erikson calls fidelity, then we can assume with confidence that they will respond to our faith in them and our concern for them. Not every day, of course. Some will not respond on many days. Sometimes it may take several weeks, perhaps a whole term, to break through the walls that some people bring with them. But if we bring with us a full commitment to the concept of an open class, and patience— from a source that never runs dry; if we can live with the recurring frustration that closes in on the days when nothing's happening for nobody, and the recurring feeling of impotence that could be dispelled in an instant by simply asserting our authority; if our egos can stand the persistent, uncomforting feeling that we have not yet achieved what we hope to achieve, then we can keep on responding to the unresponsive ones. And eventually, either teacher or classmate will ask a question or make a suggestion that will evoke a response that will bring them into the *community of learners* the class is or hopes to become. But until and after that happens, the trusting teacher must also be a demanding teacher.

Usually the hour ends before we can consider all the questions and suggestions that grow out of class talk. And just as often it's obvious that nobody has the quick and easy answer or an obvious plan of action. Again it's time to form small task groups. The task: to explore some aspect of the situation being discussed, to search together for some answers to some of our questions. Next day, or a week or two later, the group can report their findings to the class and the class can ask more questions. We may never decide on the "right" answers, but shallow conversation becomes serious discussion as we explore the possibilities.

But we do not push the class into subjects that require close analysis and extensive reading until most students can talk freely and easily in small groups and are no longer afraid of speaking out in full class discussions. For they cannot effectively handle questions about conflicting issues and values when they are tied up in emotional knots. Most classes are over that by midsemester, but even then we do not require anyone to perform for the class if he is obviously not ready to.

I hope it's clear that our small group work is not an attempt to turn the class into an encounter group, where all or most of the emphasis is on discovering and expanding self through *intensive* group experience. Fifty minutes a day, three or four times a week for one or two semesters gives us *extensive* time, not the kind needed for a group brought together solely for psychosocial purposes. Though I am obviously committed to an approach that centers on self and others, though I believe our best writing comes from intense awareness of self and a highly developed sensitivity to others, in the open class for rhetoric *that* emphasis can always be coordinated with the writing and talking students do in response to each other and the teacher.

Though every class sometimes wants and needs to analyze what's happening, the small groups are not for the purpose of *studying* group performance or interaction. All the research that has been completed and all the scholarly and popular books that have been published on group dynamics, communications theory, and interpersonal relations are certainly relevant. But if that became the content of the course, the emphasis

could no longer be on each person and the group *talking*, in class and on paper, about their own ideas and concerns.

Breaking the class into small groups is only a means for releasing more talk, from everybody, and for giving each person maximum feedback on the ideas he expresses. Analyzing and evaluating group interaction is only a means of asking why we are not achieving what we are trying to achieve. Mastering all the popular techniques of group interaction might make me a better composition teacher; it might make my students better composers. But whether or not we pursue that interest, we can go on interacting with each other. As a relating, communicating psychosocial being called teacher, I spend a lot of time trying to relate to and communicate with a lot of psychosocial beings called students. Which means, I hope, that we have learned *to ask each other why* when we feel we are not getting through to each other, as persons or as a group; *to ask each other how* we can break through the barriers that separate us from each other.

Any approach to composition that begins with free writing elicits one sure question: how do you get them to turn the corner to writing (or speaking) that is thematic, analytical, tightly organized, and fully substantiated?

To answer that question I must first be repetitious. Begin by *hearing and responding* to what each person is saying. I make no corrections, no comments on how the ideas are expressed or developed, no long response of any kind on the early writing. Maybe my Lab students' negative reactions to the teacher comments on the papers they bring with them have made me overanxious. No matter how kind or cogent I sound to me, I wonder how the student will read me. Would any of them ever spend as much time thinking about my long comments as I would spend writing them? There's also the problem of *my* time. When students are talking to me on paper, I want to read every word everyone has written before I see them again. I want to hear how everyone is responding to the first days of class and to me. But I say enough in class and on paper to let them know that I'm connecting what they write with the persons I see and talk with in class, that I want to know each person better, that I enjoy their writing because I can visualize a unique human being and hear the sound of a unique human voice as I read the pages they fill with words. And I ask questions. First, the questions that say I want to hear more. Then, the ones that will, I hope, lead each person to a competent and creative telling of his own thoughts and feelings.

In the guidelines we offer young teachers the focus moves from the writer's own "Voice" and "Perceptions" and the "Values" he lives by, to "Questions" which help him see that the rhetorical structures many texts and syllabi prescribe are not unlike his own natural thought processes. But we do not make assignments on certain days to "teach" those concepts. Instead, we introduce linguistic and rhetorical principles whenever somebody's response to a piece of writing shared with the class, or somebody's question or dissatisfaction with his own writing, makes a little lesson by the teacher or a reference to the text relevant and therefore meaningful.

The traditional patterns of organization are easy "to cover" in the open class because much of the talking on paper that students do provides examples. They relate experiences or describe processes that can be classified as narration or time sequences; they describe people or places; they explain the cause of their joy or despair; they compare and contrast what's happening to them now with what happened to them last year. For some, of course, everything comes out hazy and confused. But for almost all of them, if it's something they are *ready* to share, what they say is forceful and coherent. When they *know* what they want to say, there is no hassle about organization or content. Each is part of their knowing.

To make the students' writing a part of the dialogues going on in class, we begin "publishing" excerpts or whole pieces as soon as possible. But I never share a person's writing with the class without his consent. And I never discuss a piece of writing as if I am grading it. I do not ask What do you think of the Introduction? or Does the writer include a sufficient number of representative examples to establish his credibility? or What's wrong with this paper? Those questions and many others may be considered in personal conferences or in small groups later in the term, but we never talk in class about published writing unless someone, including the teacher, wants to respond to something somebody has said. Like, I know what you mean because this is what happened to me. . . or No, man, that's *not* the way it is because. . . .

To ditto the lone A paper to show everybody else what the teacher wants, or to distribute inadequate papers so one student can tell another what he did wrong or how he can improve his paper is asking students to talk to each other as teachers have always talked to them. It is asking them to evaluate each other as they think we would. It is asking them to compete with each other as they try to meet prescribed academic standards, as they try to fulfill teacher-imposed requirements. They learn far more, I think, by responding to each other's ideas as they would in a nonthreatening situation outside of class.

All students—the brilliant and the slow, the enthusiastic and the indifferent, the aggressive and the meek—need to be assured that they know something that teacher and class will value. So we ask them to write and talk first about what they know best, what they enjoy most. I have never known a student who could not choose something that class and teacher knew very little about. Which means each student becomes a teacher. Explaining his special knowledge and skill. Answering the questions asked as he talks or as he reads something he has written. Restating sentences that are not clear. Seeing the need for logical order if his audience cannot follow what he is saying. And when someone says, "But I don't see what you mean," he adds some concrete details or visual images that help us see what he is trying to explain. And when someone says, "But I just don't get it. What is it really like?" he tries to think of an analogy that will help us understand. And sometimes, even the ones labeled slow, come up with a striking metaphor any writer would be proud of. When convinced that somebody wants to learn what *they know*, they learn what we want to teach them.

Wha'd'y'mean is the question our students ask each other most frequently if their writing is full of vague and ambiguous words or if their opinions are always stated in meaningless generalizations. When the person challenged cannot come up with a satisfactory answer, a classmate may be able to help. Or the teacher can respond with a quick and easy lesson on definition or supporting

evidence. Or we can cite books, periodicals, or people who might be helpful in the search for answers that will help one person or the whole class extend and develop their ideas in well-supported essays.

When a student makes a generalization, in class or on paper, that is obviously a strong conviction, an attitude fixed in and by his own experience, our natural response is Why? And his natural response to that question is an attempt to analyze what he has said. Which means he will either state some supporting reasons for his opinion or he will begin to question it. Whichever, he will be going beyond his easy generalization. He will be analyzing what he thinks. He will be organizing his thoughts. In the natural give and take of conversation, he will be setting up a plan for an essay.

Instead of trying to teach everybody how to make outlines or giving them assignments that designate the way they must order their ideas, instead of giving them external forms to fill, we raise questions that we hope will help our students analyze and understand their own lives, their own beliefs, their own values. Questions that only they can answer. And with their answers they build coherent verbal structures; out of the meanings and the relationships they find, they learn to analyze, organize, and substantiate their ideas.

And they learn—through their own writing—that a person's attitude toward self, subject, and audience can control (that is, help him, sometimes quite unconsciously, organize) whatever he wants to say; that he can create the sound of his own voice on paper by re-creating his experiences—external and internal—with facts and details so graphic, with images so visual, that readers will *see* what he means. He learns through the ongoing interaction with teacher and classmates without which an open class cannot be.

Though we reject the notion that students cannot produce "college level" writing unless we feed them "college level" ideas from anthologies of nonfiction, fiction, or poetry, the class that does not read may bog down in ignorance or boredom. The importance of reading in the open class can be clarified and emphasized while first discussing class objectives and expectations, or when the teacher casually asks about their reading habits, past and present. We can make reading part of our dialogue with each student, by asking each person to talk a while on paper about each piece of reading he does for the class. Adding to their unrequired reading lists throughout the term becomes a natural part of the conversations going on in class and on paper if we share whatever we recall from our reading as we listen to their discussions. But a forceful comment need not become a lecture. Whenever we come to class excited or angry about something we have just read, we can talk about that— as we would with a group of friends. But we must always remember that students get bored more quickly than anyone else. Unless they ask for more, we should shut up before they shut us off.

Sometimes we can help someone discover reading as we respond to the bits of experience he shares with us in writing. Maybe the feeling he expresses recalls a poem that expresses a similar feeling. Or what has happened to him parallels the experience of a character from a short story or novel or play. Or we know a book or essay or an anthology that deals with the problem he is facing.

The aim: to help all our students see reading as an extension of, or another kind of, personal experience instead of a drudging academic requirement; to let reading become meaningful and involving, an integral part of what's happening in the *community of learners*.

When class talk peters out because no one can answer the questions they are asking each other, or because no one can support or refute the generalizations and opinions they are tossing about, the teacher again acts as a resource person, citing periodicals and books they can turn to for the information they need. That usually leads to small task groups that assume the responsibility of finding what they or the whole class wants to know. Again, just as in class talk and writing, students move toward the kind of reading performance we hope for when the small group work becomes a self-involving, pervasive experience. For now they are dealing with the realities of a human situation. They are a group of people brought together to look for answers to human questions, to look for solutions to human problems. So they read with a purpose. And they try to read critically. And they try to synthesize what they read with all their other experiences.

And the teacher, listening to them talk on paper and in class about their reading, responds not only to *what* but also to *how* they are reading. He responds by setting up individual conferences or small task groups for those who can not comprehend the basic meaning of a selection and for those who are ready for close analysis or critical appraisal of what they read.

If we can break through the student's concept of English teacher as corrector-grader-judge of writing and writer, he can then see us as teacher-editor, the person who can help him learn to say, with clarity and force, whatever he wants to say. Then he sees how we can help him achieve a smoother flow of words, how we can help him see the implications of his own ideas and experiences, how we can help him develop a strong and clear voice that diverse, even hostile, readers will hear and understand.

For most people, talking on paper eliminates the phoniness that sets the tone for a lot of published and unpublished writing. It also exposes the stuffy and pompous writing many students think teachers want. They can hear the difference between the dull, dead papers that attempt to sound academic and the sound of their own voices on paper. But they learn to write graceful instead of cumbersome prose, they learn to write with clarity and force, only by working with their own writing. For me that means reading their writing aloud. First, so the class can hear and respond to what the writer is saying. Then, in student-teacher conferences or small nonthreatening groups, we talk about specific ways to make the ideas in specific pieces move from page to reader's mind. When the emphasis is always on *hearing* what they write, they become sensitive to the patterns and rhythms of their sentences. They also learn to spot the repetition that bores, the vagueness and ambiguity that confuses, the generalization that weakens, and the simplistic, limited point of view that expresses no awareness of how readers may disagree.

As each person covers a wide range of thought and feeling in his dialogues with teacher and classmates, he discovers, if he does not already know, that he has many voices. He hears them as he reads aloud what he has written. And he sees that the voice that "comes naturally" in a given situation controls *what* and *how* he writes about that situation. He learns from his own writing that he can define

and enlarge his resources of self-expression by exploring and expanding all the possibilities that lie within the *self* he is or is becoming. And in his own unique way, within the limits of his own linguistic competence, he is developing a personal style.

Because I do not separate style and content as I write, I make no attempt to do so as I try to help people become better writers. If pressed to define style, I would say it is the total impact of a piece of writing. And I would say playing with stylistic possibilities includes the whole complex process of putting words together to say what we think and feel.

But that process does not include spelling and punctuation and "correct" usage. We have not thrown out those social conventions. We have simply put them where they belong—in a totally separate and final stage of the human (or academic) activity that ends in a paper for somebody to read. We call that final stage *copyreading*. Our student writers learn "correctness," not from a book of rules, but by building their own Copyreading Guides with examples from their own writing. But we never ask anyone to spend a lot of time working on copyreading until he can fill a page with some ease and with much pride in the sound of his own voice on paper. Which means someone may wish to share a paper that is full of glaring errors that might diminish him or his ideas in the eyes of someone in the class. Then the teacher becomes the copy editor, eliminating mistakes *without changing* the form or content of what the writer is saying and *without changing* the sound of his voice. Seeing and hearing the difference in his copy and the "published" one often means he sees a reason to learn something he has for years rejected, and he begins his Copyreading Guide with some enthusiasm and determination.

If reading the papers your students write is a drudge instead of a joy, perhaps you should explore the possibilities for creative interaction the open class offers. When a student is free to write about what's going on inside his own head instead of hacking out 500-word themes, when everything he writes is part of a dialogue with other human beings, the teacher's homework is not the boring, endless grind it used to be.

What would happen if I talked on paper the way I talk on the street? I somehow think of "blackmail" against me. Especially from English teachers.

When one is thinking, he shares his thoughts with no one but himself. When he has to put these thoughts down on paper for someone else to read, he tries to change them so that the other person will like him. It's almost impossible to put down on paper just what I think and not have my thoughts degraded.

I think it is impossible for a student to put his own voice on paper and to give his feelings and views. We have been indoctrinated ever since we learned to write that we should try to please the teacher. To receive the good grade is what students want.

When engaged in a conversation that I enjoy, the words just flow into sentences. This is so because I know what I want to say and without hardly thinking about it, it just comes out. But with writing, I sit and think about what I want to say and it always comes out wrong. Because it's not the real me. It's the me that has been conditioned through twelve years of school to form sentences the right way, to make sure spelling is correct, to make sure all punctuation is perfect. When I'm concentrating on these things my ideas just don't come out on paper like they do in conversation.

In high school if I liked the subject—Trig or Biology or Chemistry—I would look into the whys and wherefores of problems and see how the masterminds developed their hypotheses. But English was always a drag. I just didn't dig all those dumb-ass poets and all that hidden meaning. It was always the same old shit. My senior year was the worst because it was all those old English writers trying to write all that *elegant* shit. Now that I think about it, my junior year was worst because the whole year was spent on poems. *God* do I hate poems. I hate English and everyone keeps making me take it.

Writing to fill a required number of pages—this is what I usually end up trying to do. Counting up the number of words after I write a sentence and adding unnecessary words and straining to get out every word I can think of so I can reach the required number of words. Quickly I stick a period at the end of that sentence and start in on the next one.

I've been watching everyone else as we sit here writing and they all have at least two pages. Do you really mean we can stop when we have nothing else to say?

I feel happy, at ease, and at home. Reading what I just read made me feel as though I were talking to my friend, shooting the bull. It also took me back to high school, my senior year, when I was writing papers for Mrs. B. She really pissed me off. I would write what I really thought and she would cut me down and give me a D or F on the paper. It really made me turn against her.

Right now, though, that isn't what I'm feeling. I'm sweating something furiously writing this. As though I'm working in art. Letting myself go. Free as a bird. It's great. I can't believe how wound up I am. It's like racing against something or someone, going faster than I can get the words on paper. I feel like I'm being rushed—by myself. And I grow impatient trying to continue because I want to say so much.

I'm sitting here trying to think of something that I have convictions about. But nothing is coming; I just feel null and empty. Is man capable of ever feeling nothing? Possibly I'm proving in these sentences that he cannot. When for a second I felt that I was thinking and feeling nothing, I suddenly started coming up with thoughts. It would be some accomplishment to be able to create nothingness in our minds. Like a vacuum. To flush everything out. To ease the mind of trouble, worry, and frustration. To momentarily establish peace and calm.

I'm confused. I wonder at what stage in a person's life he stops asking the questions and starts receiving the answers. I'm trying to etablish the values that are really important and relevant to me. But about the time I decide what is most important, things change. I meet new people and experience new situations, then I change my mind.

You can learn by being helped—shown another way. But you must have the freedom to accept or reject that other way, or to modify it to fit your own style.

When I was learning to ride and race a motorcycle, a friend of mine showed me a better way to hold the clutch lever while starting the cycle. I was holding it back with my whole hand, at least the full four fingers. That made starting awkward, because as soon as the starting flag drops you must accelerate as quickly as you can and still keep the bike under control. Which means hanging on with both hands. And that's hard to do if you have a good grip in only one hand. My friend showed me that it is better to grip with three fingers and use my index finger to encircle the hand grip. I tried that way and it was better. But then I tried it using just two fingers on the clutch lever. That was better—for me.

But not for him because he had shorter fingers. My friend helped me, even though I already had my own way. A poor way, but it was a place to be helped from. When he showed me his way, I tried it, found it better, adopted *and* adapted it. Then it was my way.

Can that kind of learning take place in this classroom? I'm skeptical. But hopeful.

A patient at the University Hospital. This cat is nuts; he's sitting there having a debate with the opposition and there is no opposition. I went over and rapped with him. This cat thinks I'm a member of the House of Representatives. Man, we're debating whether or not 18-year-olds should be able to vote in major elections and I win.

Now he's a pastor and he's preaching to me about not running away from my master. If he calls me a nigger I don't know what I'll say. I think I better switch subjects before he gets out of hand. What can I change to? The cat's well educated so anything would probably be okay. Think.

Girls! No, too old.

I guess I better go; it's almost suppertime anyway. Mom was just cracking her side all the time I was talking to him.

When I was a little girl, I would always dream of going to faraway places . . . exotic countries . . . Sometimes I would dream of going to a place where the people were living on clouds. These people were dressed in beautiful costumes and were handing out candy to all the boys and girls. Whenever I wanted to be near the water, I would turn on the television dream set in my head and be on a beach, wading in the water and building sand castles. Sometimes I would feed the birds on the beach and talk with them. After a while though, my dreams would end because I had to finish my math or do some chores around the house.

My dream is to become a doctor. Not because it means money and an easy life, but because being a doctor means giving of yourself to others. I want to work in the ghetto, and instead of making a lot of money my pay will be the pleasure of helping others. Many doctors have this same feeling before med school, but after they get out into the materialistic world they are just like bankers or businessmen. Money is all that counts. You go to a big new medical office and you sit in the lounge for an hour, then some nurse takes you back to a little room. For another hour you wait, then the doctor comes in with your file. Without asking if you're in pain or anything, he looks at your file and knows what's wrong. To him you are file, not a person. He's there for at least ten minutes, not to help you, but to make money. His profession has become a business. I would like to help doctors find their lost identity.

My father said to me, when he was bringing me down to school, that I should not become involved in anything. He said the people who are going to make the changes in the world will have to sacrifice and even suffer. But he said I was not to become that kind of person. I should be greedy and secure my education. Then later on in life I could contribute my share.

A lot of kids in the class give me the impression that I'm in that little crushable box they'd like to step on. I don't give a damn 'cause I treat people the way they treat me. Step on me and I'll step on you if I can.

I really dug what Jane said about not accepting her parents' prejudices toward Blacks. She made a friend quick. I hope she never changes her ideas. I dig everybody and I wish everybody dug me. But tomorrow is another day. I'll go out in the world and people will stare at me as usual, like they wonder what a Black boy is doing on a University campus.

What is the feeling of hate? I really don't know but the other night for the first time in my life, I felt this feeling or close to this feeling. I felt like an animal trying to escape but couldn't because my hands were tied. For the first time, I felt that Blacks do have a right to do the violent things they do. I now know how they feel when people that aren't black think they're better because of the color of their skin. I now know my family has been treated like shit through the years. But my parents never told us that people think we are not white because we are Mexican. Then one day I came home from the Army and I couldn't believe what I was seeing. Everything was wrong. My brothers had been treated like criminals. Then I didn't only see it, but I felt it, too. I was arrested and hit on the head more times than I could count. And they call this *justice*. I have to laugh when I hear this word *Justice*.

I just came back from the Air Force where you don't wonder about something but accept it. Because if you don't accept it, there are 138 articles in the USMJ and someone will use one of them to lock you up. Authority exists to perpetuate the development of humility.

As I browsed through a magazine yesterday, a full-page color photo of Sister Corita's striking painting of a Disraeli quote stopped me: "From the people and for the people all springs and all must exist."

Since I saw the quote first as a picture, I saw it as "From the people all springs." And I thought—all people are necessary for anything to develop. Or, for something to develop you need all people. Then I asked, why do you need all people? And I knew it was because all people see things differently and react differently to what they see.

Then I started thinking about our class and how each person is different and carries around with him a different set of thougths. But all of us, all people, are interdependent on the thoughts that each expresses. It's like each person pulling something out of a box and offering it for consideration as part of a developing idea. So each person, all people, are responsible for everyone else's ideas. And the only way ideas can develop or change quickly is for all people to express their thoughts.

After thinking all that, I realized I am afraid of you all. Then I thought maybe someone is afraid of me. I am part of someone's fear. Which means I am inhibiting him and therefore I am inhibiting myself. I am hindering someone's development and therefore I am hindering my own development.

Each person is afraid of something. To deny that is to deny that there is anyone in the world who can hurt you. There is. You know it. But ideas and people develop a whole lot faster when everybody is aware not only of his own ideas but also aware of the ideas of others.

Whatever level of competence your students have, whatever "track" the entrance exams place them in, I believe they will respond, and learn, in an open class—if you can engage them in student-student dialogues and student-teacher dialogues. But they won't learn unless we who would teach them start where they are. They can't understand new ideas unless they can relate them to their old ideas. They can't develop new attitudes and skills unless they can fit them into the whole set of attitudes and skills they bring with them.

The least competent may need to try to talk on paper two or three times a week for a full semester before they can fill a page with ease and confidence. But when teacher or classmate asks Why or What do you mean, they, too, can give clear and forceful answers—if they believe we really want to hear their answers. And if everybody becomes involved in finding the answers to the questions raised about the experiences

shared, we do not have to "teach" them how to organize and support their ideas. They will learn to—experientially—in their dialogues with teacher and each other.

But changing the way we think and talk and write is a slow, sometimes painful, process. Some students may need a third semester of talking and writing in an open class. In fact, I believe we should provide the opportunities for them to continue the dialogues begun in English 101 in every course we offer. If we don't, college, like high school, will be little more than a place where they collect credits toward graduation, a place where they will again be denied the experiences that are essential to everyone's development as a thinking, feeling *literate* human being.

I like to think—perhaps only hope— that the open class offers a new direction —a new hope—for all the people who dread freshman English, especially the ones who might otherwise fail the course or drop out in frustration and despair because what they are being "taught" has little or no meaning for them. For I believe they will never learn what they need to know by sitting through lectures or class discussions dominated by the teacher and a few of their classmates; they will never learn to put their thoughts and feelings onto paper by filling blanks in workbooks and programmed texts; they will never know the joy of writing for others if they spend their class hours with learning systems and learning machines that provide "individualized" instruction in lonely carrels.

We must reject all the software and hardware that offer us new or old ways of *pouring* grammar or rhetoric or great ideas into the student's head. We must permit, we must help *all* our students bring the reality of their own lives, their own language, into the classroom.

No book can tell us how to do it. Nobody can answer all our questions about the open class.

With the human resources our students bring with them, with the human situations that develop within the group, we make whatever we can. For teaching is a creative act.

PETER ELBOW

A Method for Teaching Writing

The Problem

"Is English really your native tongue?" So wrote a Dartmouth Freshman English teacher on his student's essay. English teachers try not to think about how often this comment fits the essays they grade. My hypothesis is that students seldom learn to write in these courses as well as one could expect them to do as natives. They write essays which lack the skills and competences that they seem naturally to possess in their normal command of language. Of course there are important differences between what students are naturally good at with language and what is required for college essays. But these differences are not so complete as some maintain. There could be more transfer of learning than there usually is.

Writing as Producing a Specific Effect in the Reader

Two common criteria for judging writing:

1) Is the writing *true*? does it embody good reasoning (valid inferences and adequate documentation) and good ideas?

Peter Elbow teaches Humanities at the Massachusetts Institute of Technology; he is completing his Ph.D. at Brandeis. He is the author of the 1966 English Institute prize essay on Chaucer.

2) Is the writing good, effective, pleasing in the sense of being "*good style*?" This judgment emphasizes form more than content, but not trivially: "He can say whatever he wants, *but only* if it comes in clear, strong sentences; unified, coherent paragraphs; and total essays that hang together around a clear progression of ideas with a beginning, middle, and end."

But there is a third model or criterion for judging the quality of writing: whether it produces the desired effect in the reader. Teachers tend to use the first two criteria, but this third is the one that people exercise, whether consciously or not, from the day they begin to use language at all. Everyone learned to use language almost automatically in his first years and has learned—unless there is brain damage—to be very skilled at using words to make certain things happen, i.e., to make people respond to him in certain ways. He may not consciously attend to the effects he is trying to produce nor the techniques he uses for producing them; and if he is neurotic the effects may even be opposite to those he consciously desires. But the skill with language is invariably there. Writing courses need to *use* it and transform it for new ends—not work against it.

What is called for then is a writing course which ignores, at least initially, the first two criteria—whether the writing is true or good style. (This would not be a course for students who are already excellent writers.) The point is to try to build from strength and only gradually to proceed toward areas of weakness. We can try as much as possible, thereby, to avoid the common school situation in which the student is trying to satisfy criteria that he doesn't know, feel, or understand, and thus cannot really accept, even if he wants to.

Judging the *effect* of a piece of writing, however, is a subtle business. The effect tends to be intangible and difficult to specify. But we can simplify the matter. The student writing will be designed to produce a specific piece of *overt behavior* in a reader. Whether it succeeds or not is therefore readily observable.

In the first meeting of the course the teacher presents the problem of writing to the class in exactly these terms. He asks the class to reflect on situations—past or present—of putting words on paper to produce a desired behavior. It is important at this point that this conception be fleshed out from the class's own experience and speculation—not the teacher's. The class must think of assignments: it must come up with instances it can take seriously. For when I produce examples—e.g., how to get a refund on a faulty product, how to get a letter with a certain thesis into a certain newspaper, how to get a certain service from a government official, how to get a raise from a specific employer—many people find them crude, artificial, and corny. I find them clean, solid, and extremely interesting because I feel the need for solid, empirical bedrock in this mysterious matter of words on paper—even at the cost of some gentility or sophistication.

So let the class invent its own assignments. If it wants more sophistication, fine. So long as it keeps to this empirical model of writing. Perhaps it will want to pick some member of the class or some member of the college administration with a given opinion and see what words on paper have any effect in changing it. Perhaps an essay or story for a certain magazine. Perhaps words on paper to help in a specific situation of grief or anxiety—words written either by the person himself (diary or journal) or by someone else to the troubled person. Most classes will come up with far better ideas than these. But "better" is misleading: the right assignments are simply those that the members of the class can take seriously. The teacher must be firm in throwing this matter into the lap of the class. If the class takes time to handle it, that time will not have been wasted. If the class cannot come up with any cases of words on paper it can take seriously then it has specified its situation rather well. If it did not deal explicitly with this situation it would be neglecting its main business.

The teacher gets a new role by this shift of criteria from truth and good style to effect. He is no longer the authority on standards of excellence. For though he may know more than most of his students about truth in writing and good style, he is not the authority on whether writing produces specified behavior.

Indeed, the class must try to be completely empirical in its judgments. It will not only send off letters to the newspaper and see which ones get published, but also invite businessmen, officials, etc. to reveal their responses. Many will come to class when invited. The person whose mind was to be changed must be persuaded to come to class and tell the different effects of the papers. The role of the teacher will be to help students achieve the goal they specified and to help students discover why some things worked and others did not. (Empirical does not mean simpleminded; though the empirical class is not free to conclude that certain businessmen, teachers, or editors behave differently from the way they in fact do behave, it is of course free to conclude that their behavior is contradictory, that they should behave differently, or that they are insensitive to certain properties of words on paper.)

But the whole point of empirical feedback is to learn to judge for oneself. Therefore every member of the class will judge all the papers. First the class must agree on an assignment: a problem, a piece of desired behavior, and perhaps an agreed-on set of facts that all writers must stick to. Then all papers are photo-copied so that all students get copies and judge their effectiveness. (The plan requires access to inexpensive photocopying.) The class hour is used to discuss differences of judgment. The teacher's role is primarily to see that the class performs this function: fighting out disagreements and mutually explaining why some think one paper is better at producing the given effect and some another—and what things in the writing had what effect. (People without conventional "English teacher" training might do an excellent job teaching this sort of class.)

I see four reasons why it is crucial for the students all to be readers and judges. 1) It means starting with skills that students *do* possess. It forces the student to realize that he does in fact have standards and criteria for judging writing. And it requires that he develop them. The procedure should prevent a common dilemma in which the student becomes completely disoriented; he feels he's lost all idea of what is good and what is bad; he loses all confidence in his powers of responding validly to the quality of writing. Perhaps students do not possess exactly the criteria for evaluating writing that college teachers feel are the right ones: "they prefer bad writing"; "they have bad taste!" "Good" and "bad" writing, however, are not absolutes. The question is "good for what" and "bad for what." The student's best hope of learning the teacher's criteria will come from enhancing and building up his *own* tal-

ents for distinguishing certain kinds of goodness in writing from certain kinds of badness. His criteria can be naturally developed and expanded. (And there may not be such a large gap—in terms of development—between the student's "bad" taste and the teacher's "good" taste.) But if the student's ability to judge according to his own criteria is stamped out and he is asked to start from scratch in learning the teacher's criteria, he is apt to be stymied and even permanently damaged in his ability to write well.

2) I don't mean to imply all students as fine, intuitive sensibilities and all writing teachers as rigid ogres. A student will often enough be baffled by the judgment of his classmates on his paper as much as he might have been baffled by the judgment of his teacher. Yet it is better this way. For students seldom 'really *believe* what the teacher says about their writing. They may say "Oh, I see now" to the teacher's explanation. More often they make do with a glum sigh of ostensible assent. Of course they have to put up with the teacher's judgment; but really it is often resisted—especially because the teacher is a repository of authority and this gets mixed up with his also being the repository of standards for excellence. Where the adverse judgment of a class on a paper may occasionally seem high-handed and dictatorial, yet the beleaguered student's plight is better in two ways. First, he can resist it better. He can say "What do they know! I know as much about writing as they do—more in fact!" But second, he is coerced to assent to their judgment more powerfully yet more validly than he is apt to assent to the teacher's judgment. For there is no right and wrong in this business. It's just a matter of whether something works. If he cannot get his classmates to think it works—and especially if outside validation confirms the class—then he has not in fact succeeded at that assignment. But the process of outside validation will

muddy the water and force the class to try to be flexible: it will discover that different readers—e.g., different business-men—are affected by different qualities of writing.

3) It is terrifically helpful for one's writing to read a stack of papers of very mixed quality all on exactly the same subject. This is an experience that all teachers have. Most realize how much they learn from it, even if they wish it happened less frequently. But it is an experience that students never have. If you read only competent writing it is hard to know or feel what makes it so.

4) It is simply fun and interesting for the class to read and discuss its own papers.

This strategy consists, in short, of starting from strength—starting from the criteria which the student already instinctively uses—and only moving toward new or different criteria as the students discover them and accept them. I am not meaning to imply, condescendingly, that many students are complete novices in satisfying the criteria of truth and good style; but I sense that the strength and guts of most students' real skill with language is tied in with the use of language that has received their commitment for the last sixteen years—language designed to produce an effect on an audience. Correspondingly, the disturbing characteristic of much student essay writing is precisely its lack of force or guts.

But the important thing is that the criteria of truth and good style are not wholly different from the third criterion being exercised in this course. The proposed strategy will mobilize natural skills in language and then develop them so that they come to include the first two criteria. Before long, students will themselves invent truth and good style as two—but not the only two—special subsets in the problem of producing a desired effect. The class will end up talking about all the aspects of good reasoning and good style that any teacher could

desire, and techniques for achieving them —and in the process will probably *accept* more learning from the teacher than before. They will also attain a realistic appraisal and understanding of the role of "correctness"—spelling, grammar, etc. They will learn that for certain kinds of writing it is not so important, and this will better free them to see how it is necessary in most other situations to produce certain effects and behaviors. The strategy would prevent a situation that is not uncommon: students sometimes feel that criteria for good writing are imposed from above by the teacher, and therefore they naively blame and resent him for what are simply conventions of correctness. Students will be forced to derive trustworthy criteria for themselves. The strategy here, in short, is that "producing an effect" is not really a criterion in itself but rather a neutral rubric which contains all criteria.

Students will not take long to specify writing problems closer to the classroom, e.g., how to produce the behavior in a history teacher of giving an A on a fresh-man history essay. All will write an assigned essay for the history course and ask a history teacher to grade them and come to class to explain. When the class does this a number of times, students will begin to attain a sound understanding of the problem of writing satisfactory college essays. For example, they might well develop real misgivings about the criteria used by a teacher—and conclude they had attained much sounder ones in their course's explorations. They will nevertheless see that the teacher is a teacher and that they will probably have to write essays for him. But they will understand what his criteria are and see them as one set among a wide range of possibilities— and be able to decide freely and realistically how to respond to the teacher's demands.

Inviting teachers in will be very interesting for the teachers as well. It will sharpen their perception of their own criteria. I can well imagine a teacher saying his criteria are x, y, and z, and the class replying that really he uses v, w, x. However the argument ends up, everyone will learn a lot.

It may be objected that this program spends too much time exploring criteria and too little time learning how to *satisfy* the new and difficult criteria that a college student must meet; that the program neglects the brute necessity of learning skills—correct syntax, clear paragraphing, good style, coherent reasoning. I do not wish to imply that these skills are easy—far from it. Yet I am sure that learning them is far easier than it often seems. But these criteria must be clearly seen, and above all, realistically accepted. I am sure that when a student seems unable to learn some of these skills—when he goes on for months or years without really mastering them—often he is covertly refusing to accept them. He may say "I guess I just don't have good study habits," or "I am just too lazy," or "I just can't seem to *get* writing," or "I guess I'm just not verbal." But covertly he may be saying "I'm damned if I'm going to give in and play word games according to the rules of those goddam teachers." Notice that his humble or contrite assessment of why he doesn't seem to write well blandly lacks the natural force he possesses as a person; his real juice is bound up with the resentful refusal that he does not express—probably not even to himself.

Until students have discovered, felt, and accepted the criteria, a teacher simply wastes his time trying to teach students to satisfy them. And once a student has accepted them he gets on rather quickly and forcefully with the business of learning how to satisfy them. In the procedure I am advocating it would be quite natural for a class of poorly trained students to decide at some point in the middle of the course to devote the next three weeks to grammar drill. They finally can see it is worth their time. In those three weeks they will learn more grammar than if the whole term had been devoted to it.

In recent years teachers of writing have begun to learn how immensely it helps a student's writing if he imagines a specific audience. Better yet if he has one. This can be seen as support for my hypothesis: the student's best language skills are brought out and developed when writing is considered as words on paper designed to produce a specific effect in a specific reader. Other excellences in writing are best produced as developments from this model.

Writing as Revealing the Author's Self in His Words

Two experiences have recently given me concrete meaning for what was previously a vague concept—the self revealed in words. The first experience was literary: trying to understand what made *Moll Flanders* a better book than my existing literary criteria seemed to suggest it was ("*Mol Flanders* and the Problem of the Novel as Literary Art," unpublished essay, Honorable Mention, English Institute, 1967). One of the important things about that novel is the way you can actually hear Moll speaking in the words on the page. Robert Frost made the specific connection between this phenomenon and a good prose style:

> Everything written is as good as it is dramatic. . . . A dramatic necessity goes deep into the nature of the sentence. Sentences are not different enough to hold the attention unless they are dramatic. No ingenuity of varying structure will do. All that can save them is the speaking tone of voice somehow entangled in the words and fastened to the page for the ear of the imagination. That is all that can save poetry from sing-song, all that can save prose from itself. (From the introduction to "A Way Out;" quoted in "The Speaking Voice," Reuben Brower, reprinted in *The Study of Literature*, Sylvan Barnet, Morton Berman, William Burto, eds. [Boston, 1960], p. 160.)

When words carry the sound of a person —whether in fiction, poetry or an essay —they are alive. Without it they are dead.

Now this capacity to write words which contain a voice may not be everything. We all know students who have it and yet still write poor essays. But it is a lot. I think it is a root quality of good writing and that we should try to teach it. A student who has it may make spelling and syntactical errors, he may organize his papers badly and reason badly; and his sentences may contradict all the structural canons of what is currently called good prose. But there is a real sense in which he already has the main characteristic of good prose: his words hang together into felt syntactical units whose meanings jump immediately and automatically into the reader's head. And from what he has, the other excellences can grow more naturally, organically,— and usually more quickly—than in the case of the student whose words on paper are totally lacking in life.

A student who has a voice in the words he puts on paper can be said to "have words" or be able to "find words" in a way that the other student cannot. This can be quite literally the case: many students without a voice simply have an agonizing time *finding words*. They struggle over each sentence, break down in the middle, and sometimes cannot even produce at all. It can be a kind of muteness or radical incoherence. Others who lack a voice can find words but those words are not strong and centered. Such persons are often those who cannot, in fact, stop the words from rushing to the page, but the words are flaccid and without force or point. Of course the student who has a voice must often struggle too. He struggles to decide on the best word; he struggles especially in revising; but he hasn't the terrible struggle simply to emerge from silence—or from the functional silence of empty wordiness. The student who has a voice can "unlock his word-hoard." The connotations of the poet's kenning are appropriate. Everyone does have a "word-hoard": a collection of words that are connected to his strong and primary experiences in the world—as opposed to words which (putting it inexactly) are only connected to other words. (Cf. L. S. Vygotsky on "spontaneous" and "scientific" concepts in *Thought and Language* [Cambridge, Mass., 1962].)

How to teach students to write with a voice is difficult to know. Frost emphasizes what we already guess—that we miss the whole point if we concentrate on tricks of structure. But the following procedure would help. The students read a writer with a particularly strong and obvious—"loud"—voice and then try to write something that produces the same voice. The object is for the student to "get inside" the self of the imitated writer by getting the sound of his tone of voice. It is an exercise in producing words that sound like a person and not merely like meanings. The class tries this assignment with various writers. Here again the class would serve as the official judge: the judgment of all the readers in the class is in fact the best judge of which papers get the imitated writer's voice into the words on the page. The teacher—or any single person—is in danger of prejudging the question because of conventional parameters for defining style. For the assignment is to get the *sound* not the style. I think I can imagine two papers of which one seemed closer to the style of the model, and yet the other attained more unmistakably the sound of the model. That is to say I don't know where the sound comes from. In the class judgment there is not likely to be tidy agreement about the matter. But that's as it should be with something not fully understood.

The second experience to give me a sense of what is really meant by a self revealed through the words on the page is not literary but pragmatic—the experience of being a draft counselor trying to help conscientious objectors in their preparation of #150 forms for their draft boards. The CO who wants to be classified as such by his draft board must answer questions about his beliefs. Ostensibly his answers tell the draft board whether or not he has the right belief. In order to be recognized as a CO, the man must have a belief that is *religious* and it must compel him to refrain from fighting in *all war*. But draft boards do not give the classification to everyone who describes such beliefs. There are too many. The Supreme Court's Seeger decision in 1965 defined as religious any belief which occupies a central place in the life of the man (like the belief in God of the traditional CO). And nuclear weapons have increased the number of people who cannot support any war. (Cf. my article, "Who Is a Conscientious Objector?" *Christian Century*, August 7, 1968.)

Therefore draft boards now rule more and more frequently on the question of sincerity—whether the person really *does* believe the things he says he believes. And so questions which look as though they are meant to reveal whether the man has the right belief are in fact crucially used to reveal whether he has the belief he says he has.

Students I have counseled seem to be strikingly bad at this test. In the first place they tend to start by describing something which is not really their belief at all. (I can speak freely because I did the same dance.) It seems we come out of our educational process thinking that when we give an account of what makes sense—of what we feel we can ask others to assent to—we have stated our belief. The absurdity of this notion is clear when it is stated so badly, but it is amazing how many persons give this kind of answer when asked to tell their beliefs. We are slow to realize that belief is what you call on when action is required and knowledge and evidence do not provide certainty. (And they never do: philos-

ophers demonstrate how "is's" cannot give birth to "ought's.")

Perhaps the difficulty is that the registrant wants to show that his belief makes sense—that it holds. But whether the belief holds is irrelevant. Draft boards are not asking to be proven stupid or evil—which is what follows from a demonstration that the CO's belief holds.

The only issue is whether the applicant *holds* his belief. And so even after he succeeds in really determining what his belief is, there is the mysterious matter of how to state it in such a way that the reader believes that he believes it.

Literary critics have tended to assent to the exorcism of "sincerity."[1] But the draft counselor has his nose rubbed in it. He's faced every day with the difference between an answer that makes him respond "I'm not at all convinced this guy believes this stuff," and one which makes him respond "Yes. It is clear he believes these things." And it has nothing to do with the content of the belief: some-

---

[1] It is a corrective simply to spell out what follows from the premise that there is an unconscious. (A) Intention becomes messy: in our use of words, as in other behavior, we must sometimes distinguish between what we thought we intended and another intention we were not aware of. (B) What this means for the interpretation of literature is that we are cowards to decide there is no intention just because we cannot be certain what it is. Besides, with certain kinds of evidence, tact, and practice, we can sometimes have a pretty good idea. Of course anyone who wishes may decide that the intention is not part of the *work*. But most readers—even if they see the sense in which a work of literature is a detached, timeless piece of significant form—nevertheless cannot refrain from also responding to literature as they respond to words uttered by whole men living in real time and space: "Am I sure he means what he seems to say he means?" (The concrete advice of Wimsatt and Beardsley—in effect not to trust the teller but the tale—was more right than wrong since it made us see intention as more complex than what the writer said he had in mind.) (C) What this means for rhetoric is that we are not always right when we think we are sincere. We can make good use of the ears of others in trying to determine what we really mean.

times the sincerity of the most outlandish belief is beyond question, while the statement of a "tame," almost universal, belief carries no conviction; sometimes *vice versa*.

The situation forces out into the open an important criterion for writing: one must refrain from considering these pieces of discursive prose in terms of whether the assertions make sense or are consistent, and judge them instead in terms of whether they reveal a person who holds the assertions—whatever the assertions may be. I realized I was faced with a pragmatic but pure instance of the problem that critics of literature and teachers of writing have talked of for so long—whether writing is "alive." If the teacher of Freshman English does not teach his student to write "lively" prose, the student is likely to get lower grades for the rest of his college career. If the draft counselor does not succeed in helping the registrant write prose which is "alive" in this primary sense—prose which contains not just propositions but a person—the man is likely to have to go to jail.

Teaching Freshman English may be trying, but this situation is downright frightening. After more than a year of it I still haven't a clue as to the objective ingredients of this "aliveness." The only thing I have learned is to say to the man who lacks it, "Look, I don't believe you! I can't feel any person in these words! You've made all these interesting statements but really I haven't the slightest idea who you are. I can't *hear* you." But this helpless response turns out powerful. It forces the man to look at what he has written from a point of view he is unaccustomed to. He struggles and flounders and is baffled. But he is finally forced to realize that he has left out the main thing—even if he doesn't know what that main thing is. The situation is grave enough that he knows he has to go home and try to put himself into his words. The new product—to the extent that it

is an improvement—may not be objectively more graceful, correct, or logical than before. But it does have what writing teachers are most eager to produce—writing that is alive and reveals a person.

Thus even though I don't understand the observable ingredients of this aspect of good writing, and therefore haven't any theoretically justifiable rules for teaching it, I nevertheless end up teaching it (or rather helping others to produce it) more consistently than anything I ever taught as a Freshman English teacher. The moral seems to be that asking for the right thing may be better than knowing how to explain what you ask for: i.e., even if x, y, and z are all valid ways to conceive the capacity that you are trying to teach, and even if you understand x and y much better than z, nevertheless you may teach it better by asking for z.

Therefore I propose reproducing this situation for our writing course. Students will be asked to write pieces for which the test is *not* whether the assertions make sense or are consistent but whether the reader feels the writer in the words—whether the reader believes that the writer believes it. (For irony, a more complex formulation is required.) Again the best yardstick in this imprecise matter will be the judgment of all the members of the class. This is really a subset of the category of writing designed to produce a certain effect in the reader. But it would be aimed at a particular root capacity in writing—the ability to have a voice, to find words; not to be incoherent, tongue-tied, or emptily verbose. In short, to write from within the self.

What would these writing exercises be? Wouldn't they be invasions of privacy inappropriate to school? Some exercises might seem personal. For example, the questions relating to conscientious objection seem very rich and useful writing problems. But if some students felt lack of privacy as a problem, papers need not be signed. As long as the student gets feedback on his paper—which he would do from class assessment and discussion—there is no need for the teacher or the class member to know the author.

But I am not talking about intimate, autobiographical "self-exposure" when I talk of "revealing a self in words." Writing in words which "reveal the self" has nothing necessarily to do with exposing intimacies—undressing. For I am talking about the sound or feel of a believable person simply in the fabric of the words. The most intimate revelations can be put in words that are not alive and have no self; and conversely, the most impersonal reasoning—in lean, laconic, "unrevealing" prose—can nevertheless be alive and infused with the presence of a person or a self. It would be important, therefore, to have some exercises about matters which are relatively impersonal but to judge them solely in terms of whether conviction is displayed—whether the writer is *in* the words. This would teach the students that this quality is not to be confused with undressing. (Actually the person in the words need not be the "real" self of the author; it is the gift of truly creative writers to reveal different "selves" in written words.)

The notion of judging an essay solely on whether it contains conviction and a self will set some teachers' teeth on edge: "This kid has plenty of *conviction* and *self* in his words—too much! What he needs is to reason carefully and write a decent sentence." This response is difficult to avoid. But maybe it's necessary to go *through* conviction and self rather than away from them or around them. Maybe the quickest path to good reasoning and decent sentence writing—and we must admit that we haven't yet found quick ones—is through learning better how to write words that reveal conviction and a person. And it is important to remember that the class's judgment here may be more accurate than the teacher's: it might not agree, for example, that "this kid has plenty of conviction and self in

his words." It might see the paper as pretty fake—as in fact *lacking* conviction and self—and be right. When it got the student to burn through the prose he had been using in his words, I suspect he would reason better and make decent sentences.

Summing up

It will be objected that I am abandoning the teaching of what is observable and explainable—truth and good style—for what is mysterious and unexplainable—whether it affects the reader in the desired way and whether a self is revealed in the words. Though the terms of the objection may be true, I don't think the objection holds up. *Perhaps* we have better rules for manipulating propositions to achieve the truth than for manipulating words to produce specific effects in the reader; *perhaps* we have better rules for building words into a clear and effective prose style than for putting down live words to reveal a self. But these indeterminate and unexplainable qualities may still be more worth concentrating on. It may be that the most characteristic use of language—the use of language that will permit people to liberate and develop the greatest skill—is language for the production of certain effects in readers and the presentation of the self. It may be that teachers put students into a trap by telling them to do x and y and not z, when the best way to do x and y is to do z. It is a common idea that freshmen have too much sincerity and too little sophistication and tough-mindedness. But I wonder. Ostensible sincerity may mask a fearful avoidance of the real thing.

Some readers will notice that I am disguising as iconoclasm the wisdom of tradition and common sense. But the essay would never sell under the title "Getting Aristotle Back into Freshman English." Yet it will be recalled that Aristotle devotes far more space in his *Rhetoric* to the speaker and the audience—and begins with these topics—than he does to the speech. He understands rhetoric as a transaction between the self and the audience—the two prior realities in the human activity of verbal composition and communication. He recognizes that this activity is not the same as that of determining the truth. C. S. Baldwin describes Aristotle's approach:

> Aristotle's division and its order are the division and the order not merely of analysis, but of much the same synthesis as underlies the actual processes of composition. I begin with myself; for the subject-matter else is dead, remaining abstract. It begins to live, to become persuasive, when it becomes my message. Then only have I really a subject for presentation. A subject, for purposes of address as distinct from purposes of investigation, must include the speaker. It is mine if it arouses me. I consider next the audience, not for concession or compromise, but for adaptation. What is mine must become theirs. Therefore I must know them, their $\eta\theta$os and their $\pi a\theta$os. My address becomes concrete through my effort to bring it home. The truth must prevail—through what? Against what? Not only through or against reasoning, but through or against complexes of general moral habit and the emotions of the occasion. I must establish sympathy, win openness of mind, instruct in such wise as to please and awaken, rouse to action. My speech is for these people now. Only thus am I ready to consider composition; for only thus can I know what arguments are available, or what order will be effective, or what style will tell. (*Ancient Rhetoric and Poetic* [New York, 1924], pp. 12, 13.)

Cicero and Quintilian carry on this tradition.

If we leave tradition and look to common sense we notice how students who don't write well can miraculously achieve a high degree of truth and a strong, clear prose on certain occasions when they somehow involve their selves and get turned on: sometimes on an exam, sometimes very late at night on a paper due next morning, and sometimes in personal communications like important personal letters. Sufficient pressure has built up to force the student finally to put himself into his words, and there is usually a strong sense of desired audience response which focuses the words and thoughts. Is he not, on such occasions, finally doing precisely what we are talking about here? Working for a specific effect and revealing himself in his words?

From here, in fact, we may even wonder about those rules for truth and good style. Are they really so trustworthy? Those rules only approximate the outward characteristics of the prose of writers who excel at using language to produce desired effects and reveal the self. For such writers can depart wildly from these approximations and still produce good writing. These rules ignore the generative principles which *produced* the truth and the good prose.

In short, this is a proposal to teach writing from the hypothesis that true writing and good prose are only end products and are—from the standpoint of development—almost epiphenomenal. Producing an effect in a reader and revealing the self in words are prior achievements in the process of learning to write well. The use of all the members of the class as judges is not merely a strategic nod towards participatory democracy but rather the most valid way to exercise these essential prior criteria.

Final Considerations

In thinking about this approach I have had college freshmen in mind simply because my experience in teaching writing has been with college students. But I don't see why it wouldn't be at least as appropriate to high school.

It would be easiest to point this proposal at very poorly prepared, "disadvantaged" students. With them, the inability to transfer obvious linguistic skill to the production of good written essays is most glaring. But I suspect that the loss is just as great in competent, well trained students.

I don't wish to diminish the validity of other models for the use of words. For example, words can usefully be thought of in a way that has little to do with a self, an audience, or an effect. That is, we can think of words as approaching the blessed condition of number—as a truthseeking machine, a prosthesis for the brain: writing thus can usefully be conceived as the manipulation of propositions according to the rules of grammar and logic—and according to the (half) rules of association and metaphor—to see what new propositions can be made to emerge. This is a model which emphasizes the use of words as thinking.

But thinking is not the same as writing. It is true that they vastly overlap. Words in the human head tend to be accompanied by concurrent thought; but thought tends to come in the medium of words. Or more concretely, nothing helps in writing an essay like having an idea; but students think amazingly better when they finally mobilize their natural skill with language and learn to write from inside a self. But in spite of this overlap, being able to think well is *not* the same as being able to write well—and certainly not the same as being able to have a voice, find words, and produce a desired response in a reader.

Of course thinking ought to be taught to freshmen. Perhaps there should be one term which stresses writing and another which stresses thinking. Since the former is too important to be left to English teachers and the latter too important to be left to philosophers, why not have all departments staff these courses and keep class sizes down to ten or fifteen?

But it may be a mistake to reduce to one term the amount of time devoted to writing. For if there is any validity in this essay it points to the conclusion that we are hasty in our teaching of writing. Freshman English courses have tended to try prematurely to induce the outward manifestations of good writing—control and self-conscious clarity. But real writers have constantly stressed how long it takes to learn to write; and most have recognized that good writers may have to write very badly for a long time— usually purple. If a whole term does not fill most essays with excellent reasoning and a good prose style, it will be too soon to call it the wrong path. It may still be the shortest one. After all, under present techniques, few are satisfied with the writing even of seniors and graduate students.

If a college didn't want to commit more than a term's worth of money and effort, it could adopt the following plan: The course would run all year but meet only once a week for one and a half or two hours. Students would turn in papers to an office three days before the meeting and pick up the complete stack of photocopied essays two days before the meeting. The classes wouldn't require a great deal of teacher preparation beyond reading the stack of papers and trying to think about responses. Indeed this would be a good place to begin experiments with teacherless classes.

What about grading? What I propose in this article suggests experimentation: since the class's job is to figure out different ways in which writing succeeds in being good, the class might play an important part in grading. But even if it is not possible or desirable to depart from orthodox grading, it would make sense to treat the weekly assignment not as grade-determining tests but rather as exercises in getting feedback and therefore learning how to write better—i.e., as *preparation* for grade-determining tests. Why not grade the student on, say, five essays he chooses to revise on the basis of class feedback and hands in at the end of the course? This would make the grade more nearly a measure of what the student has attained over the period of the course.

W. E. COLES, JR.

The Teaching of Writing as Writing

"*Give me a sentence which no intelligence can understand,*" *says Thoreau.* "*There must be a kind of life and palpitation to it, and under its words a kind of blood must circulate forever.*" *Perhaps these strange words open up the possibilities for a writer in a way that Unity, Coherence, and Emphasis can never do. Perhaps writing may be seen as somehow the expression of the imagination, and imagination itself may be mysterious and wild.*

Theodore Baird, Amherst College

THE TEACHING OF WRITING as writing is the teaching of writing as art. When writing is not taught as art, as more than a craft or a skill, it is not writing that is being taught, but something else. To teach writing as something else, to teach art as non-art, is to make impossible the conception of art as art. On the other hand, art because it is art, cannot be taught. What is wanted then, for the teaching of writing as writing, is a way of teaching what cannot be taught, a course to make possible what no course can do.

With the help of innumerable col-

William E. Coles, Jr., is Assistant Professor of English and director of a special writing program at Case Institute of Technology of Case Western Reserve University.

leagues and students, most notably those of Amherst College where the course I am teaching had its inception under Theodore Baird, I have developed an approach to composition which I believe approaches the teaching of writing as writing. The evidence of my students' papers, the only evidence, finally, which matters, is the vindication of that belief. And what it is possible for me to have achieved as a single teacher, it is possible for others to achieve.

The composition course I teach is a departure from the traditional college freshman English course, if for no other reason because it is a course the students and I take together. It is not a repetition of what we have already done in high school. It does not consist of a smorgasbord of assigned readings in required texts. Its nucleus is not the Theme. It does not depend upon a handbook or an anthology, a formula or a gimmick. It does not, in the ordinary sense, depend upon a syllabus at all. It is neither a course in methodology, although it is concerned with the development of certain basic skills, nor a course that serves as an introduction to other courses given by an English department, however it intensifies a student's awareness of the relationship between language and experience. Its subject is writing, writing

Reprinted from *College English*, Vol. 29, No. 2, November 1967.

conceived of not as a way of saying something but as something being said, as an action, an extension of being at a moment in time.

The course is based on several assumptions: that the only way one learns to write is by writing, and that a course in Freshman Composition, therefore, ought to be a course in writing, not in something else; that writing is an art and deserves to be treated as an art, by teacher and student alike; that it is a writer's responsibility to improve his writing because no one else can do it for him; that a writer can be led to understand he cannot live anywhere but in the languages he knows; and that if a student cannot make himself into a writer, he can at least have some intelligent awareness of what a writer is, imagine what he could do if he were a writer. Above all, the course aims at shattering the illusion that learning about writing is Easy, or Menial, or Dull. Although these ideals, I realize, are large and loud, the work of my students has demonstrated that they are neither factitious nor extravagant.

I can describe the organization and administration of my course more easily than I can its content, its purposes, its results. It is a one semester course running for twelve weeks in which I meet my students for a regular period of fifty minutes three times each week. I work with two classes of about 25 students each who are selected only in the sense that as a group they are a microcosm of the Case freshman profile as a whole. Each period, the students turn in a paper for a writing assignment given them the previous meeting, receive another writing assignment for which they write a paper due the following period, and get back the papers they have turned in the period before. The class meeting is devoted to a discussion of mimeographed samples of unidentified student writing and is confined solely to a discussion of that writing and the assignments to which it is addressed. We use no books of any sort. At no time do we invoke a text outside the one we are in the act of creating. I mark the student papers not with standard correction symbols but with metaphors evolved from our class discussions. After four or five examples, no student is in any doubt as to what is meant by such terms as "bulletproof," "cocoa-marsh," "sky writing," or "mayonnaise."

Each student writes thirty-five papers: an autobiographical introduction of himself, thirty-two regular assignments, a long paper at the end of the term, and a final examination. These can be any length the student cares to make them, and he is free to rewrite any paper as many times as he wishes. Although I keep a record of each student's progress through the term, I place no grades on individual papers, and I ban grades as a possible source of conversation along with two other subjects: the sequence of assignments and the matter of how a student can improve his writing. Since these last two subjects are the course, there is no point in conferences about them—a policy which produces almost no students for conferences at all. I allow no unexcused absences and no late papers.

The student supplies the material for his own discourse, while the assignments are contrived both to define a way of thinking and writing about something and to direct our general movement from day to day throughout the term. Every year I make a new sequence of assignments dealing with a new and different problem, so that for all concerned, this is always a new course, a fresh progression in thought and expression, a gradual building up of a common vocabulary, a more precise definition of terms. The assignment usually puts the student in a position to isolate a bit of his experience, and then asks him something about what he has done in this act of separating one thing from another, of arranging what he knows in some sort of pattern. Subsequent assignments question this pattern, ask the student to reexamine it from this perspective and that. As the year advances, he makes increasingly complicated statements about his own activities as a composer, problem solver, knower, writer. Whatever continuity he constructs from one paper to another, from one class discussion to the next, is his continuity and his alone.[1] There is no verbal formula to memorize, nothing to catch onto—except the fact that with writing there is nothing to catch onto. Whatever the student learns, *he* learns, and by himself, even if he does not do it alone.

Perhaps I can best explain what I try to do with a subject by recalling sets of assignments I have worked with in the past. I have asked what it means to wear a mask. What correctness is. How you solve a math problem. What it means to lie or to be logical. How the present can contain the past, or the past the future. How you operate a machine. Whether there is such a thing as non-linguistic experience. I have never had more than a tentative answer to any of these questions. But I take comfort in the knowledge that no one else seems to have answers to them either, even though these same questions in different forms have occupied the acutest minds I know.

I devise each new set of assignments, ask each new set of questions as another attempt to make some communication work between teacher and student. Though I am in pursuit of an idea when I make one out, I do not know whether that idea is communicable outside the form that my questions have as questions. If it were, there would be

no need for the questions in the first place, and I certainly could not use them to run a class. My object is to keep things open, to pursue an idea in such a way as to allow a student to have ideas of his own, to find himself in the act of expression, to become conscious of himself as becoming through the use of language or languages. No set of assignments which fails to pursue an idea can allow for these possibilities. No set of assignments which closes an idea, which has a "point" to get, or moves to a predetermined conclusion, can allow for them either.

I ask the questions I do then not because I know the answers to them, not even because I do not know the answers to them, but because though I know that they do not have answers in the conventional sense of the word (what kinds of questions do?), it is only the dead who cannot be brought to see as alive a subject through which there is the possibility of self-definition. For this reason, though I have never repeated an assignment, every assignment I have ever worked with, every question I have ever asked, involves the same issues: where and how with this problem do you locate yourself? To what extent and in what ways is that self definable in language? What is this self on the basis of the languages shaping it? What has it got to do with you?

I wish to make clear that the self I am speaking of here, and the one with which I am concerned in the classroom, is a literary self, a persona, the self constructible from the way words fall on a page. The other self, the identity of a student, is something with which a teacher can have nothing to do. That there is a relation between writing and this other self, between writing and thinking, a confusing, complicated, and involving relation indeed—this is undeniable, but it is a relation that only the individual writer knows about, and it can hardly become the province of

---

[1] Several of the sentences of this paragraph appear in a slightly different form in a mimeographed description of English I written and distributed by the Department of English of Amherst College to the students taking the course.

any public intellectual discourse without a teacher's ceasing to become a teacher, a student's ceasing to become a student. Ideally, hopefully, primarily, our concern is with words: not with thinking, but with a language about thinking; not with people or selves, but with languages about people and selves. If I refuse to be moved by tears idle tears, to talk about or sympathize with the self apart from the words it has chosen to have being, it is because I believe that my students are students, and that I am neither equipped for nor ready to assume the responsibility of posing as a priest, a psychoanalyst, a friend. I am a teacher of writing. No more. And, I hope, no less.

The sequence of assignments I used Fall Semester, 1965, was on the subject of Amateurism and Professionalism. I began the assignments with the problem of definition (assignments One through Six) by asking the students to find, as Wittgenstein would put it, "a substance for a substantive." I came at this slowly and with deliberate repetitiveness in order to allow for the necessary street-cleaning that has to be done before anyone even begins to think about writing anything. Assignment One reads as follows:

> Here is a statement:
>   A professional, whether paid or unpaid, is the man that counts. An amateur is a clumsy bastard.
>   Stanley Woodward, *The Paper Tiger*, 1964.
> Where do you stand on this issue? Begin your paper by explaining what you mean by the terms professional and amateur. Do you respect one more than the other?

Here is Assignment Two:

> Make a list of some of those people you consider to be professionals and of some of those you consider to be amateurs. Using one or two people from your two

lists as examples, explain what you see as the chief advantages and disadvantages of being a professional and of being an amateur.

Assignment Three asked whether and in what ways amateurism was preferable to professionalism; Four had the students create a situation defining an amateur; Five a situation defining a professional; and so on. The notion of definition as a way of seeing, as a description of the definer rather than the defined, takes time to understand the implications of, has implications only if a student discovers them on his own. I then moved to the seemingly unrelated subject of what it means to give or take advice and asked questions intended to complicate the student's notion of the role of a definer depending on whether he is the subject or object of an action, or both.

Assignment 9

> "Come, there's no use in crying like that!" said Alice to herself rather sharply. "I advise you to leave off this minute!" She generally gave herself very good advice (though she very seldom followed it), . . . for this curious child was very fond of pretending to be two people.
>   Lewis Carroll, *Alice's Adventure in Wonderland*
> Describe a situation in which you gave yourself what you consider to be very good advice that you did not follow. Who was there? What was said and done? Did you pretend to be two people? Explain your answer.

Assignments Thirteen through Seventeen asked the students to compare the advice of some professional writers on how to write about science (J. D. Thomas, Sir Clifford Allbutt). We then explored some of the resources of language available to a definer in terms of the concepts of amateurism and professionalism. In Assignment Nineteen the students were presented with a paragraph from *The Catcher in the Rye* and the directive:

> Describe the voice you hear speaking in the passage above and its ideal audience. What is it you call professional here? What do you call amateur?

By Assignment Twenty-Two we were in the midst of the subject of nonsense:

> Ideally, this story [Edward Gorey's *The Willowdale Handcar*] ought to be presented to you in its original form. Each paragraph is accompanied by an illustration drawn by the author and the whole arranged in a format reminiscent of a child's picture book. But your concern on this assignment is with the words alone.
>
> Begin by making clear to a reader your understanding of this story. What is the relationship between the various characters? What "happens," exactly?
>
> You may express your understanding in any way you wish: by means of equations, through the construction of a diagram (using color if you find it convenient), with a chart or graph, by re-telling the story in your own words.

The last series of assignments in the sequence, seven of them, had to do with the place of the humanities at an institute of technology and with the relationship between the humanities and science. The students then were asked to make an order of their experience with the course:

Assignment 32

Look back over the assignments given you this term, the papers you have written addressing yourself to them, and the papers mimeographed for discussion in class. Recall any conversation you may have had about the course, either in class or out of it. Where did you start this term? Where do you seem to come out? Do not simply arrange the course in chronological order; put things together in a way that will enable you to say what the real subject of the course has been.

The real subject of the course, of course, no one has any trouble naming as language, but every student writes out his relation to that subject differently and with a differently heightened self-consciousness of his identity as a reflex of the languages he commands—whether they are of mathematical or chemical symbols, gestures, words. This awareness is also differently come by, and in this sense the chronology of the course as I have presented it is misleading. I have not detailed the several logics of the assignments nor the way in which classroom conversations can be manipulated to exploit them. I have given no evidence for the possibility of connections other than my own. Above all, I must here rest the claim of the success of the course I am teaching, and of its superiority to the traditional approach of the standard college freshman English course, on naked assertion. With world enough and time, I would make the case differently.

That the course does work is, I think, particularly important to have substantiated because of what may be argued from its having worked. Indistinguishable from my imagining the place of such a course in the evolution of a student's awareness of what it means to write a sentence in English, and the extensions of that awareness beyond the issues of an assignment, a course, a curriculum, is my belief in the power of that knowledge collectively shared to establish an institution as a school; to create that impalpable, indefinable, and yet unmistakable presence of tone without which the curriculum is no more than an aggregation of courses, the campus a group of buildings, intellectual community an empty phrase. A tone emerges from the collectiveness of any institution simply as the result of its being an institution, but the extent to which this tone is worth standing by as well as for is a matter of what that collectiveness incorporates and how it incorporates what it does. A community is made; it is not just there.

I know that the course I am teaching would work as successfully at a business school or a university as it has at a liberal arts college and an institute of technology. What I imagine is that course taught wherever it is taught as a required course for all freshmen, whatever their aptitudes, whatever their future areas of specialization, and the course subsidized, respected, as one which is a field of its own. I imagine such a course taught by teachers, and not necessarily members of an individual department or of a single discipline, by colleagues who with the same set of assignments, devised cooperatively, are teaching different classes, making different connections, developing a different metaphoric relation to their subject. I imagine a communal effort which is more than a cheap or shallow concession to Togetherness in that the necessary collaboration of a faculty to teach is reflected in the opportunity given the students to relate the various areas of their experience at a college of, by, and for which they are the incorporation. I imagine the individual's search for self-association by connecting the laboratory with the dormitory, by relating the writing of a sonnet with the writing of an equation, by harmonizing the requirements of a course with what has to be required of the self, giving birth to a spirit of inquiry developed as a tradition and enriching all disciplines of a school. I imagine the creative act, even in a Freshman English course, even on the part of first year college students, seen as an act of self-identification inviting self-identification, and as such both noble and ennobling. In imagining that this course could provide the syntax for the vocabulary of the college experience and thereby create the tone of a college community, I imagine another way of evolving that end in which all of us as teachers and students have our beginnings.

GEORGE STADE

Hydrants into Elephants: The Theory and Practice of College Composition

I

No DOUBT college composition is in a bad way. Everyone says so, even people who are responsible for its being as it is. The course for years justified its existence by disenchanting more students, harrying more administrators, breaking in (or down) more apprentice teachers, and enriching more publishers, than any other; but it has suddenly become as embarrassing and superfluous as it is difficult to part with: our feelings towards it, that is, are like a bridegroom's towards his pornography collection.

Freshmen do not write very well and the composition course does not get them to write much better: this mismatch between ill and remedy is what high-minded hysteria calls "The Crisis in Freshman English"—a subject that has been drawn into the polemics of the cold war and the conservative revival, as it's called, or was called. The New Left, as it's called, answers, "Let them write poetry instead," as though poetry were a kind of radical prose. McLuhanites would have them tune in on the air waves of the future. But right, left, or imploded, everyone agrees on the ultimate cause: the times they are a-changing.

Mr. Stade, who has published a study of Robert Graves and who edited, with F. W. Dupee, Selected Letters of E. E. Cummings, is head of the College English Department at Columbia University. This paper was first presented at a meeting of the Conference on College Composition and Communication.

Colleges, students, their teachers, the national environment are not what they used to be—not what they used to be sixty years ago, say, when only those with money to spare could afford to attend colleges and only those with even more spare money (or a taste for genteel poverty) could afford to teach in them. No doubt students and professors spoke a common language in those days. But I doubt very much that the students learned to speak it in college. Possession of the lingo went along with whatever it was got them admitted in the first place. (Immigrants' sons with new money either never learned the language or sopped it up from the ambience.) It follows, presumably, that teaching composition then amounted to giving directions for the pouring of a kind of class cement into two thousand-year-old rhetorical molds.

But we no longer much care whether or not our students speak *that* language; and the molds have finally been shattered. The traditional rhetorical categories no longer seem capable of describing what happens when people write, let alone capable of prescribing what should happen. All of which leaves us with a course built on a double paradox: the content of the course is form, but all the old forms have lost their content. What we talk about in class, that is, is how to talk; we are, at least theoretically, concerned with how students write, not

Reprinted from *College English*, Vol. 31, No. 2, November 1969.

with what they write about; and if we give them something to write about it is only because we know that outside of God and French symbolist poetry there is no such thing as form without content. They learn, we hope, a manner which is applicable to all the matters of discourse under the sun. But no one has yet been able to describe any *one* manner, or any system of manners, that satisfied anybody but himself, if indeed it did satisfy him—which is the sort of thing that always happens to manners of all kinds when a ruling class loses both its self-confidence and the emulation of inferior life-stylists.

So we do what we can: we do patchwork; we make the students learn a grammar also two thousand years old and also believed in by nobody, least of all by the students; we put before them techniques, tricks, turns, models, rules of thumb, conventions, anything we can think of—all of which we somehow expect on the one hand to instill in them that sense of their audience's needs we might just as well call decorum and on the other to provide them with the means of escape from the Spanish Cloister of their own inarticulateness. And in our moments of greater academic self-absorption, we further expect that we are at once helping students to help themselves to the good things of our culture and placing before them the means and desire to add to these good things. The least guarded among us might claim that we and our colleagues in other departments are acculturating our students; our job, we might claim, is to cultivate a style of writing that will reflect and encourage a style of thought and a style of life; and all these are either to embody and further the best that has been thought and done in the West, or, depending on the instructor's politics, to be directed toward undoing what has been thought or done in the West.

Well, that's claiming a good deal, nor is there any reason why we should not claim as much, or more, so long as we admit, at least to ourselves, how short the achievement is of the intention. If the teacher of Freshman Composition really feels that the course can accomplish any of what we claim are its goals, the teaching of it should provide him with occasions for self-justification and grounds for hope, if not for faith. But we all know that, in fact, teachers of Freshman Composition feel less justified and less hopeful in direct proportion to the number of years they have taught it, and that their ruling attitude toward the course is usually some mixture of cynicism and despair. For all that, the goals are the right ones, and even if they were totally out of reach we should have to work toward them as the determinist acts upon his choices—with instinctive, but absurd, determination.

The question is not *for what?* but *how?* especially when we recall—and this is what *we* learn from freshman composition—that there is no teaching, only learning, and that people only learn for profit or through play. Any honest appraisal of the results of Freshman Composition (as we see them in students who in their sophomore slumps return to us in other courses) must convince us that, outside of the truly secondary motive of a good grade, the course must seem to students singularly devoid of either the profitable or the playful.

How about the readings? you may be thinking at this point. How about those collections of essays collected from other collections of essays? They, one supposes, *do* from time to time provide the subjects about which students very much want to say something. And they are profitable, not only because of their content, but because students can learn from them by imitation. In the best of them, we might add, the authors' concern with style, structure, and embellishment provides object lessons in the forms of literary play.

But the essays are not in fact models we want our students to use as such if they are pursy translations of sturdy originals, or shards broken off some well wrought design, or examples of the botched prose the students are perfectly capable of writing without reference to a model. And most of the exhibits in most anthologies are just such specimens. Further, my earlier remarks about teaching, learning, and motivation apply to learning by imitation as much as they do to learning through exhortation.

The unhappy truth is that the best imaginable collection of essays would impede our aims more than it could further them. First, because they are not examples of form without content. A student who has been stimulated (I may exaggerate here) by Bacon on dissimulation, or by Milton on censorship, or by De Quincey on murder, or by Mary McCarthy on Vassar, wants to talk about dissimulation, censorship, murder, or Vassar, not about Bacon's false antitheses, Milton's inspired use of the non sequitor, De Quincey's polytropics, or McCarthy's epitropes. And the instructor who cuts off the student's legitimate desire to misconstrue and argue aside from the point usually winds up displaying his authors' beauties of style before a class of doodlers and windowgazers. The split between the content of the essays and the content of the course (that is, composition) is the main source of the schizophrenia that is everywhere the badge and stigma of Freshman English.

And because the essays themselves are about a variety of subjects and by a variety of writers, the half of the course they comprise is further fragmented, until by the fourth week the course has settled into a hebephrenia beyond therapy. The readings, in short, do not provide Freshman Composition with what every course needs: a subject that reveals itself in stages. The course does not develop or progress, but like Eliot's silent vertebrate in brown, it contracts and concentrates, withdraws. There is not the sense from class to class of new accomplishments, intellectual or practical, that confirm the validity of the old ones, impart morale to student and teacher, establish rapport between them. It boils down to this: the course we think of as having form for its content has no content at all. Freshman English as we teach it is not a subject.

This absence of a subject encourages certain distempers of teaching. Each college has a prevailing intellectual climate that determines what kind of instructors are likely to seek and find jobs there and which rounds off any square pegs, except for the most seasoned knotheads, so that in each college, Freshman English will precipitate a certain range of compensatory teaching styles, as I call them. (In Columbia, for example, I have seen no instance of the droning bore who fastens onto the minutiae of grammar as a sinking skipper lashes himself to the mast or of the indomitable anachronism who teaches Freshman English as a substitute for finishing school, a course in literary manners.)

But from staff meetings, from the confessions of colleagues who have more honesty than discretion, from students who by sly confidences about other members of the English Department wish either to puff me up or put me down, and, most of all, from reflections on my own behavior in the classroom, I have decided that three compensatory styles of teaching composition prevail at Columbia (for example).

The first presents us with the instructor as shaman of the modern variety, like Cipollo in Thomas Mann's story. This type fills in the vacuum left by the absence of the subject with a concitation of the group mind. He conducts his class through an extraordinarily sensitive attunement to every nuance of emotion and attitude on the part of the student general will, which he comes to embody, so that no matter what he says, the students hear their deeper selves talking, and are convinced. The classroom atmosphere becomes quickly charged with the crackle of over-loaded psyches, which the slightest ebb of nervous energy on his part will short-circuit. An hour's teaching leaves him exhausted and his students dazed, let down, as though they had just come out of a trance, which indeed they have.

The second compensatory style is that of the teacher who reveals himself as his own subject. The elements of style become stages in his autobiography and testimonials of character. Students quickly understand that a B paper is a loyalty test safely passed and a D paper a guilty confession of unrequited love. To the sophisticated but modest student, attending such a teacher's class is like reading D. H. Lawrence on togetherness or F. R. Leavis on Lawrence—the student begins to fear that the degree of earnestness being demanded of him is forever outside his range.

The third compensatory style is that of the teacher as ironist. Every non-remark he makes on his non-subject is undercut by a hollow intonation or a *risus sardonicus*. It's one joke, he implies, that a man like him should be non-teaching Freshman English. It's another that students like them should have to nothear him do it. It's a bigger joke that he knows that they know that he knows that they are in on the joke. But. the biggest joke is that although he knows that they know he knows it is all a joke, he also knows that they know he knows he takes it very seriously, and has grave doubts as to whether he can carry it off.

All three styles provide the teacher with opportunities for self-expression and the students with out-of-the-way excitements. And clearly they result more from an excess than a deficiency of good intentions. But as the teacher measures his exhaustion and the students estimate how much each hour's entertainment at approximately five dollars a throw has subtracted from their patrimonies, teacher and students might separately wonder whether giving and taking the course hasn't been like taxi-dancing with a transvestite: amusingly weird at first but finally stale, flat, and unprofitable. And the conscientious teacher will realize what his students may not, that he has committed the one unforgivable sin of teaching: he has deprived them of an opportunity for the development of intellectual autonomy—the magician by a Negative Capability that removes from the classroom landscape any steep or unfamiliar ground they might pit themselves against, the autobiographer by an Egotistical Sublime that confuses personalities and issues, and the ironist by a technique of equivocation that makes a figure of fun out of any student who asks for or gives a straight answer.

The only way out of all this, it seems to me, is to make Freshman Composition into a subject, or to give it one, or to take one more look from another angle, just in case it does, after all, already have one, one that need only be unearthed and nurtured.

II

In the spring of 1966, at the encouragement of my English Department, I went to Denver in search of a subject— to Denver, because that was where the Conference on College Composition and Communications was holding its meeting. There I joined hundreds of men and women from all over the country in search of a revelation that did not seem to be anywhere near at hand. The lack of confidence, agreed purpose, and economy of effort that were to characterize the two and one-half days of speeches, panels, demonstrations, seminars, and conferences made themselves felt immediately, from the very opening address, which was given by three speakers, none of whom agreed about anything—except that Freshman Composition was in a bad way.

The schedule of activities, however, reflected the history of attempts by members of the CCCC to find a subject for the course that had brought them together in one body of many minds. The five panels on "Issues in defining the aims of Freshman Composition Courses," for example, were as follows:

1. With Emphasis on Rhetoric
2. With Emphasis on Literature
3. With Emphasis on Language
4. With Emphasis on Communication
5. With Emphasis on Ideas and Issues of Human Society.

In other meetings advocates of stylistics, semantics, linguistics, logic, and the study of mass media had their say. And there were dark rumors of something called the "Voice Project," inspired, I was told, by madmen who wanted students to write like they talk, like. It began to seem as though College Composition, to the members of the CCCC, was like the gold doubloon in *Moby Dick*—something by violence yoked to an unnatural vehicle, in the process transformed from an object of uncertain but assured value into a goad and a lure, its aspect to be determined by the special interests of its fellow travellers. So far as I could tell from the number of long arguments and short tempers during, and quick drinks between, meetings, none of

the special interests had anywhere been the salvation of Freshman Composition, any more than the doubloon had saved the sinking ship to which its ambitious master had nailed his hopes.

Literature, for example, is the worst subject for the composition course, because it is (to English teachers anyhow) the very best otherwise. It is the English teacher's own special interest. What student or teacher will want to concentrate on student prose when they can attend to the lessons of the masters? Nor does dedicated study of the greatest instances of English prose guarantee the student even a modest grace in exposition, or PLMA style would not be what it is. And there are great novelists, like Joyce, whose expository prose is utterly without distinction. The fictional and expository uses of words are not the same. Lastly, although no teacher of good will can want to turn all college students into literary critics—he does not want the student, that is, to approach all problems as the critic approaches his—that is exactly what making literature the subject of Composition encourages.

"Communication Skills," a much-advertised but mysterious discipline, which seems to be concerned with the philosophy and techniques of reading, writing, talking, and listening, was the coming thing during the fifties, but for some reason it never arrived. Though it still has a large number of champions, its best known theorists are now working either for the CIA or with porpoises.

Rhetoric is, once again this year's coming thing, if I read the signs aright, and anyone who knows what it once accomplished must feel the force, largely sentimental, I am afraid, of its appeal. There was much passionate talk of it at the last three meetings of the CCCC, but no one could explain to me what it might now mean. From the kinds of texts that have the word in their titles I gather that a rhetoric is a book, written by two authors, that comes out in a new edition every second year, and that, after a one-hundred-page exordium on outlines, moves to a cautionary narration on the evils of mislaying modifiers or falsifying antitheses, to a confirmation of a sublimely naive paragraph-mystique, on to a refutation of such words as "complected," to, finally, a peroration on the research paper. Traditional rhetoric, alas, is tied to a world-view, a model of the mind, a theory of language, a pedagogical method that not even Jesuits can really make themselves believe in.

Linguistics is a valuable discipline for the composition student to know something about, because it might lead him to ponder the awful fact that experts on language are seldom expert writers. The scientific study of language no more guarantees good writing than musicology will refine your cadenzas or economics will put money in your purse or ornithology will teach you to lay eggs. Writing, like making money and playing the piano, is an art, not a science. There were men who wrote well before there was linguistics; to this day, there are few good writers who can tell an allomorph from a murmur-vowel; and linguists who write well do not write well because they are linguists.

The *Voice Project*, I believe, is concerned with making students learn to write from how they talk, with developing in each student a prose voice modeled on his speaking voice, as he himself hears it. There clearly is something in this project. Prose cannot be heard unless it speaks in a tone definite enough to rise above the static of a reader's interior monologue. Officialese, and the kind of prose in, say, textbooks for education courses—or wherever the absence of matter had to be disguised by a pseudo-scientific manner—might best be called noise, or sound not directed by intelli-

gence. It is audible enough, but one can attend to it only with a kind of numb and mindless passivity. Every good writer, then, has a voice in the sense of a recognizable style that reflects his personal and characteristic way of thinking in words. But one's speaking voice is not one's prose voice. Prose and talk, that is, obey different rules. M. Jourdain speaks prose only because he is a character in a play.

We can learn something else from M. Jourdain. The sound of one's voice is largely a resonance fed back from an imagined or real audience. A writer, like a speaker, becomes aware of his own voice by listening to the way it sounds to an audience, not from introspection.

I would say that a writer develops his own voice in the first place by working as hard as he can at saying exactly what he means. He will only discover exactly what he means in the process; and since he will never quite mean what anyone else has meant, he will never find anyone else's constructions, rhythms, range of diction quite what he needs. He develops a voice, secondly, by saying what he means in a way that reflects his awareness of an at least hypothetical audience. Prose is at once expressive and communicative, a private and a public possession, something that allows for self-revelation, but on a stage already set.

Logic of a certain sort is part of what the composition course requires. The logic required, however, is not of either the formal or symbolic sort, but the kind that is logically, historically, experientially, and methodologically prior to it, even in the work of logicians —the logic of ordinary language. The logic of ordinary language is formally illogical; it catches up what formal logic must leave out to remain logical. That is what the major work of Russell and Wittgenstein was all about.

There are similar arguments against

pumping the life of other subjects, such as semantics or pop sociology, into Composition, as there are similar arguments against fastening it as a sort of remora to a general education course, such as Humanities, Contemporary Civilization, or the survey of English literature. But the argument prior to all others, and to me the conclusive one, is that Composition has a subject of its own; it is a necessary part of any general education program in its own right.

The subject I have in mind, the one that suddenly came over me in Denver, is so simple, so natural, so obvious, so fruitful in its implications, that it must be the right one. It is, in fact, what everybody knows is the proper subject of college composition. *The subject of the course is the students' writing.* It is secondarily their thinking, to the extent that their thinking expresses itself in words. The aim of the course is to make the students write better, or to put it another way, to improve their verbal thinking, to extend their ability to capture and create experience with words. A number of subsidiary aims, which many teachers consider important for political or ethical reasons or because of their understanding of what a liberal education entails, naturally follow.

We want to help our students transform experience into knowledge, verbalize whatever they have done or undergone, so that they will know what these are. The one unambiguous sign and probably the *sine qua non* of someone's *knowing that* something is the case is his ability to say it in his own words, just as the proof of someone's *knowing how* to do something is his ability to do it. We want to give our students the *know how* for saying whatever they *know that*. No doubt teachers of other subjects want the same, for the transformation of experience into knowledge is the goal of education in general; but

the composition teacher wants to provide his students with something prior to, less specialized than, more nearly indispensable than, the analytic and descriptive tools of the various academic disciplines—he wants, say, to train the fingers that bring the speculative instruments of other disciplines into focus; he also wants to provide the materials out of which those instruments are made.

We want, then, to help the students towards exploring, defining, and so in part mastering themselves and the world around them, which is largely a world of words. We want them to be a larger part of the world and we want the world to be a larger part of them. We want to enlarge their boundaries—not just the boundaries in which they think, but also those within which they act. A person is, at least to others, what he does, how he acts, and a large part of what anyone does is to use words. What one does with words is to a large extent what he is, to himself as well as to others.

We should like to lead students toward the means through which they might escape their inarticulateness, no matter how fluent it is, because inarticulateness, as we all know, has political, as well as psychological consequences. All people, including those who, like many of our former students, look daggers from out of their silent, suburban rage, want a "voice." They want to be heard, but first they must learn to speak, and here the teacher of composition can be of use.

He can also be of use in extending the student's social, as well as political and intellectual, boundaries. He can introduce students to verbal communities—communities of ideas, of manners, of cultural style, of ideologies—other than these into which they were born. He can help to free them from provincial bias, which takes rumor for truth and takes tribal prejudice for the limits of choice;

he can help to free them from the historical fix, which takes the reflexes of the present as the first and last word on how to say and do. The composition teacher, in short, would like to introduce his students to the infinite universe of words, which, because it transcends and incorporates the social and historical worlds, provides a perspective from which to judge them.

We should like the composition course, finally, to provide the student with verbal and intellectual tools for criticism and self-defense. We should like to provide him with means to combat or evade propaganda, whether from Washington, Madison Avenue, Peking, quadrangle orators, Hugh Hefner, or professors. We should like him to be able to distinguish among arguments based on evidence or experience or observation or logic from those based on conventional usage, on authority, and on appeals to semi-conscious fears or desires. We should like our students to feel the force of a remark of Sartre's: "We are no better than our life, and it is by our life that we must be judged; our thought is no better than our language, and it ought to be judged by the way it uses it."

The most difficult questions of all remain to be answered. How is Freshman Composition to achieve its aims? What should happen in the classroom? What should students read, if anything, and what should they write about? According to what standards should the teacher evaluate their writing? On the basis of what assumptions should he construct his schedule of assignments and of topics for discussion in class?

I said before that the main aim of the course was to improve the student's writing, and his thinking so far as it is verbal. Everyone tacitly admits as much, but no one can say what the principles of good writing, in the abstract, are. No one can

say before it appears what good writing on any subject would be like. One can point to pieces of good writing and say that they are good and point to bad ones and say that they are bad, and one may even be able to say a little about just what is good and what bad, but no one has been able to deduce rules of either a predictive or prescriptive sort that even commonly, let alone universally, apply.

But the teacher of Freshman Composition does *not* need to know in the abstract or in advance what good writing would be like. He need only, to begin with, recognize bad writing. He need only be like the jazz musician who can play, but not read, music. The musician knows perfectly well when he hits a clam, as Dizzy Gillespie puts it, even though he may not be able to explain what is fishy about the note. The teacher, likewise, need only recognize verbal clams when he sees them, need only *feel* their wrongness, as he need only, feel the adequateness of other expressions or their felicity.

And the teacher does recognize these things, if English is his native language, and what is more, the student does too, once they have been pointed out to him. Eighteen out of twenty students, even if they habitually make the mistake in question themselves, will recognize that something is wrong and know more or less how to put it right the minute the teacher says, "Look here, there's something wrong." The average teacher of composition has been speaking English for twenty-five years, the average student for fifteen. During these times each has developed a language sense, a sense of idiom, a feel for the logic of ordinary expressions—the expressions from which all extraordinary ones are derived. This sense, or faculty or "dispositional property" is at once generative and critical: it enables us to combine words as fast as thought, but without a thought for the rules according to which we combine them; it enables even an illiterate to spot incongruencies among the words in any expression, and enables him to do it as fast as the musician who plays it by ear can spot a flatted fifth in a diatonic progression; it is more subtle, complex, inclusive, and useful than any grammar. You cannot speak without it; you cannot write well without developing it. This sense, to begin with, is composed of knowledge that is tacit only—you can only tell it is there by its effects; and it is accumulated by what some psychologists call subception—we take it in while our attention is focused on something else. It is on this tacit knowledge, this sense, that the teacher both relies and goes to work; it is, in fact, the ultimate subject of the course, as life is the ultimate subject of a course on animal biology and history is the ultimate subject of a course on the French Revolution.

The teacher of composition, then, is one who can recognize clams and pearls when he sees them, the student one who can recognize them once they have been pointed out. Ideally speaking, the teacher's language sense is more finely sifted and more shaped, is based on a greater number and a larger variety of linguistic experiences, and above all, is more conscious than the student's; and his job is to make the latter's sense of English idiom as alert as his own. His job is also to make his students conscious of the relations between speaking informed by this sense, these habits, and idiomatic writing. Once students become just a little conscious of the logic of ordinary language, they are quick to see how grammar, punctuation, and syntax can do for writers what tone, pitch, pause, facial expressions, and gestures can do for speakers.

The student develops his written idiom as he developed his spoken one—he practices and has his practice corrected by a more experienced practitioner, his teacher, and has it tested by measuring it against the practices of his peers, his fellow students. After the student's sense of the logic of ordinary language has emerged into his consciousness he can transform it from the determinant of his verbal behavior into the ground of verbal action; he can play with it, trim it, build on it, decide how much of it to put under the tension of his personal idiosyncrasies, so as to establish what relationship he will between linguistic tradition and his individual talent.

To get the course under way, then, the teacher does not need any ideal of good writing toward which he will direct his students. All he needs is a sample sentence that does not quite feel right. He need not know what is wrong with the sentence: in fact, he will never in any final sense know what is wrong. The ultimate source of his feeling will be some relationship between the perceptual and nervous apparatus he began with and all that has happened to him, and with some relationship of all this in turn to the history of the English language down to the first barbaric yawp from which it evolved.

The teacher begins by putting his sample on the board: "Shakespeare certainly had the knack for writing": or "Man, in the modern America of today, is alienated; they don't like their jobs." He nods toward a student: "Mr. So-and-so, what do you think of that sentence"? (He does not say, "what's wrong with that sentence"?)

Mr. So-and-so will probably say something like, "It looks all right to me," but by then two hands will already be up and waving: one from a student who will try to find something wrong with the sentence because he thinks his so doing will please the teacher; another hand from a student who will insist that the sentence is perfect because he thinks his so doing will displease the teacher. No matter—once the teacher has gotten a student to make a definite assertion for or against, he will have no trouble finding other students ready to argue. Disputatiousness is the glory of the current generation of students and the salvation of their teachers.

During the discussions of students' writings, which should occupy at least one class-hour each week, the teacher should get the students themselves to work towards establishing nothing so grand as canons of right and wrong, but rough standards of effectiveness, of the satisfying, of, above all, appropriateness, so long as he remembers that there is inappropriate as well as appropriate appropriateness. (Even the logical is finally a category of the appropriate.) Good prose, my students, for example, have told me, is characterized by *density*: more things happen per word than in unsatisfying prose; by *clarity*: the things that happen do not suspend, short-circuit, or muddy each other—the associations, the overtones of the words, so to speak, have a harmonic relationship, are not in a class conflict, unless conflict and dissonance are the appropriate effects; by *shapeliness*: the words and ideas are arranged in intelligible units and memorable rhythms; by *felicity*: the expectations aroused are satisfied in an unexpected but apt way. And, of course, there are other qualities, such as interest and drama, as there are other ways of formulating these; but these are the kind that naturally arise out of discussions with students of their own writing, so long as the teacher restrains his understandable impulses to exhort or coerce.

On the first meeting of each week, then, the instructor should discuss with his class representative samples of student prose. In my experience the students

enjoy such discussions and through them quickly develop a sense of themselves as a group. As critics of each other's work the students tend to be more generous in their praise, more severe in their adverse judgments, more patient, and more courteous, than their teacher is likely to be. They become feelingly, and unprofessorially, distressed by old mistakes newly made, and become communally proud over individual displays of verbal dexterity. On each first meeting the students will bring in new pieces of writing, not necessarily full length themes, for next week's discussion.

During the last meeting of each week, the instructor probably ought to open up the topic on which students will write their next papers. His proper method is some form of dialectical analysis. His materials are the academic and other experiences stored in his and his students' minds. His working assumptions are as follows:

1) "Our common stock of words embodies all the distinctions men have found worth drawing, and the connections they have found worth making, in the lifetimes of many generations: these surely are likely to be more numerous, more sound, since they have stood up to the long test of the survival of the fittest, and more subtle, at least in all ordinary and reasonably practical matters, than any that you or I are likely to think up in our armchairs of an afternoon—the most favored alternative method." (J. L. Austin)

2) "When we examine what we should say when, what words we should use in what situations, we are looking again not *merely* at words (or 'meanings,' whatever they might be) but also at the realities we use the words to talk about: we are using a sharpened awareness of words to sharpen our perceptions of, though not as the final arbiter of, the phenomena." (J. L. Austin)

3) "The meaning of an expression, or the concept it expresses, is the role it is employed to perform, not any thing or person or event for which it might be supposed to stand.... To know what an expression means is to know how it may and may not be employed.... [Further, as] we could not learn to play the knight correctly without having learned to play the other pieces, we cannot learn to play a word by itself, but only in combination with other words and phrases." (Gilbert Ryle)

4) People know things they do not know they know. Students can intelligently discuss justice, piety, imagination, conscience, proof, civil disobedience, Eros, comedy and tragedy without in advance reading essays on these subjects. They can work towards definitions of the proper functions of these words, the logical boundaries of these conceptions, their interrelations with other words and conceptions, through the dialectical examination of things they already in some sense know but are not fully conscious of. I. A. Richards used to say that a genius is unlike other men in that his experiences are always available for instant application. There is a method through which people can develop the latent genius in them. Dialectic is it.

The instructor, then, will begin a class by asking a student to consider, say, the distinction between *sincerity* and *honesty*. After some preliminary distinctions have been made, he might ask the students to write a "character" (in the Theophrastian sense) of the Sincere Man or the Honest Man. Or the instructor might ask his class to distinguish among actions performed *willingly, on purpose, deliberately*, and *intentionally* and ask what the distinctions imply about common sense notions of volition, action, and responsibility. When a student explains that he hasn't been doing his work

because he has been trying to find himself, you can put it before the class: ask them, who, is such a situation, is trying to find whom? He can ask students to talk about the subjective-objective hoax, and devise exercises to expose it. He can ask his students to explain why it is that the languages of description and of evaluation are so often identical, why we can say that a sum in arithmetic is *wrong* and also say that it is *wrong* to torture children.

The language of description seems to me the natural starting point of the second-meeting discussions. The instructor might begin by asking the students to describe something as neutrally as possible and then by question-and-answer lead them to the discovery that no matter how hard they have tried to be "objective" every word in their description will express an attitude or evaluation. He might for the next assignment ask them to list everything discernable about their left knee caps, or, say, a banana peel,—anything they are all likely to have nearby—with the proviso that they must list at least one hundred items. Once they have gotten beyond the obvious they will find that they have to make finer and subtler distinctions, draw on more original and complex figures of speech to express what they perceive, be ever more clear about the point of view from which they are examining the thing, and, best of all, they will find that a perception is not really fixed until it is expressed, that the attempt to find verbal equivalents of a perception changes the perception and leads to new ones, that clear writing is not only the product of clear seeing, but a cause of it. After the students have been trained a bit by exercises of this sort, the instructor might tell them to go out and stare long and hard at a fire hydrant until it begins to have the aspect of a hallucination. Let them imagine it transforming itself into an elephant. Have them describe what they imagine. The results are invariably a revelation. Some students spread out the transformation in mental space as an architect spreads his blue print on a drawing board. Other students see the metamorphosis in the jerks, pants, and dramatic rhythms of some animal or plant or insect breaking out of its old carcass into some gorgeous and sunlit affirmation of its rightful identity. Other students see the transformation in slow motion, with portentious and technicolor shapes gliding effortlessly into position. In the discussions of these descriptions the instructor might have his students pin down exactly which uses of words created the various effects.

Everything (almost) depends upon the assignments; if they are interesting the students can be relied upon to respond interestingly. And a loose schedule of concatenated assignments is something any composition staff ought to work up together, preferably with student participation. Such a schedule should include assignments leading to definitions of invention, amplification, point of view, proof, evidence, narration, figurative language, the aphorism, logic, rhythm, and so forth. But (1) more than half of the second meetings of the week should be devoted to the kind of dialectical analysis outlined above; (2) the schedule should be thought of as merely a guide for instructors who have not on their own worked out a sequence of assignments that exactly reflects their individual interests and predispositions; and (3) the schedule should be suspended whenever some kind of improvisation seems likely to accomplish more.

In sum, if my scheme is adopted, each week the first meeting of the course will be devoted to a discussion of things the students wrote during the previous week; the second meeting will be devoted to something about which the students are to write for the following week. The classroom procedure will be the dialectical analysis of terms and concepts. During the class on clichés, for example, the instructor will get students to work toward a definition of verbal and intellectual clichés. He will ask how one recognizes them, what is wrong or right with them, how one goes about finding substitutes for them. On another occasion he will ask them to work toward a definition of the rhythmical. He will ask what is rhythm in prose, how does one recognize it, how does one go about writing rhythmical prose. He will ask to what kinds of things we properly apply the "logical." He will ask what we mean by the word "structure," and work toward methods of putting together words so that they seem the constituents of a structure rather than a heap. He might, if he is ambitious enough, have the students develop a theory of the paragraph, a matter more full of intellectual traps than the question of the "out there."

The virtues I claim for this way of conducting the course are that it will improve the morale of students and instructors; release and form the huge hoard of experiences lying like the nagging ghosts of unfulfilled promises at the back of the students' and instructor's minds; develop methods of analysis and exploration that will profit both students and the instructors who will work with them in other departments; improve the students' writing.

KENNETH A. BRUFFEE

Collaborative Learning:
Some Practical Models

IN THE WORLD which surrounds our classrooms, people today are challenging and revising many social and political traditions which have heretofore gone unquestioned. They are making this challenge not as individuals alone, but as individuals working together in collaborative ways. The social organization they are substituting for traditional forms is likewise in many respects collaborative. Indeed, classrooms remain today one of the few places where people do not organize themselves for collaborative activity. On campuses everywhere, right outside the classroom door, students form their own academic clubs for collaborative study, organizations for self-government, "free university" classes, social groups, film societies, political discussion groups, and activist organizations. Elsewhere, everywhere, collaborative action increasingly pervades our society.

The Commissioner of Indian Affairs, Louis R. Bruce, has begun a fundamental reform of the Bureau of Indian Affairs that is intended to put the future of the nation's Indians into their own hands. . . . The Commissioner . . . said it was acknowledged that Indian communities

and tribes had the right and the authority "to take part in the planning and the operation of activities that touch their everyday lives." (12/3/70)[1]

All traffic was halted for nearly four hours tonight on a 25-mile stretch of the New Jersey Turnpike by about 1,000 antiwar demonstrators returning home from Washington. (4/26/71)

Mutual funds will apparently be required, in the future, to let their shareholders vote on whether fund managers should consider the social policies of corporations before investing in their stock. (5/11/71)

Dr. Harvey B. Scribner, the Chancellor of the New York City school system, proposed today that students—along with parents, teachers, and supervisors—participate as advisors in the selection of high school principals. (2/15/71)

City planners have begun to use the term "charette" to describe "a new technique of 'total community planning.' This technique calls for the bringing together of an area's residents for discussions on designing a facility, such as a school, to serve as a multi-purpose center of activity for their community. . . . 'There was never anything like this before,' said one participant. 'Everyone was involved, from white gun clubs to Black Panthers.' . . . The ideas that the

Kenneth Bruffee is Associate Professor of English and Director of the Freshman Writing Program at Brooklyn College. He is author of "The Way Out" (CE, January, 1972) and a textbook, A Short Course in Writing, published by Winthrop.

[1]The quotations are from The New York Times. The irony of the first one is, since the Indian action in Washington last fall, all too apparent.

charette developed proved so innovative that they have astounded and excited a number of city planning officials." (1/6/71)

To reduce the dehumanizing effects of modern factory life, . . . two Swedish automobile makers, Volvo and Saab, have begun to eliminate that pillar of mass production, the assembly line.

As part of a growing emphasis on team production methods, the parts will be brought to the cars and installed by semi-autonomous groups of workers instead of the cars being transported through a gantlet of men, each of whom performs a single, monotonous job. . . .

A spokesman "noted that management was often cool to such programs because, even though productivity may increase, 'humanizing work gives more initiative and autonomy to the worker' " so that " 'he or she becomes less controlled by the manager.' " (12/28/71)

Some activities similar to these have particular relevance for education. In the women's liberation movement, for example, people have begun to work collaboratively in support groups—sometimes called "rap groups" or "consciousness raising groups"—which subordinate figures of authority during the process of self-development. Likewise, peer-group counseling is helping many young people burdened by such problems as drugs, homosexuality, and parental neglect. In some instances, collaborative learning has also occurred on a massive scale. The Cambodia-Kent State student strike three years ago became one gigantic, nationwide, impromptu seminar in collaborative action. The quality of learning in that seminar is evident in the disciplined and thorough book which emerged from it, *The Organizer's Manual*.[2] In such

ways as these, people have created, outside classrooms, structures in which learning is integral both with human interdependence and with private inner experience and feeling.

Here and there even teachers have struck on the principle of collaborative learning.

As part of "a growing number of health education programs around New York state, designed to teach preventive medicine concepts to school children . . . new programs are trying to involve pupils directly and to channel peer influence, on the theory that if youths can teach each other bad habits, they can also teach each other good habits.

"The schools . . . put about 30 high school pupils to work last semester as volunteers in the local hospital, doing clerical work, talking to patients, even collecting bedpans. . . . They trained another group of youngsters to counsel their fellow students about drug information, and a third group will be trained as general health counselors.

"There is a real responsibility here. The kids had better learn their lessons well," a spokesman said. . . . "I don't know of a better way to make education relevant. . . . I don't know of any better way to turn kids on than to make them helpful to other people." (6/72)

"Officials of the [New York] State Department of Education said today they were studying a new method for teaching reading which in the last two years has raised the reading scores of students. . . . The system relies heavily on family and community involvement, with students teaching their younger brothers and sisters and slow youngsters in the learning group being assisted by the faster pupils." (3/9/72)

In this second instance, officials would have been neither surprised at student progress in collaborative learning, nor startled at the "newness" of a "method" by which children teach other children, had they read the following passage in

---

[2]"By the O. M. Collective," a Bantam Book (Q6516), 1971. Another useful and influential book, indirectly related to the strike, is Saul Alinski's *Rules for Radicals* (Vintage paperback).

Thomas Wolfe's *Look Homeward Angel*.

He learned to read almost at once, printing the shapes of words immediately with his strong visual memory; but it was weeks later before he learned to write, or even to copy, words. The ragged spume and wrack of fantasy and the lost world still floated from time to time through his clear schoolday morning brain, and although he followed accurately all the other instruction of his teacher, he was walled in his ancient unknowing world when they made letters. The children made their sprawling alphabets below a line of models, but all he accomplished was a line of jagged wavering spearpoints on his sheet, which he repeated endlessly and rapturously, unable to see or understand the difference.

"I have learned to write," he thought.

Then, one day, Max Isaacs looked suddenly, from his exercise, on Eugene's sheet, and saw the jagged line.

"That ain't writin'," said he.

And clubbing his pencil in his warted grimy hand he scrawled a copy of the exercise across the page.

The line of life, that beautiful developing structure of language that he saw flowing from his comrade's pencil, cut the knot in him that all instruction failed to do, and instantly he seized the pencil, and wrote the words in letters fairer and finer than his friend's. And he turned, with a cry in his throat, to the next page, and copied it without hesitation, and the next, the next. They looked at each other a moment with that clear wonder by which children accept miracles, and they never spoke of it again.[3]

Learning Collaboratively

It seems reasonable to suppose that what young children are capable of in this regard, adults and near adults must be capable of as well. It would seem that college students—Freshmen, Sophomores, Juniors, Seniors—can also learn with one another and from one another.

Yet students do not as a rule learn collaboratively in our classrooms. We do not ordinarily recognize collaboration as a valid kind of learning. Traditionally, indeed, collaboration is considered irresponsible; in the extreme, collaboration is the worst possible academic sin, plagiarism. We ordinarily expect a student to talk mainly to the teacher, write to the teacher, and, surely, determine his fate in relation to the teacher, individually. Among students we recognize few relationships in the learning process itself. More accurately, we tend to preserve a negative relationship among students. Officially, students are anonymous to one another, and isolated. We turn our back on collaboration which does occur in learning, or we penalize it, or we simply refuse to see it. The odds are very good that Eugene's teacher never knew who taught Eugene to write. Had he known he might well have punished the two boys for disturbing class, or for "cheating." For the children, collaborative learning could be nothing but a clandestine "miracle."

But the examples I have given suggest that in reality collaborative learning is no miracle. No productive, satisfying collaborative activity is miraculous. As Durkheim puts it, collaboration is unquestionably "a very rich activity . . . periods of creation or renewal occur when men for various reasons are led into a closer relationship with each other, when . . . relationships are better maintained and the exchange of ideas most active."[4] And collaborative activity hap-

---

[3]Thomas Wolfe, *Look Homeward Angel* (New York: Bantam, 1970), p. 79. I am indebted to Anthea Hemery for pointing out this passage to me.

[4]*Essays on Sociology.* Quoted by Edwin Mason in *Collaborative Learning* (New York: Agathon Press, 1972), p. 26. A very practical book on collaborative learning is Charity James, *Young Lives at Stake* (New York: Agathon Press, 1972), especially Chapter 3.

pens willy-nilly, even in an educational tradition which militates against it. It will certainly happen at an accelerating pace whenever a teacher conceives of teaching as a process of creating conditions in which collaborative learning can occur.

To create these conditions is not simply a matter of deciding "how much" freedom or discipline a teacher should "give"students. The teacher must reconceive his role. He must become an organizer of people into communities for a specific purpose—learning. He must re-apportion freedom and discipline within the class, thereby establishing a "poly-centralized" collaborative learning community in which the teacher moves to the perimeter of the action, once the scene is set. The central action then is people learning. It is important to see that the teacher does not simply take a laissez-faire attitude, abrogating his responsibility to educate. He reinterprets this responsibility. The teacher understands that his primary job is to organize the learning community, because, as Dewey points out, "community life does not organize itself in an enduring way purely spontaneously. It requires thought and planning ahead."[5]

Generally speaking, the kind of community such a teacher organizes is composed (depending on class size) of an indeterminate number of self-governing, self-teaching, mutually responsible groups of four to six students each. Here are several examples of how teachers have applied this general principle under widely varying conditions.

(I) Recently a young community college teacher[6] told me she had in effect re-invented collaborative learning herself. In despair, faced with an introductory literature class of over 130 students meeting in a gym, she divided the class into groups of five to seven people each, scattered the groups around the gym, and told students to discuss the assigned story among themselves.

She gave them a question or two to start with each class hour, and throughout the term she visited each group in turn for an hour or part of an hour each, giving each group a small but intensive and valuable portion of her undivided attention. She lectured to the class as a whole three or four times during the term to give people additional background or ways of approaching the work. In this way, everyone in this gargantuan class had a chance to discuss literature in a fairly intimate and yet guided way three times a week for three months. Under such adverse conditions, "literary study" could hardly be more immediate or intense.

(II) Last year I had a class of fifty-five people in an elective course in Romantic poetry, which by trial and error I turned into a collaborative class in a similar way. I lectured occasionally, usually for the first and last class hour to be spent on each poet. The other classes were devoted to discussion in collaborative groups. I tried at first to change the makeup of the groups from class to class. In failing this I discovered how fundamental and important the coherence of each small group is, especially in a setting of large impersonal classes. Although I had composed the groups arbitrarily at first, after a week or so during which a few people migrated from one group to another, the groups became settled and loyal.

During the collaborative classes, I visited the groups in rotation, working with

[5]John Dewey, *Experience and Education* (New York: Collier, 1963), p. 56.
[6]Ms. Fraya Katz Stoker.

each small group intensively—sometimes in a strongly directive way, especially when I found that people were failing to read carefully. During the first weeks of collaborative work, also, I offered each group a set of questions at the beginning of each class hour to get them started. This gave students a greater sense of security and direction. In addition, before the end of the term, one group began meeting voluntarily outside classtime. They prepared a difficult poem (Shelley's *Prometheus Unbound*) and, splitting up, became leaders of the other groups when the time came for the class to discuss that work.

Every person wrote two papers during the term, and each one read and wrote an evaluative critique of at least four papers written by fellow students (two evaluations each assignment).[7] The students thereby became familiar with each other's work, and not incidentally, familiar with additional works of the Romantic poets. They also developed through practice their critical eye. And the final evaluation of each paper was not based, then, on the views of a single judge, the teacher, but was comprised of the views of a small jury of students as well. Also, two pairs of students wrote their papers in collaboration; in each case, the pair accepted equal responsibility for the result.

[7]To help students learn the evaluative process, I offered them the following optional set of four questions as a guide:
1. What is the "point" of the paper? What does it say? What position does it take?
2. How does it make its point? What does it do to defend or explain its position?
2. Is the paper related to any issue raised so far in this course? If so, which? If not, what context of issues is the paper related to?
4. What are the strong and weak points in the paper? What do you like about it? If what you read was a draft, what suggestions would you make to the writer for revising it?

A curious thing happened in the final exam. Some students felt, because of the way the course had been taught, that they should be allowed to discuss the exam questions in groups before writing the exam. As an experiment, I concurred, giving them the first half-hour of a two-hour exam period for discussion. Two-thirds of the class refused the option. The remaining third formed into two groups. One group was made up of well-prepared students who had been active in group discussion all term. They talked for fifteen minutes and dispersed to write. The other group was made up of students who had been inactive or frequently absent. They spent the better part of the allotted time picking each other's poorly furnished brains, before setting reluctantly to work. The net result of the experiment was to dissipate exam-panic for almost everyone. The one bad effect I half expected did not happen. Unprepared students did not become the parasites of better prepared students, who had neither the time nor the inclination to indulge them.

(III) The year before, I conducted a more advanced and smaller class, a senior seminar in the novel. Less certain of myself at that time, I organized the class more formally, according to the following written "convention."

A Collaborative-Learning Convention

1. The purpose of this convention is to organize class members to teach one another and support one another in learning. Mutual interest and responsibility—affinity, rather than autocratic control—is to create coherence among the members of the class.

2. The first week or two of the term may be a period of orientation. The teacher may direct the meetings, intro-

duce the subject matter, and provide basic concepts which class members are likely to find useful in exploring the material, and in developing their own line of thought regarding it. Students will then declare their interest in units of the subject matter. The teacher will divide the class into collaborative groups of four to six students each, according to the interest declared by each member.

3. Each collaborative group will be responsible to the rest of the class for its own unit of material. Members of the group will decide how to teach the material to the rest of the class, and the emphasis to be made. The group will then direct and govern the class for one to two weeks of the term. Groups may aid discussion by providing supplementary information in written form.

4. Each class member will be responsible individually to the group which is in charge of the class. Each member will also be responsible for his own preparation and for contributing to class discussion. And each member will be responsible for the work his group undertakes in preparing material and directing the class.

5. The teacher's responsibility will be to determine before the term begins the subject matter and written requirements of the course. Both may be revised in negotiation with the class. The teacher will also provide orientation, and act as mediator, as judge in the process of evaluation, and as the class's resident resource. The teacher will provide resources and advice on request, to the limit of his ability, and may also provide unrequested resources he thinks may be useful to the class in their work. The teacher will be available for consultation on request to the class as a whole, to each learning group, and to each individual member of the class. He will hold individual conferences with members of the class at least once during the term. Any class member at any time may choose to learn independently with the teacher's guidance.

6. Class members will be responsible to each other and to the teacher for evaluation. Each student paper will be read and evaluated, in writing, by a jury of at least two class members; hence, each student will read two papers as a juror for every one paper he writes himself. After the student jury has considered each paper, the teacher will read and evaluate it, weighing student critical opinion with his own, providing his own written comment, and assigning a grade if necessary.

7. Twice during the term (mid-term and end of term) class members will evaluate their own work, the work of their group, the class as a whole, and the teacher's contribution. Also at these times the class as a whole will recapitulate the subject matter covered. Discussion of the nature and process of the course will be channelled to these limited periods in order to insure coherent, uninterrupted consideration of the subject matter during the balance of the term.

The last sentence in paragraph 5 of this convention is important because it leaves the door open for students to choose alternative ways of learning—in particular, more individual ways—if they find collaborative learning emotionally intolerable, too academically demanding, or not demanding enough.

The convention is admittedly unwieldy, or is likely to seem so at first, because it necessarily specifies many of the social and learning processes which we take for granted in a traditional classroom.[8] It is designed, furthermore, for the rigor of advanced study, in order to satisfy the following criteria:

a. Subject matter. A primary consideration in college study. Students should gain an understanding of subject matter which is at least as thorough as the understanding they may be supposed to gain through traditional teaching.

b. Direction. Students should gain increasing confidence in their ability to learn on their own. They should learn how to develop worthwhile purposes in learning, and learn to develop and pursue questions and problems of their own devising.

c. Evaluation. Students should gain increasing confidence and ability in critically evaluating their own work and that of their peers, as well as the subject matter studied.

Learning to Write Collaboratively

The principle of collaborative learning is applied somewhat differently in a composition course than in a literature course, although the assumption remains the same, that students can learn with and from other students. In a composition class, the possibility that collaborative learning is a case of the blind leading the blind is more apparent. But students can be of immense help to each other in learning to write, for several reasons.

One reason is that learning to write is not much like learning anything else. There are few important facts we must learn in order to learn to write. In learning to write, we learn to *do* something,

as we learn tennis, carpentry, or the violin. Yet unlike learning these activities, in learning to write we do not start from scratch. (I am speaking at the moment of native speakers of standard English.) We use a language which we have been fluent in since we were about five years old.[9] Furthermore, because this language, our principle resource in writing, develops during our earliest years, it is associated deeply in us with feelings and experiences we can hardly ever be fully conscious of.

A good deal of learning to write, then, requires us to become actively aware of what as native speakers we already know. It also requires us to overcome the resistances which seem inherent in writing because we are working consciously with something we would ordinarily prefer to be as little aware of as possible. Therefore for adults or near-adults—that is, for college students—learning to write is in great measure a process of gaining new awareness. Gaining new awareness of any kind is likely to be a painful process. People need some kind of support while undergoing it. And the evidence provided by collaborative activity in the society at large suggests that people can gain both awareness and support as adequately in a small group of their peers, as from the ministrations of a teacher.

Another reason students can help each other learn to write is that a person is, or can learn to be, an astute and demanding audience before he becomes a clear, effective writer, just as a small child becomes an astute and discriminating listener before he can speak. Thus read-

---

[8]For an analysis of the traditional teaching conventions, see "The Way Out," *College English* (January, 1972), pp. 458-461. Some introductory and articulatory material in the present essay appeared in different form in this earlier one.

[9]For the amount and types of language learning which occur after five, see Carol Chomsky, "Stages in Language Development and Reading Exposure," *Harvard Educational Review* (February, 1972), pp. 1-33.

ing their own work aloud to each other regularly helps students learn to write. The listeners become increasingly capable of detecting lack of clarity, organization, logic, and substance, a development which leads eventually to the ability to write clearly, coherently, and logically themselves. When one student tells another he can't understand what he's heard, that criticism sticks. On the other hand, in practicing listening, as well as in practicing reading aloud, the weak writer begins to develop his own ear for the language, becomes more aware of the criteria of judgment he already maintains, and begins to learn and apply new criteria. In this way, both reader and listener become more demanding of one another's work, as well as of their own.[10]

This spiraling effect is typical of collaborative learning. It is the third reason students can help each other learn to write. People themselves learn, when they teach others. Chances are Max learned as much teaching Eugene to write as Eugene learned—maybe he even learned more. What we have all experienced as new teachers, students may also experience when they teach each other. They gain an active knowledge of what they had before known only passively, and they become aware of their ignorance in a practical way, which is the necessary first step to learning more.

The following, and final, example of collaborative learning shows how one teacher applied the principle in a class of freshman composition.

(IV) Recently I visited a colleague's

class.[11] To prepare for this class hour, the students had been asked to write five questions, drawing on their reading of a set of assigned essays. About half the students attending (19 that day) had done at least part of the assignment. The teacher divided the class according to that criterion, and then divided the students who had done the assignment, again into two groups of five. She asked the students in these groups to pool their material and agree how they would conduct a discussion of the essays if they were to lead the class. These groups then went to work on their own. Once during the hour the teacher asked each group how they were doing, encouraged them, and answered questions. Throughout the hour she was available to them for information and help.

She formed the other half of the class —those who had not done the assignment—into a single group of nine. She assumed, implicitly, that these people had not completed the assignment because for some reason they were unable to. She sat with the group and led a short discussion of the essays, trying to find out how much each student had understood in reading them. Six of the nine responded readily to her direction, and before the hour was half over, they were completing the assignment on their own. This left the teacher twenty minutes or so to work individually with the three students who had the most difficulty doing the assignment. Thus her students had the option of working collaboratively with other students, or of working alone with the teacher, to get special, individual attention. In the collaborative groups, students could work without instruction from the teacher, at their own pace and drawing on their own re-

---

[10]Reading aloud as an aspect of collaborative learning is discussed further in *A Short Course in Writing* (Cambridge, Mass.: Winthrop Publishers, 1972), pp. 71-73, 282, and 287-9; see also pp. 290-301. A related discussion of the "psychological" (that is, emotional) difficulties people have in learning to write may be found on pp. 7-8 and 66-70.

---

[11]Ms. Pamella Farley.

sources, or they could reach out to the teacher for help, depending on their need.

The Stress of Change

The examples of collaborative learning I have presented here have all been successful to a marked degree. But teachers vary considerably in their ability to organize classes successfully in this way. The ability can be developed, but it may take time. It took me personally several years of wrestling with my own compulsion to Teach as I was Taught. On the other hand, some of my colleagues seem to have taken to it with little or no inner struggle. Similarly, many students welcome collaborative learning enthusiastically. It is a fact, however, that some feel "forced" if asked to learn collaboratively. Many feel bewildered at first. Few students will know immediately how to go about it. Some will distrust it, or reject it entirely. Teachers should realize that students are uncertain and distrustful for good reason. In being asked to learn collaboratively, they are being asked to do something their whole education has not only left them unequipped to do, but has actually militated against.[12]

Teachers should be prepared, therefore, to help students learn to learn collaboratively. Having set up a collaborative class structure, the teacher might begin by posing problems of increasing generality for each learning group to solve. Beginning with specific questions on the material at hand, the teacher could then pose broader questions, and eventually propose that groups begin discovering the important problems and questions on their own. Finally, the teacher could face learning groups with the problem of reaching other people with both the questions and the answers they have come up with—that is, offer groups the problem of creating conditions in which others could learn what they have learned.

This gradual process is one way a teacher may go about progressively "demythologizing" himself as The Teacher in the traditional sense. Students must see their teacher differently if they are to learn well collaboratively. But it is important to keep in mind that the teacher must see himself differently too. Like students, teachers also carry with them "the influence of failed institutions . . . when [they] set out to create anything new."[13] The teacher will have to be wary of his own tendency (and that of some of his students) to lapse back into the traditional patterns of dominance and passivity. He will find it tempting to "declare [his students] children, rather than adults." This relationship, "which emphasizes and accentuates the [teacher's] strength and the student's weakness . . . the same relationship that exists between an adult and a child,"[14] is at the bottom of the human relations which are normal in a traditional class. It is an attitude which is disastrous to collaborative learning.

At the same time, teachers who are willing to encounter these difficulties may find help in *The Anatomy of Judgment*, by M. L. Johnson Abercrombie.[15] This book discusses a course established to improve significantly the diagnostic

---

[12]See "Comment and Rebuttal," *CE*, December, 1972.

[13]Adrienne Rich, *New York Review*, June 15, 1972, p. 35.

[14]These phrases are adapted from an eye-opening short essay on college admissions procedures by a recent high school graduate, Ethan Gorenstein, on the Op-Ed page of *The New York Times*, July 10, 1971.

[15](New York: Basic Books, 1960).

judgment of medical students. This improvement could be accomplished, Dr. Abercrombie discovered, only through collaborative learning. Similarly useful is *The School without Walls*, by John Bremer and Michael von Moschzisker, which describes an urban high school based in part on principles of collaborative learning. These two books also suggest the range of education—secondary school to professional training—in which the principles of collaborative learning must play an increasingly important part. Regarding the importance of these principles, Abercrombie clearly implies what Bremer makes explicit: "no changes [in education] will be of any significance unless the social organization of education is totally changed."[16]

---

[16](New York: Holt, 1971), p. 7. I am indebted to Ronald Gross for directing me to these two important books.

Timothy E. McCracken
W. Allen Ashby

The Widow's Walk: An Alternative for English 101—Creative Communications

---

I

The Quaker Graveyard in Nantucket

This is the end of running on the waves
We are poured out like water, Who will dance. . . .
Here in Nantucket, and cast up the time.

Robert Lowell

Who should determine what a student needs to know? Four of us have carried this question and its correlates, a stack of books, a box of groceries, and two bottles of bourbon and brandy to rest here on this island. We are looking for an answer.

The fall was an experiment that we fell into. Nancy got an abortion. Joanne tried to kill herself. Rose and Mary got engaged, and Cindy got a divorce. By the end, Steve had flunked out (it was his third school in two years), Bill had had his first affair, and Alan had wrecked his car. In addition, Marcy suffered her second nervous breakdown while Maryann's father had a heart attack; so did Claire's. Every other day Dawn would go home and put her father on the kidney machine.

We had expected it to be a bit of fun for both of us—five sections of English 101, team taught. We were just preparing ourselves for some team teaching in the spring—a sophomore course called Literature and the Arts. This accident was a dry run, warm ups, nothing exceptional. At least we expected that. We nearly died. Today on our break between semesters we are resting, secluded here on Melville's island off the coast of Cape Cod, reviewing. It is our widow's walk, and from this vantage point now we want to look out over the long sea run of last semester.

In September we began with just another course in English Composition. By the middle of the semester we had been forced from composition into a series of experiments dealing with communication. By the end we were just listening to our students, wondering if their value-free language really belonged to them.

Timothy McCracken and W. Allen Ashby are both Assistant Professors of English at Union College, Cranford, New Jersey.

Reprinted from *College English*, Vol. 36, No. 5, January 1975.

What we found surprising when we listened was that many of them (of those we got to know, nearly all) were going through experiences which we would have found difficult to handle, and yet they, for all their anxiety, did not appear to be suffering.

Now, looking back, we are more surprised to find that during the course of the semester those personal adventures from their lives rarely if ever appeared in their writings, even in a disguised form, although frequently in their formal writing there was a structure that encouraged their discussion. Of course we recognized that Nancy's abortion, for example, was out of the purview of English composition and except that it was volunteered, none of our business. This was our presupposition. Now we are not so sure. We still don't want to enter their personal lives without knocking, but we're not sure that we are adequately fulfilling our tasks if the problems of their lives don't at least appear coded in their speaking or writing.

So we have retreated here to our island to see if we could find the bones of a course which could serve as an alternative to English Composition. Ideally, what we want is a course which would still be a "required" freshman course taught by English department personnel and yet nevertheless be a valuable offering to the students. Looking through our questions and doubts, it is this problem that we are trying to solve.

II

Voyages

The waves fold thunder on the sand;
And could they hear me I would tell them:
. . . .
Permit me voyage, love, into your hands . . .

Hart Crane

We have been walking on the beach. It is winter and so the island is empty. In a myriad of forms one question keeps recurring in our conversations: "Who are these kids we have left behind?" We want to know, for they are not in college for the reasons we were, and though both of us feel closer to them than to the universe of our colleagues, neither of us feels close enough to understand why they lack motivation and seem unable to participate in lives of joy and suffering.

To be sure, they can follow directions. Tell them what an image is and they can reproduce it by the thousands. Show them a descriptive paper and they can write one. But ask them three weeks later to do the same and they withdraw into silence. Why doesn't anything seem to carryover in their lives? This is what frightens us. Their *Weltanschauung* is not ours, and this is not sour grapes. If they have a better world we want to join it. If their lives are more rich, more varied, more creative, then we are prepared to set sail with them. But are they?

Walking along the beach we recall Sylvia Ashton-Warner's new book that we have brought with us, *Spearpoint: Teacher in America*. In it she observes that the American first graders she worked with for a year have a vocabulary unlike children in any other part of the world—a vocabulary that is at the outset emotionally and personally rootless. Her children live in an external world—an object among objects. They also, she notes, live solo; do not ask questions; have fleeting attention spans compared to other children; do not like to write; and have perhaps lost their potential for imagery. For her it is the latter that is distinctive and critical because her prescription for teaching is: "Release the native imagery of our child and use it for working material," or "Touch the true voice of feeling and it will create its own style and vocabulary." And yet without this functioning native imagery, teaching as we have know it is not possible. For our job, we remember, is language and imagery, and if Ashton-Warner is right about her children and if we already have them in our classes—this year firmly and clearly for the first time—then we've got fifteen years of kids coming whose lives are divorced from their feelings and their bodies separated from their minds. We have students who are not in touch with themselves or their world because they are not in touch with the language and images which compose their own personal world.

Like Ashton-Warner's children our kids don't carryover. For them each new experience, new fact of knowledge, new feeling is an island unrelated to the next, to the one before, the one to come. They seem determined to repeat themselves; endlessly wafted on the wind like Francesca and her lover.

But is this really true? We are stretching out footprints along the shore, the ocean always on our right. We wanted to know and then we recalled an experiment we had tried midway through the semester in which we had asked the students to focus in on themselves by finding the five words which they thought best described themselves. And when they came to class that next time we asked them to put their words on the board with their initials under them. So they filled the board and every student looked like every other. All of them alike: "sensitive," "lazy," "optimistic," "emotional," "moody." It was terrifying. They were carbon copies of each other. Xeroxed humans. But now on this beach in our winter walk we are not as surprised as we were then. Then we felt panicked and we pushed them. We would say: "Talk to each other. Interrogate each other. Joan ask Mike what he means by sensitive. See if it is the same as Susan's." Joan would ask Mike. Mike would say: "Well ya know, I get hurt easily." Joan says, "Yeh, I know." We would ask Joan if she knows what Mike means. She says yes. Susan says yes. Mike asks Susan what she means. Susan says: "I like to help others." Everybody nods. Everybody understands. We ask: "Are they different? Did everybody understand before? If not, why not?" We read Hayakawa. Hayakawa says there is an abstraction ladder. We tell them they are nearly cumulous in their abstractions. So begins our litany: "Come down. COME DOWN the abstraction ladder." We quote Henry James: "Show me. Don't tell me!" Don't tell me red is a color. Tell me it's a fire truck or a stop light. Don't tell me you are emotional. Tell me about the time you hit your brother and broke your mother's favorite vase over her knee. They told us red was a spectrum of light—a wave length—and that they cried a lot. We knew we were in trouble. We had found our elephant and every time we tried to shove him out of the way (and get back to composition) he would roll over on us. That was the beginning of a series of lessons in humility, testing our capacity for continuance.

Yes, composition is not our main problem. We wish it were. But here along our sea walk we now believe that it will not be enough simply to change English Composition to another course unless we also grapple with the altered way the students feel and perceive, for they can't carry over, can't play, and have lost the vertical dimension of life. They live almost entirely on the horizontal—the flat opaqueness of the T.V., the movie screen. This life that lives on two dimensions, but with the illusion of three.

> And under the oppression of the silent fog
> The Tolling bell
> Measures time not our time, rung by the unhurried
> Ground swell.

They live in this fog: Chief Bromden's fog, Eliot's fog. It seems to be a world where feeling comes in vague oversized blocks: "I'm moody." "I'm sensitive." "I'm quiet." But our colleagues tell us this is nothing new. They tell us that students have not changed, that they have always been lazy, bored, numbed. They tell us you have to keep after them, that's all. But since when, we wonder, did you have to keep after anyone who is in love? Since when, they ask us, was the student in love with education? Yes, we reply, since when, and why not?

But we will not mask this issue. It is loving that is the problem. Here on the beach at this distance, alone, looking back, we see it clearly. Our students are not in love with anything, not even with themselves, because they have lost contact with the ground swell, the force that tolls the bell. They are unable to work naturally in images, are suspicious, weary, distrustful of authority yet easily intimidated and quickly obedient to any orders or directions. They dislike reading and hate writing. They seem to have no driving passions, no desire to create worlds either with their hands or in writing. Their lives are a movie, trailing without stops, without depth, without a time for reflection. Besides this they are losing the capacity for wonder, for extended periods of wonder and awe, even in the act of touching another person. Their language reflects this lost dimension of exaltation, of personal creation. They "ball" rather than make love; they "rap" rather than talk; their lives are "heavy" but never tragic.

The point during the semester at which most of our male students grew enthusiastic was when the Grateful Dead gave a concert over in Jersey City. One fellow even went four out of the five nights. It is this group sensation-oriented experience that moves them. Feeling in blocks. Nothing private. Nothing personal. Nothing individual that makes them individual. Nothing that cuts deeply into the fabric of their own lives a living pattern of feeling to which they can return and clarify their world and aid their friends.

Tentatively, we are almost ready to assert that their sensory systems have changed, that our students have altered the very coding process that records their experience. An experience comes into their lives in a concrete manner and then is coded in the memory as a general impression—a block, nothing more. It falls into a zone of sensation rather than a private area, into a field of feeling rather than a concrete or particular place. It is this, we believe, that allows them to live without being haunted by their personal tragedies. Nancy got an abortion. Joanne tried to kill herself. Bill had an affair. All turned into nothing. Nothing to build on. Nothing to remember.

And in English Composition what is the world we confront them with but this same world devoid of feeling, unhaunted by the tragic? No, we are farther down the beach, animating to each other our joint feeling; if we want to be faithful to the roots of our own discipline, to the sea of our own ground swell, then we must sound deeper than we have. We can no longer expect them to love Sophocles, or Dickens, or Stevens simply because we love them, because Sophocles and Dickens and Stevens present an alien world to them. And it is not a matter of simply learning the language anymore, for they are losing contact with the very process upon which the language is based. They are losing the entry into the imagination itself, and into the capacity for self-directed imaginative re-enactment. And so our task must be to reach deeper and restore the lost connections between the sources of all love and the objects of love, for it is these that have been severed—and the gap grows wider each year as the waves wash behind the boat.

Originally, when we began, we thought that if we just quit telling them what to feel they would begin to tell us what they feel. Now at this far point—the island's western extremity—we are not so sure that if we left them alone they would even know how to feel, or to play, or to love. And how can we transmit our heritage to someone who cannot *feel* the ground swell that underlies the realities we are trying to transmit through our language?

> They're so different from other children with whom I have worked around the world. Usually it takes no time for children to find in themselves something important, but with these it is a long time and a long way inward . . . where are the fear and sex words or, put it this way, where is the evidence of their instincts?
> "What are you frightened of, Peter?"
> "I'm not frightened."
> "Whom do you love, Rocky?"
> "Nobody."
> "Whom do you love, Peter?"
> Blushing, "Not love . . . *like*."

Why won't they acknowledge the reality of loving and hating? What is the cause of this terrible silence that lies at the center of their lives? Here on our island we are a bit frightened by what we see, nothing coming of nothing. The sun is setting over Madaket. The wind has changed to the north. The sea has begun its night roar. We turn on the sand and retrace our footprints back to the cabin, to the fire, and to help our friends fixing dinner.

III

The Waking

This cove the sailors knew. Here they drew in,

and the ship ran half her keel's length up the shore
. . . .   They bore this treasure
off the beach, and piled it close around . . .
That done, they pulled away on the homeward track.

Homer

The meal is over. It is late at night. Regina and Katie are in the other room, reading. We throw another log on the fire. Now we are ready to talk. We know that we must enlarge that diminishing space where the ground swell still lives if we are to authentically transmit our heritage, and in order to enlarge that space we must first let each student find his own vocabulary that will unlock his own feelings for himself—break his own block patterns of feeling and coding.

We know too that as teachers of our language we have long been too narrowly concerned with making our students into competent writers. But competent writers don't necessarily make good writers or sensitive readers or happy human beings. For generations we have prepared the student to write competently, but for what purpose? He must live before he can write and writing is only a small part of the communicative process. Tonight we believe that English departments have sold themselves too short when they have settled for and then asserted as a made-in-heaven objective, the making of competent writers.

Yet we do not want to disparage writing but only to put it into a larger context. For us it should come out of a self and clarify a world, but they apparently have nothing to clarify. And besides, when we bring it all home, *they don't like to write*. Why? We see two major reasons. First of all, it might be because writing is unpleasant; it is a confrontation with a very confusing world. And it takes a discipline and creativity that T.V. hasn't and wouldn't give our students to adapt and change to our ever present flux. To know who you are is to give up who you are not. And this is frightening in the conformity of personality most education encourages. We are enforcing standards which in fact don't exist and are molding our students to sound and look alike in their writing and thinking.

This brings us to the second reason: grades. Anytime student writing is given a grade, it evaluates the performance of the student. Yet student writers are not performers but learners, and we insist that there is not and should not be any way to evaluate writing! How would you evaluate a life? And we also insist they be allowed to fail and succeed without a letter being attached to their state of awareness. Thus, in terms of student writing the teacher should be primarily a reader and not a grader or marker. And we need to remember that every time we make a notation, respond to a line, or correct a sentence we are saying in effect; "This is important."

So as readers our responses should be individual and personal. In addition, it is apparent to us that most discussions about writing should be done outside of class and should be largely tutorial. If we really see our students as individuals, writing individually, their problems will probably also be individual. So an entire class directed to any composition problem will be largely a waste of time.

Now, in front of the fire, things are beginning to clear. It is apparent that if we follow our own line of reasoning then *writing is now no longer the center of the Freshman English classroom.* What then is the center? This, we now realize, is the question we have been working towards. We sit in the silence around it until one of us rises to go out into the dark for wood, while the other continues by the fire and reflects.

We begin to talk again and it is clear to us that we must start with our differences. It is time, we feel, to adopt an existential approach to student communication, an approach which asserts that the experience of learning is more important than what is learned. We poke the fire and continue the conversation looking now for the wood to lay this keel with. Gradually our thinking revolves around five elementary aims:

1. To reunite the senses and feeling;
2. To emphasize self-definition and self-actualization;
3. To create an atmosphere where failure can be seen as a natural part of the learning process;
4. To develop a problem solving methodology through a question-centered rather than an answer-oriented environment; and finally,
5. To encourage creative rather than standard or linear responses as necessary for survival in a complex world.

What we need, we now know, is a new course, a course devoted to Creative Communication. With this title and these aims we look back over the semester trying to distill more of what we have learned.

Being uncertain of most things we begin to feel confident about at least three things: 1) That nobody learns anything unless he feels the need to learn it; 2) That there are some necessary steps before abstraction; and 3) That the discovery process should begin by using what the students know rather than what they don't know.

In front of the fire with our feet propped up on the coffee table we begin to go over our five elementary aims, one at a time, seeking to understand them and to make them clear for ourselves. Our first hypothesis is that when students are able to plug themselves into their own experiences the more articulate will be their questions, the more specific will be their responses and the broader will be their alternatives. So, where we need to begin is with perception and the senses since that's where all learning begins. For example, we postulate that the making of analogies is an important step in the thinking process for it shows a person's ability to unite sensory perception, feeling, and idea in one linguistic construct. An analogy is the synthesis of what the body experiences with what the mind thinks. And without this ability to draw analogies it is probably impossible for higher thought to occur. During the semester we saw this in one startling situation. Borrowing an idea from William Schutz (*Joy*), we asked each member of the class to bring a piece of fruit which reminded them of their favorite person. One girl brought in a banana and said: "This reminds me of my boyfriend because he is tall and skinny and pale." When we asked "Does he bruise easily?" she looked perplexed and got very silent. She was lost. She didn't understand. It was at this point that we learned that our students are losing the capacity to make analogies. They are becoming ametaphorical and see no connections between things and their life. Tonight we think that this is probably due to the fact that they are basically hostile, suspicious, afraid, or simply unaware of the messages from their bodies. In short, we believe that students don't know that when their ass hurts they are probably bored. So the plug must be pulled out at the sensory end of the analogy cord. What needs to be relearned is that the body is the initial starting point in the learning process, that it is in concrete, specific, sensual experiences that ideas begin and that the senses are the key to creative behavior.

So, if we want to put together a course with this new emphasis in mind one of the first things we would want to dispense with is the instructor-generated assignments. In their place the first part of the semester should consist of student-teacher conferences in which each student evolves his own concepts as to what he wants and needs to know. Thus, through this conference the student will determine his own grade by setting his learning objectives for himself. Does he want an A? Alright, what's an A? Yes, one should learn how to write a research paper, but does he feel the need yet? Practically, we see this as a process of decision making and concrete thinking which should manifest itself in a contract in which the student states the numbers and kinds of things he hopes to accomplish during the semester. This exercise in self-definition is, we believe, a crucial key in Creative Communications.

Next, failing must be brought into realistic focus. We recall that Jerome Kagan has noted that: "Educators have been guilty of minimizing the cultural role which a child's expectancy of failure plays in shaping his behavior in a school situation." Kagan links the expectancy of failure with "decreased involvement in the task and subsequent withdrawal." Often the only time we received any involvement was at grading time, and then the anxiety of failing drove them into a frenzy of short term interest.

However, the failing we are concerned about is not that of the evaluative grade. The failing we are talking about is that failing prevalent in the learning process. The doing of something wrong, the misunderstanding of a concept, the failure to comprehend, the inability to do something successful is at the heart of our approach. Because it is only through failing that success takes on definition; it is only in the little deaths of life that life itself becomes meaningful and joyous. Often in learning what you can't do, you can discover what you can. So we speculate, we ought to provide an atmosphere in which failing is seen as a natural part of the learning process; an atmosphere in which the student is encouraged "to live, to err, to fall, to triumph, to re-create life out of life." For us, honesty is more important than positive reinforcement. We remember that we are working with individual human beings in search of their individual destinies. Under such a banner what does failure mean? And if for whatever reason we are not honest with them— one person to another—in this search, then what are we there for?

In the light of this impulse it is obvious to us that our new course should be question- rather than answer-oriented. This means that the teacher in Creative Communications must be first and foremost a listener and not a talker. Our function in the classroom is to supply the learning situations, not the conclusions about what there is to learn. We should ask the evocative questions, not supply correct answers.

Here on our island what is evident to us is that we must stress creativity and freedom in the classroom if we are to help create vital human beings. We have gone too far down the path of mediocrity, conformity, and standardization. We have produced children who fear failure of any kind, who resent the arts, who "ball" people they don't love, and fight in wars they don't believe in. We must encourage creative responses to a complex world. From this island window the stakes are very clear to us: we must learn to respond creatively or perish.

We put the last log on the fire and remember Chomsky's paraphrase of Rousseau that: "the essence of human nature is man's freedom and his consciousness of his freedom." We feel that we should no longer profess a belief in freedom with our values facing in the opposite direction. We feel that the present way of teaching English with its concentration on writing skills, correctness, and logic is a dead-end street, an anachronism with no future and a dismal past. Now we would want for ourselves and all English teachers to embrace the art of our endeavor, and to admit to ourselves and our students that we too are deeply troubled, deeply confused, but equally deeply hopeful. Now is not the time nor is the English classroom the place to retrench in tradition, to claim a duty beyond the student sitting before us, a duty beyond the face, that stares back in the mirror. The teaching of English now badly needs to take on the open-endedness, the ambiguities, the emotionalism, in a word, the spirit of art.

Thus we envision our new course, Creative Communications; a course where every utterance, gesture, action, every sound and piece of writing, everything we call communication becomes a potential learning situation. In short, Creative Communications is a model of the learning process: organic, open-ended, and as experimentally free as anything can be that admits that learning, like life, is an adventure that begins in wonder and ends in freedom.

IV

Terminus

And every wave is charmed.

Ralph Waldo Emerson

It is morning although off and on you can still hear a hiss or a crackle from an ember in the fireplace. Outside a fine snow has fallen, half concealing the winter grass. We come down to breakfast, still talking. We think we know something: we think we understand our students better than we ever have before, and that from within this understanding we have evolved a set of philosophical objectives which ought to guide us in restructuring our course. We believe that these objectives have bequeathed us an approach, although it is perhaps more a methodology than an approach. Concretely we feel that the key to this method probably resides in the initial student-teacher conferences in which the student sets his goals and grade objectives for the semester. At least as an image it is certainly the clearest representation of how we have relocated the center of our course, as well as the clearest gesture we know that will communicate to the student that, in Creative Communications at least, he is expected to make the major decisions about his own life and his own needs. What we have done, we realize, is to shift the grade pressure from an external judgement to an internal motivating force belonging to the student. But where do we go beyond that?

Setting the table we decide that we now have two major problems: 1) If, as we believe, instruction ought to be individual then does the classroom make any sense any longer; and 2) Even if we keep it, what practically are we going to do with it?

So we start at the beginning and probe: "Why not eliminate the classroom and the class hour altogether? Why not set up special office hours and let the students come to us with their problems and their papers?" At this open speculation Katie and Regina both begin to laugh from the other room. Both of them are still students, having taken off a year or two in the middle of their college careers because they felt a certain dissatisfaction with their educational lives. We ask them why they are laughing, and they tell us it is because we are so funny. They tell us that we call ourselves teachers but that we are prepared to do away with the heart of teaching. We try to remind them that we think that education is a personal affair, and ideally ought to be a one-to-one situation, and they laugh again.

Katie says that we've been out so long that we don't know which way is in. She says that what we don't understand is that the classroom is the source of energy which must set off the chain reaction of interest and enthusiasm, and that without this source of energy nothing can get accomplished. She says that she does her best work for the classes she finds the most enjoyable. Regina agrees and adds that not only is it the source of the enthusiasm, but it is also the place which frequently gives her the first shape of an idea and the first form to a feeling. It is a threshold of thought, not its terminus. Mostly, she says, she uses it to collect ideas that she wants to work on later by herself—books to read, thoughts to follow up, opinions to examine.

Then Katie reminds us how impersonal much of education is becoming. "It's why we left," she states, "and the English classroom is one of the last free playgrounds where a real discussion and dialogue can occur." The classroom, she asserts, is the real place of community within the university. If we take it away then the students will have no reason to come to see us, and we will have no place to see them in—no way to maintain contact with them. While they are talking we remember how empty our halls are becoming, and now we begin to get a feeling for why that is. "If you don't teach what you love," Regina warns, "then they won't learn to love what you teach."

"O.K., O.K." we say. "We'll keep the classroom," but that leaves us with our second problem: what are we going to do with it? We have our five philosophical objectives, but how can we get them to directly manifest themselves in the classroom? So we sit down to breakfast and we begin to talk. Before we are finished it is early afternoon, but we have some feeling for what might be done. We are the first to admit how tentative this exploration is (especially since we haven't tried it yet!), but we also believe that this restructuring of the classroom experience is the major challenge confronting us.

We attack the problem theoretically at first, struggling to understand ways in which we might concretely realize our principles in the classroom. We recall that our first objective was to reunite the senses and feeling, to restore this severed connection. Reflecting on this we remember a heated discussion the class had had endeavoring to make a decision as to how to use an upcoming class hour. They had suggested many alternatives and there seemed to be five or six major possibilities which were being vociferously argued among approximately half the class. However, after a while the discussion reached a point where they started to repeat themselves, and the decibel and pitch levels were rising. So we stopped them and asked what the quiet half of the class felt.

At this point Kevin, a talker, reminded us (with gentle humor) that the quiet students were protected by the Constitution (no less) to remain silent. He was right, but this fact didn't get us any closer to a decision either, and so we asked them how someone might tell what a person felt without using words. Peter said; "Just look at em." "But where," Bobbie teased, "at their faces, their hands, their eyes, their posture?" Someone else noted that as the discussion had degenerated into an argument, Jack (a quiet student) had gotten progressively closer to the door. "What did that mean?" Mary Jane wondered. Interpretations ranged from a lover's anxiousness, through Jack's possible inability to handle arguments, to a lack of interest on Jack's part. Bonnie asked Jack for the right answer and he merely shrugged his shoulders.

We suggested that since we were sitting in a circle and Jack's gestures were visible to every member of the class, that he was, in fact, communicating his feelings to the class. Suddenly everyone was looking at everyone else to gage where they stood on the decision. They began asking questions and probing, taking anything and everything as a message. Quickly they became aware that there were no silences, that they all felt something and it could be seen or heard. Interestingly, after this Jack became (against his will) a barometer of class feeling. Whenever he inched toward the door someone would note that apparently the subject was getting nowhere.

Recalling this experience we realize now that what we need to do in the future is to make their feelings break through this threshold of insentience into awareness—to continually help them to see how their visible gestures are communicable vehicles. We need to help them see that while Jack's gesture reveals something about the way he feels, that it can also reveal to each of us something about the way we feel, just as the fact that Mary Jane starts swinging her leg whenever the discussion picks up, reveals that we are on the right track again. And then we need to attune ourselves to the possibilities inherent in our own gestures and to connect these attenuations to language so that Jack can say (as he feels himself moving toward the door): "Hey follows, I'm bored!" Or that Mary Jane (legs swinging) can say: "Now we're getting somewhere!"

Our second elementary objective was that of self-definition and self-actualization. Here we believe decision making is the key. Every choice between alternatives, where the choice matters, further refines who we are. Thus our responsibility as teachers will be to create situations where choice is necessary and the object of choice a valuable addition to one's life. This is, perhaps, the role of art and literature in the classroom, for it is in these as Louise Rosenblatt says in

Literature as Exploration, that the student can be freed from "anachronistic emotional attitudes" by "imaginative participation in the wide variety of alternative philosophies and patterns of behavior. . . ." (275). But here Katie and Regina were quick to warn us that we must be careful not to let literature become a room with set pieces of furniture. A great deal, they stressed, depends upon the way in which we explore the ambiguities in art, and they both urged us to use art and literature to explore the creative possibilities of living (our objective # 5) as well as to expose the students to alternative philosophies.

A more natural view of failure was our third aim. The quest here is for a proper atmosphere, and once again decisions and choice play a prominent part. We realized this concretely when we played volleyball with them, for we saw then that the game was less exciting when no one kept score—that there ought to be a winner and a loser, and that failing was an integral aspect of participation. In the classroom failure most commonly manifests itself when a student makes a foolish statement. And here it is not a matter of learning how to treat the student, but how to utilize the aspect of failure in his response. This was brought pointedly home to us once when we asked Brenda to name everyone in the class and she did except that she omitted us and no one bothered to correct her. We realized then our own failure (and the greater failure of twelve years of educational conditioning) and we saw immediately how at least this one failure could lead us on to further productive insights.

We believe that this attitude toward failure is closely linked to our fourth objective of question making and problem solving. Regina reminded us of a line from e. e. cummings that she had always liked: "Always the beautiful answer who asks a more beautiful question." Now we think that maybe our function in the classroom is (1) to ask questions to which we don't have an answer, and (2) to insure that those questions are honest questions—that is, that we are really interested in the answers. We wonder privately if it wouldn't be advantageous for a while to use only literature that we have never read before (or only read once). We speculate that this might provide an atmosphere in which we could discover along with the students what genuinely and spontaneously confuses and interests us in a given work.

Finally, there was our last aim of creative behavior. Immediately we can think of a number of devices which could be used to encourage the student to think off his normal pattern. One would be to have a student defend a position or view that he doesn't believe in. Carol says that Dickens' *Hard Times* is a bad novel, and so rather than work out what she doesn't like about it, we could have her defend the proposition that it is a good novel. What is important here is the element of playing and the student's willingness to be able to play—to speculate and come up with things that are absurd, funny, or challenging, and to be willing to fail and understand the nature of his failure.

Well, these are the objectives and a few general ideas, but concretely what are we going to do with the days of the week? The classes meet Monday, Wednesday, and Friday for fifty minutes each and Katie suggests that we let each day develop a purpose of its own. So we explore that idea, like it, and decide that we will experiment with our three days.

Monday will be our art day. In it we will stress creativity and non-linear responses. Rather than let a poem mean one thing we will encourage it to mean 6½ things. Rather than ask what this abstract painting means, we'll ask: how should it be hung? We are aware however that we must always keep in mind that the art must connect personally and concretely to the students' lives. Thus, we would ask Joan: What do *you* feel about this piece of music? And then: Who feels something different? And, how many different feelings are there? That's Monday.

Wednesday will be our Board day. We think that we need one day a week generated almost entirely by the students' interests. And so on Wednesday before the class begins each person present (teachers and guests included) must write something on the board and put his initials under it. It can be anything. But it must be something (and it should be something of immediate and genuine interest to the writer). A word, a comment, an opinion, a piece of a poem, a drawing, an album cover. Anything. Then the class can go where it wants. It is a free day of discovery. For us it will be a day of listening, where we see our responsibility as that of sharpening their questions and interests and sharing with them our honest opinions.

Friday will be Court day. What we need is a book which gives us issues that require decisions. Perhaps actual court cases on important questions. What is essential is that the two distinct sides be represented, and that a vote be taken in the class at the beginning and at the end of the hour, and that during the hour the discussion consistently strive to sharpen the areas of disagreement. Ideally perhaps the students should select the problems themselves. Beyond that it is clear that at some time during the hour everyone should voice his opinion and have to make a stand.

Three days. Three aims. On Monday our desire is to spiral outward increasing possibilities, encouraging creative behavior, and striving to establish a pattern in which a number of responses are created for a problem before the choice of one response is taken. On Wednesday our endeavor is to assist them and ourselves in discovering what our real interests are—both on a short and long term basis. And on Friday we want to constantly engage them in a problem, moving inward, refining and clarifying it, all the while encouraging decision making and choice.

This then is our projected week, and with its elaboration our circle of conversation comes to an end. Besides, we are hungry again. In the afternoon all that will be left to do is to put together a tentative syllabus and then wait for the fall and the crucible in which all theories are finally tested. For the present we want a bit of fresh air and a break in the run of our lives, some laughter and perhaps a walk by the sea.

Take Two

A Syllabus for Creative Communications

Well, to begin with, this is an experimental course (we couldn't hide that from you even if we wanted to). And although it's our second time around team teaching this course, it is still experimental. What makes it so is rather simple: namely that we are going to take a journey whose destination we do not yet know. In fact, the course itself has been designed as a dual journey. With us and the class you are to take an outward journey; while with yourselves you may make a personal exploration. For your own explorations the methods of travel and the points of interest will be largely individual. This part of the course belongs to you, although we will want a copy of your Itinerary before you head out on your own. Within the classroom the journey will be a collective venture and we will all be on the same boat together. But that's for later and the fun we hope will follow.

In order to participate then in both of these journeys there are only four requirements:

1st. *Communications*:

Since we call the course: Creative Communication, we want each of you to communicate with at least one of us, Tim or Allen, at least once every week in whatever manner you want. If you are creative, you won't use the same method twice, but in any case we want to feel your presence, once a week, on fifteen occasions.

2nd. *We are to read four books*:

We will give you a list of the books and a reading schedule on a separate sheet.

3rd. *We want a copy of your Itinerary*:

We want this no later than Monday, September 30th.

Concretely, your Itinerary is: Your indication

(1) Of what you think would constitute proper and valid work for you for each of the following grades:

A, B, C, D, & F.

(2) Plus a circling of which of these grades it is your intention to work for.

You are, in essence, to select your own grade. You will hand in your Itinerary and we will either approve it or we will suggest improvements in your plans. We will never dictate to you what you are to do, but we will expect mature, college level work from you. In any case as soon as we can agree on your Itinerary the grade is in your hands and you are (as much as you want) on your own.

Now, what can be included in your Itinerary? A fair question.

Our answer: Anything can be included.

Anything?

Anything!

However, a good Itinerary should perhaps cover these five areas:

(1) Doing something you didn't want to do, like talking to your parents for fifteen minutes every day for two weeks.

(2) Doing something you haven't ever done before that you'd like to try and at which you might fail, like learning how to sky dive.

(3) Improving something you can already do, like watching TV.

(4) Learning something you need to learn, like what you want to be or how to write a research paper.

(5) Doing something wacky, like . . . well, you know, wacky!

Since, as you will discover, this is a course in problem solving, your first major problem is to get the items you want to put on your Itinerary linked somehow into a grade game plan that justifies your efforts for each of the grades from A to F, remembering that an F is not a zero but is accomplishing 50-60% of your goals.

4th. *You are not allowed to cheat.*

And this covers the requirements for the trip.

There is one other thing however. Attached to this syllabus is a sixteen page Survival Manual. It is basically concerned with reading, writing, and tests. Instead of devoting class time to these things we have attempted to put these over-emphasized items in their proper perspective by giving you their basic elements on paper. If, after reading the manual, you still feel that you are weak in reading, insecure in tests, or if you are unsure about writing something: a poem, a play, formal paper, lab report, book review, research paper, business letter, or whatever, then that ought to be a part of your Itinerary for this semester—to learn or make sure you know you know.

Our theory is that unless we hear from you otherwise, we assume you know and if you don't and let this semester slip by without learning then you'll only shipwreck yourself later. We are not trying to be mercenary in this, just adult and practical. We can and will teach you (in terms of writing) what you want and/or need to learn, but we are not going to tell you what you need to learn. That's up to you, although we will be glad to help you discover what your blind spots are if you want us to.

And one last note: We will not read anything you write for spelling, punctuation, or grammatical errors or mistakes unless you specifically request us to play "English Teacher." We basically could care less about those unless they stand in the way of a real understanding of what it is you are trying to communicate. So, write freely and write only what you want. It makes the best reading.

And finally, our second last note: Although it may seem contradictory after all of the above reminders, we want you to enjoy this course and your Itinerary. The reason we foggy intellectuals give you independent work to do is because we have an undying hope that you will teach yourself something. Despite your overwhelming feeling to the contrary, college is a personal love affair with ideas and feelings. As with any love affair, sometimes you yell a lot, sometimes you are lethargic, sometimes you are joyous. Believe it or not, any experiences you have this semester should articulate that feeling. And that feeling, happy or not, should be rewarding.

Coda

I have set sail from a leaking ship
in a gale off Cape Horn.

Herman Melville

We stare out over the sea. The week is over. The ferry turns on the waves towards Woods Hole, and we stand on the stern, the four of us watching our island vanish into the fog. It has been a good week. The empty bottles we leave are a testament to that as is the feeling we have that for the first time in a long while we are approaching an understanding of our students, and that nearing that coast we now have an active plan for closing the distance between our worlds. At least we are ready to begin again. On the boat a soft rain falls. A wind bellows. From the island the fog horn pulls once, long and deep throated across the sound. And for the first time, from this deck on the passage back home, we are reminded of Melville and of his ship that also set sail from here, and in a fit of humor we wonder, one to another, about our fate and what the future, like the fog, might hide. And just to be safe we each tap our legs just once to make sure.

R. C. TOWNSEND

The Possibilities of Field Work

WHEREAS ENGLISH TEACHERS could be doing a great deal of important teaching and learning *in the field*, so far as I can tell we are doing practically none. In our efforts to bolster the Humanities, to reach new student constituencies, or to retrieve those we used to be able to count on, at an NCTE conference, say, there will be discussion of experiments with new books, new issues, new materials, new dialects, but the assumption seems to be that all the while we remain in the classroom. There we talk, we write, maybe we view or role play; on our own, we try to keep up with the literature. That is how we work "in our field"—and we never take the metaphor seriously. It is for others, primarily social scientists, to bring the metaphor alive, to test out and give expression to ideas and feelings as they exist in the actual world.

The present essay is a reflection on the possibilities of field work in English—on what doing field work in English might mean and on what works can provide guidance or inspiration to anyone who

sees meaning in the idea of doing field work in English. It is also a report on the kind of course one might give—or at least on the kinds of specific activities one might engage in in a course involving field work. The course is one I gave last term on small town literature, one in which we read five or six books relating to small towns and wrote one of our own.

1

The aims of a course involving field work are those that Whitehead spoke of in *The Aims of Education*:

The insistence in the Platonic culture on disinterested intellectual appreciation is a psychological error. Action and our implication in the transition of events amid the inevitable bond of cause to effect are fundamental. An education which strives to divorce intellectual or aesthetic life from these fundamental facts carries with it the decadence of civilization. Essentially culture should be for action, and its effect should be to divest labour from the associations of aimless toil. Art exists that

Reprinted from *College English*, Vol. 34, No. 4, January 1973.

we may know the deliverances of our senses are good. It heightens the sense-world.

Disinterested scientific curiosity is a passion for an ordered intellectual vision of the connection of events. But the goal of such curiosity is the marriage of action to thought. This essential intervention of action even in abstract science is often overlooked. No man of science wants merely to know. He acquires knowledge to appease his passion for discovery. He does not discover in order to know, he knows in order to discover. . . .

First-hand knowledge is the ultimate basis of intellectual life. To a large extent book-learning conveys second-hand information, and as such can never rise to the importance of immediate practice. Our goal is to see the immediate events of our lives as instances of our general ideas. What the learned world tends to offer is one second-hand scrap of information illustrating ideas derived from another second-hand scrap of information. The second-handedness of the learned world is the secret of its mediocrity. It is tame because it has never been scared by facts.[1]

No educator is willing to admit to striving for decadence; all of us can so define our practices in the classroom and in our research as to make it clear that we, at least, are striving to marry action and theory. And of course in general most of us are. Scientists and social scientists, either in the lab or on trips into field, are trying to ground learning in first-hand knowledge. The humanists' passion, like theirs, may be a passion for discovery and no mere grubbing after knowledge. I do not cite Whitehead in order to surround myself with straw men. We all share his aims. I lay special claim for his support only in that I have taken him literally: I have tried to set up a situation in which a student of English may, like a student of chemistry or social relations, benefit from first-hand knowledge.

That has usually seemed either impossible or undesirable:

> Literature as a whole is independent of real experience [Northrop Frye writes] and something distinct from the passing of belief into action. Literature is a body of hypothetical thought and action: it makes, as literature, no statements or assertions. It neither reflects nor escapes from the world of belief and action, but contains it in its own distinctive form. It is this independence from real experience which the term "imagination" expresses, a term which includes both intellect and emotion, and yet is different from actual truth or real feelings. When we meet an unfamiliar experience in literature, the relevant question is not, is this true? but, is it imaginatively conceivable? If not, there is still a chance that our notion of what is imaginatively conceivable needs expanding. Literature thus provides a kind of reservoir of possibilities of action. It gives us wider sympathies and greater tolerance, and new perspectives on action; it increases the power of articulating convictions, whether our own or those of others.[2]

In English courses we literally move from book to book to book; that is the way assignments and discussions usually evolve, and insofar as we set up courses based on generic or historical or formal considerations, we tend to conceive of literature as self-contained, self-reflective—"as a whole," "as a body." But there is nothing mediocre about our subject or our task, we say, because our perceptions of the world are heightened through books and somehow (it is never clear how) our powers of expression are increased—though here we have to be tentative, speak haltingly, as Frye does: "Literature thus provides a kind of reservoir of possibilities of action."

---

[1] (New York: Macmillan, 1929), pp. 73-74, 79.

[2] *The Well-Tempered Critic* (Bloomington: Indiana Univ. Press, 1963), pp. 149-50.

But imagine moving *to* and not *from* the texts we assign in an English class. "Literature," Dewey wrote, "is the reflex expression and interpretation of social experience; . . . hence it must follow upon and not precede such experience. It, therefore, cannot be made the basis, although it may be made the summary of unification."[3] Ideally, a reader is continually conscious of the experiences being expressed and interpreted in writings, and anyone engaged in activities more social than reading is the more conscious and the more sensitive, maybe even the more humane, because his perceptions have been heightened by other men's imaginings. And ultimately it will not do to think of experiencing and then going off to read about what one has experienced, as Dewey seems to advocate. The process is never that simple. But it *is* a simple truth that one is in a better position to appreciate a work after some experience of what it is about. I taught *The Scarlet Letter* to a class that included a vocal preacher and an equally vocal woman who was bringing up her children alone and it was clear that the book meant more to them than to students for whom careers and the complexities of married and unmarried life are only possibilities. A rare occurrence, but still you may be more likely to create the desired interaction between books and "real" or extraliterary experience if you can find some way to engage students in social situations that you will want them to read or write about. We often bear in mind the experiences we think students have or should have had when we assign books and writings; we could be even more conscious and deliberate in our effort to start from experience. Stated this way the

problem is unnervingly, embarrassingly, simple. On the elementary level they bring in "real experience" in show and tell exercises; at the school and college levels the solution is only slightly more sophisticated.

How do you do this? It is true that you cannot set up an adulterous relationship for study, nor can you provide God's first born or stage a war or count on a country boy to tell of the development of his mind. Nor can you expect students to write classics before the term is over. Those you read, and you assign critical papers on them, hoping students will gain new perspectives, wider sympathies, and increased powers of articulation—"a kind of reservoir of possibilities" there. But there are other facts surrounding students and the institutions they attend. Experimenting with them can make their reading more immediate, their writing better.

I chose the town of Amherst itself. Not sure how the experiment would work, I picked an area of experience that I knew would provide a limitless number of options. I was sure of the importance of the subject, of the role that towns had played in the social and psychic life of Americans, and I was sure that there was more than enough reading to choose from. In ways that I shall describe in more detail below, students made contact with the town, gained some first-hand knowledge of "constituencies" in the town. They met with people, interviewed them, occasionally worked for them, and gradually came to know something about what it is like to live in a community that was at least a small town not long ago. (Amherst's population has doubled in the last ten years because of the expansion of the University of Massachusetts; as it turned out our subject was not so much "The Small Town" as "Amherst and the Small Town Myth" or "Coping with Change

---

[3]"My Pedagogic Creed," in *John Dewey on Education*, ed. Reginald D. Archambault (New York: Modern Library, 1964), p. 433.

in America.") I chose the town as a whole but one might choose among the constituencies themselves, among such groups as the elderly, the black population, the business community, or the street people; among institutions and associations such as churches, schools, the Grange, liberationists' organizations, or the police; among the media that interpret these areas of experience. Next year the course will deal primarily with the elderly, recording and creating their memories of Amherst when it really was a small town and their responses to its changes. Mark Twain said that "Human nature cannot be studied in cities except at a disadvantage—a village is the place,"[4] but the same and many more constituencies obviously now exist in urban areas. Field work as I conceive of it, though, does not mean simply going out and observing or participating in the lives of such groups; unfortunately we may learn very little from unmediated experience. The contact has to be coupled with, enlivened by, and it must challenge the renditions of those areas of experience as they exist in writing. To take the most obvious example, students will read *Winesburg, Ohio,* or Ronald Blythe's *Akenfield,* or Anthony Bailey's *In the Village,* after stints in the field and, perhaps most importantly, they will be writing up their experiences all the time. Their reading is put to the test of what they are concurrently discovering, their perceptions goaded by what others have reported and imagined. Out of the interaction comes writing that is different from a critcial paper on *Paradise Lost* on the one hand and an exercise in "creative writing" on the other. It is based on personal experience but it contends

against the writing of others who have to some degree shared that experience, and, as I will try to demonstrate at the end, the results can compare with books that might otherwise too easily acquire the status of final authority.

"Our goal," as Whitehead said, "is to see the immediate events of our lives as instances of our general ideas," and that is literally and easily done in a course such as Small Town Literature. What Vidich and Bensman say about the relation between small town politics and politics at the national level in *Small Town in Mass Society* was dramatized for the student working with the Town Planning Board's Project Review Subcommittee; what any number of writers, from William Allen White or Mary Russell Mitford or Anthony Bailey on the one hand to E. W. Howe or Sherwood Anderson or Sinclair Lewis on the other, have to say about the virtues and shortcomings of small town life, can be tested daily; what James Agee says in *Let Us Now Praise Famous Men* about the responsibility yet the impossibility of a writer's doing justice to the sanctity of another human being is brought home to students every time they attempt to write about their experiences in the field. The barriers between the classroom and the outside world do not come down, but there is more traffic. If students (and teachers) are impatient with the abstractions of the academic world, field work affords some relief. Through field work, life outside and a student's inner life may inform his study, his intellectual life—or so it sounds when one turns to an encouraging student evaluation of the course: "I am beginning to see my way a little more clearly. I am beginning to examine more closely the nature of community study and the relationship between human lives, my own subjective feelings, and the

---

[4]Quoted in Page Smith, *As A City Upon a Hill: The Town in American History* (New York: Alfred A. Knopf, 1966), p. 262.

words that attempt to express those lives and feelings as truly as possible for all involved."

2

Doing field work in English, then, means going out to confront the experiences the books you might read are about, hoping thereby to understand more and write more intelligently about both the books and the experiences.

In setting out to do field work, there are countless models which one might choose. Working in the general area of community studies the most obvious models are likely to be sociological or anthropological, but there are literary and unclassifiable examples that I found equally helpful. If one were to set about working within the black community, literary and particularly autobiographical works might prove more obviously and immediately helpful; with churches you might soon rely on sociological studies. But whatever the area, one cannot afford to be very squeamish or strict about the lines that separate the various disciplines.

Classic sociological studies, or sections of them, like Vidich and Bensman's book, the Lynds' *Middletown*, Dollard's *Caste and Class in a Southern Town*, or White's *Street Corner Society*, may prove helpful to students working on particular problems, but none provided the appropriate model for the kind of writing my students did. The only study made by a class that I know of, that on Chanceaux by Lawrence Wylie's students at Harvard,[5] is primarily sociological in character. But we were not working up, conducting and interpreting surveys or questionnaires, and we never sought to be more than impressionistic about the

class or occupational structure of the town of Amherst. We were less objective than that. On the other hand we were not going to reduce *Huckleberry Finn, Middlemarch,* or *The Scarlet Letter* to books about small communities in an effort to be respectably literary, nor could we take lesser works like *Our Town* or *Winesburg, Ohio* as models for our own writing. We were more objective than that for the simple reason that our primary materials were people as they existed in the real world and not as they were created by the fictive imagination. If artistic truth was to be present in anything we wrote, it was to be there because the potential for it had first been discovered in the field. For inspiration we would cite Agee's remarks on photography: "The artist's task is not to alter the world as the eye sees it into a world of aesthetic reality, but to perceive the aesthetic reality within the actual world, and to make an undisturbed and faithful record of the instant in which this movement of creativeness achieves its most expressive crystallization."[6]

No amount of defensive criticism of social scientists' occasional jaw-breaking terminology or labyrinthine methodologies should obscure the fact that the reality of which Agee speaks may be as likely to exist in their writings as in anyone else's. Indeed, as early as 1954, on one famous occasion (a review of David Reisman's work) Lionel Trilling was led to wonder if in some respects the sociologists hadn't already taken over:

> In writing about *The Lonely Crowd* I spoke of the jealousy of the social sciences which is likely to be felt by people of literary inclination—they are troubled because the social sciences seem to be

---

[5]*Chanceaux: A Village in Anjou* (Cambridge: Harvard Univ. Press, 1966).

[6]*A Way of Seeing: Photographs of New York by Helen Levitt with an Essay by James Agee* (New York: Viking, 1965), p. 4.

expropriating literature from one of its most characteristic functions, the investigation of manners and morals. This jealousy I myself experienced intensely as I read *Individualism Reconsidered.* No American novel of recent years has been able to give me the sense of the actuality of our society that I get from Mr. Reisman's book, nor has any novel been able to suggest, as these essays so brilliantly do, the excitement of contemplating our life in culture as an opportunity and a danger.[7]

For our purposes, a certain kind of sociological work was particularly suggestive. It was the kind in which the investigation of manners and morals came about as a result of an author's ability to let his materials break the mould of his well-prepared experiments and hypotheses, of his well-defined terms, in order that they might find their own truth. Thus William Whythe's "Reflections on Field Research" were encouraging: "It was a long time before I realized that I could explain Cornerville better through telling the stories of those individuals and groups than I could in any other way. Instead of studying the general characteristics of classes of people, I was looking at Doc, Chick, Tony Cataldo, George, Ravello, and others. Instead of getting a cross-sectional picture of the community at a particular point in time, I was dealing with a sequence of interpersonal events. . . . I was seeking to build a sociology based upon observed interpersonal events. That, to me, is the chief methodological and theoretical meaning of *Street Corner Society.*"[8] The citizens of Vandalia, Ohio tell more of their own study in Joseph Lyford's *The Talk in Vandalia: The Life of an American Town* than do the boys

in Cornerville, the residents of Watts more than either in Paul Bullock's *Watts: The Aftermath.* In Oscar Lewis' most characteristic work there is nothing but the transcriptions of his subjects' talk. At the heart of Robert Coles' work is that talk reshaped, recreated, so as to give a reader as great or a greater sense of the human situation in which his subjects find themselves than might be possible in the languages of social scientists. "So many reporters mistake social-science metaphor for facts," Albert Murray writes

. . .without realizing that even the most precise concepts are only nets that cannot hold very much flesh-and-blood experience. Whereas the most pragmatic thing about *poetic* metaphor is that you know very well that your net cannot trap all of the experience in question. Indeed, you often feel that maybe most of it has eluded you. . . . You readily concede that formulations generalized from scientific-research findings may be nets with a closer weave, still not only do they remain nets, but at best they trap even smaller areas of experience than literary configurations, expressly because they are necessarily in a narrower weave.[9]

It was interesting to note, too, that as artists such as Agee in *Let Us Now Praise Famous Men* or Orwell in *Down and Out in London and Paris* and *Wigan Pier* or Mailer in *Miami and the Siege of Chicago* rendered actual social situations in terms that could impress the social scientists, social scientists in turn were making use of artistic forms. A recent book by Lynn Eden, *Crisis in Watertown: The Polarization of an American Community,*[10] for example, reads, as we say, like a novel. It is a "story" of the firing of a minister in a Wisconsin town

[7]*A Gathering of Fugitives* (Boston: Beacon Press, 1956), p. 92.
[8]*Street Corner Society* (Chicago: Univ. of Chicago Press, Sec. Ed., 1955), pp. 357-58.
[9]*South to a Very Old Place* (New York: McGraw-Hill Co., 1971), pp. 59-60.
[10](Ann Arbor: Univ. of Michigan Press, 1972).

for marching with Father Groppi and generally alienating a conservative town, and it is told primarily in the words of the participants in the "drama." Ms. Eden appears like the narrator. It is clear where her sympathies lie, but the burden of response is the reader's: he does not stand on territory carefully limited and marked by sociological terminology; he must respond to a situation in its psychological, historical, political—in all its dimensions. From a medium where the lines between art and sociology are even more blurred, one thinks of Marcel Ophul's *The Sorrow and the Pity: Chronicle of a Town During the Occupation,* an extraordinary film made up almost entirely of contemporary documentaries and the talk of the people who lived in and occupied a town in the Auvergne region during World War II.[11]

One stumbles around a bit in the dark area that lies between literary and sociological studies. There is not much company and those who have ventured out have done so at the risk of being criticized for being wayward and undisciplined, Oscar Lewis for taking liberties with his materials, Robert Coles for not being scientifically (or politically) sound enough. But I sense that sociologists are discovering the advantages of more lit-

erary approaches to social situations— or that there have been "literary sociologists" since Cobbett, since Mayhew— and I know that English teachers can (like Trilling almost twenty years ago) get help from sociologists in examining the human situations that have always been their central concern. Sociologists too can help train readers and writers. Their works can also demand imaginative readings, even to the point where a reader has to be as creative, be as sensitive to the relations between himself and the world outside himself, as he must be in the presence of voices on a stage. "You feel him to be a poet, inasmuch as, for a time, he has made you one—an active creative being,"[12] Coleridge said of Shakespeare. Reading Lewis or Coles, or watching and hearing Mendes-France or a farmer in Clermont-Ferrand in *The Sorrow and the Pity,* you have to create truths which formerly did not exist and which exist only so long as you imagine them. It is the task of a reader of actual as well as of fictional events.

The conjunction of the aesthetic and the actual is even more challenging and illuminating to the writer, and my primary purpose in speaking of these relatively unclassifiable works has been to suggest the variety of them that are available as models to anyone who is trying to introduce field work into the English classroom. A student doing field work sets out to discover truths in the actual world, and in the process he may discover new truths about himself. A momentous task, it seems, but he has support in knowing about writers like Agee and Orwell, like Whyte and Lewis and Coles.

To our class no book was more helpful than Ronald Blythe's *Akenfield: Por-*

---

[11]Nor, of course, is the interaction merely formal. See Clifford Geertz, "The Balinese Cockfight," *Daedalus,* Vol. 101 (Winter, 1972), pp. 1-37, in which Geertz sees cockfighting not as a rite or a pastime but as a text in which one can read what a Balinese's "culture's ethos and his private sensibility (or, anyway, certain aspects of them) look like when spelled out externally." Thus the anthropologist too must "engage in a bit of metaphorical refocussing of [his] own, for it shifts the analysis of cultural forms from an endeavor in general parallel to dissecting an organism, diagnosing a symptom, deciphering a code, or ordering a system—the dominant analogies in contemporary anthropology—to one in general parallel with penetrating a literary text." (p. 26)

[12]*Shakespearean Criticism,* ed. Thomas Middleton Rayser (London: Everyman Edition, 1960), II, 65.

trait of an English Village,[13] and no voice was more helpful than Blythe's in describing how the class ought to proceed in its study of the town of Amherst. *Akenfield* is a book about a small East Anglian village (pop. 298). It contains a great deal of historical data; introductory sections tell of the residences, occupations and even crop yields of its inhabitants' fields. A prefatory bibliographical note lists such books as E. Morris, *History and Art of Change-Ringing* (1931), C. D. Harris, Geography of the Ipswich-Orford Area (Unpublished thesis), and W. M. Williams, *The Sociology of an English Village* (1956), but essentially the books is, in Blythe's words, "the quest for the voice of Akenfield, Suffolk, as it sounded during the summer and autumn of 1967,"[14] and most of its pages are devoted to recordings, transcriptions, recreations, perhaps inventions, of the talk of the people who live there. It is and it is not history; it is and it is not sociology; it is undoubtedly a literary performance, demanding of a reader as much creative activity, as much responsiveness to psychological and linguistic subtlety as one expects to exert in reading a novel or watching a play.

Blythe begins by sounding some of the themes that will emerge in more complex form from the voices of the villagers. He speaks of the elemental quality of the growers' life in the village and, by contrast, of the younger generation's desire to escape to Norwich by motorbike on the weekends or perhaps forever, and of the new residents' hopes of immersing themselves in a village life that has no existence other than on British travel posters. His "Introduction" ends not with a formulation of city-village dichotomies

or definitions of the new pastoralism but with Davie, a character Hardy could have used:

> The village fool? So obviously and completely not. Some slight imbalance, some occasional fall due to "nerves," as all illnesses beyond the immediately identifiable and accidents are called in Akenfield, might have placed him—might have enrolled him in the tolerated company of the "touched." Yet the one certain thing about Davie is his crushing sanity. His isolation is due, maybe, to some snapping of the communication links between his world and ours. Scraps of old farming practice can be dragged out of him—nothing special. Twenty men and boys scythed the corn and sang as they went.
> "What was the song, Davie?"
> "Never you mind the song—it was the singing that counted."

After that Blythe is content to introduce his speakers and let them do the talking.

The book is divided into twenty sections, beginning with "The Survivors" (five village elders, of whom one "had often talked with men who knew the Suffolk farmers of the eighteenth century") and ending with "In the Hour of Death," a gravedigger:

> And there was this old lady at Wickham Market and she was in three different coffins. They called her Cheat-the-grave at last. All these things happened because people will insist on checking on death with a mirror, which isn't a mite of good. The only way is to stick a shred of cotton-wool where the lips part and if there's the least little wind of life it will flutter. I can always tell if a person is dead by looking at the eyes. I never make a mistake about dead eyes. I see at once when the seeing is gone.
> Village folk have been buried over and over again in the same little bits of churchyard. You have to throw somebody out to get somebody in—three or four sometimes. I always put all the bones back so that they lie tidy-like just under the new person. They're soon all one. The parson

---

[13] (New York: Pantheon Books, 1969).
[14] Ibid., p. 18.

said to me, "How is it that you get so many in one grave?" and I always tell him that I must have disturbed a plague pit. Parsons will believe anything.

In between are such "constituencies" as people connected in one way or another with religion, "The Ringing Men" (the local bell-ringers), "The School," "The Orchard Men," "The Law," and, it seems, the only fool in Akenfield, the poet:

> After Oxford, I worked in London where I wrote a poetry of despair. It was a continuous cry for what I had lost, for the hills and fields, and the vixen wood, with the dog-fox barking at night. I imagined myself dying inside and so I came to this village to find my health. My wholeness. That is what I am here. It was not my village but to say that I had returned to it seemed a true way of describing what had happened to me. Suffolk amazed me—the great trees, the towering old buildings soaring out of the corn. The huge clear spaces.
>
> I am now at home here. I know everybody and everybody knows me. Words have meaning for me here. I am lucky, I came here to get better but I have in fact been re-born. I have escaped into reality. There are no nameless faces; I am identified and I identify. All is seen.

Each section, often each individual, is introduced by Blythe, but to the full force of every monologue and of the combination of all forty-nine, each reader must respond in his own way. (Perhaps to some the poet is a veritable phoenix!) Just as the Ricketts, the Gudgers, and the Woods in Agee's *Let Us Now Praise Famous Men* represent the life of the sharecropper to many of us, those who speak in *Akenfield* give us the history, the psychology, the sociology, the very life of the English village in our time. We are dealing in these books with poetic as well as social sci-

ence metaphor. There is always the possibility that the world is depicted as all lies, but it seems to me that in these instances the loose weave captures—mirrors—more about human nature rather than less.

In answer to the question, How do you go about making such a study?, the answer seems to be that you have to go out into the community as much as possible, know about it and yourself in relation to it, and write the best sentences you can. I asked Blythe but I never did find out what interview techniques he used, what questions he asked, or how much he edited or otherwise recreated his interviews.

> I am not a trained sociologist [he wrote instead]. I suppose I am a kind of historian-cum-poet-cum-literary critic! I didn't come to Akenfield, I have been there for centuries. Not in the actual village upon which I based my book but from the same culture. The people in the book were saying things which I had known all my life.
>
> If I had to give anyone advice on how to set about understanding or studying a small community I would tell them that there are two main paths to the interior. If that is your own community, then you must reach and identify its heart through your own experience. If it is somebody else's community, then you will never understand it if you reduce it entirely to facts and figures. The secret lies in your sentence in which you say you would like to "put together some *writing* on the small town. . . ." There are population tables, work patterns, health stats, education developments, climate and a thousand other skeletal supports to the life in a particular place, then comes an interpretation of the life itself. The latter—for me —is what really matters. One needs a real language for this. An ability to state what one feels to be the truth.[15]

---

[15]Personal correspondence, November 16, 1971.

3.

Turning now to the course itself, I had eighteen students and two auditors,[16] one of whom was on Independent Study and doing what turned out to be publishable work (in the Agee-Blythe vein) on the church communities in nearby Hadley. We met once a week, in the evening. I made my intentions as clear as I could at the outset. Somehow we are going to study the small town not just by reading about it but by putting together a book of writings that would be the result of our own contact with Amherst. And I started the course not with Blythe but with Agee.

I suspected (and evaluations confirmed my suspicion) that there was no specific way that I could prepare them for their contact with their constituencies. They had to go out and make contact and they had to make their own mistakes. To ease my conscience I handed out pieces on "Establishing Field Relations,"[17] on "Field Tactics,"[18] and on "Field Work Evidence,"[19] but if any reading had any effect on students' attitudes toward going out of a classroom and meeting people it was *Let Us Now Praise Famous Men.*

If anything, Agee is too good for these purposes. Given the caution, the reticence, the protectiveness with which our culture arms us against Other People, and given the schools' endorsement of the idea that learning characteristically takes place inside the classroom, in relative passivity and silence, the idea of going out and initiating talk with strangers creates enough fear as it is. (The fear probably is especially great at a privileged institution like Amherst, for as Irving Goffman says: "The higher one's place in the status pyramid, the smaller the number of persons with whom one can be familiar . . . and the more likely it is that one will be required to be polite as well as decorous.")[20] Agee only intensifies the problem by reminding you that to undergo the task is a sacred act and that ultimately it is impossible.

In his preface Agee defines his intentions and, with the word "divinity," prepares us for defeat:

> The nominal subject is North American cotton tenantry as examined in the daily living of three representative white tenant families.
> Actually, the effort is to recognize the stature of a portion of unimagined existence, and to contrive techniques proper to its recording, communication, analysis, and defense. More essentially, this is an independent inquiry into certain normal predicaments of human divinity.

His hope is to be able to bring us into the world he explored with Walker Evans, to make a reader an "active creative being":

> This is a *book* only by necessity, more seriously, it is an effort in human actuality, in which the reader is no less centrally involved than the authors and those of whom they tell . . .[21]

but he does not go far before he turns

---

[16]My colleague, Leo Marx, sat in regularly. His suggestions were invaluable.
[17]John P. Dean, Robert L. Eickhorn, and Lois R. Dean, "Establishing Field Relations," in George J. McCall and J. L. Simmons, *Issues in Participant Observation* (Reading, Mass.: Addison-Wesley, 1969), pp. 68-70.
[18]Anselm Strauss et al., "Field Tactics," in Ibid., pp. 70-76.
[19]Howard S. Becker, "Field Work Evidence," in *Sociological Work* (Chicago: Aldine, 1970), pp. 39-62.

[20]*The Presentation of Self in Everyday Life* (New York: Doubleday Anchor Books, 1959), p. 133.
[21](New York: Ballantine, 1966), pp. xiv-xv.

on the act of writing itself. He will hold out some hope for photography (as elsewhere, like the great romantic he is, he will aspire after musical effects), but in doing so he only brings further home the fact that the gaps between him and the tenant families, between his language and his Alabama experience, and between readers and that experience are ultimately unbridgeable:

> If I could do it, I'd do no writing at all here. It would be photographs; the rest would be fragments of cloth, bits of cotton, lumps of earth, records of speech, pieces of wood and iron, phials of odors, plates of food and of excrement. Booksellers would consider it quite a novelty; critics would murmur, yes, but is it art; and I could trust a majority of you to use it as you would a parlor game.
>
> A piece of the body torn out by the roots might be more to the point.
>
> As it is, though, I'll do what little I can in writing. Only it will be very little. I'm not capable of it; and if I were, you would not go near it at all. For if you did, you would hardly bear to live.[22]

Agee's doubts about the efficiency of his prose, his efforts to inventory every board of a tenant shack, every article of clothing, every sound ("The most I can do—the most I can hope to do—is to make a number of physical entities as plain and vivid as possible, and to make a few guesses, a few conjectures; and to leave to you much of the burden of realizing in each of them what I have wanted to make clear of them as a whole"),[23] these are familiar enough to readers of Agee, and they may not be to everyone's taste. Some may murmur, "but is it art?"; more legitimately some will say they do not like being told they could not stand up to the kind of experience Agee had or do not need to be

told that art is not life. To students, the reminder that in using language they are entering a complex relationship with the world is salutary, but perhaps Agee tends to defeat one at the start.

But what justifies Agee's presence in the course (in any course, really) is the attitude he brings to his work and engenders in students in their work. "The difficult task of knowing another soul is not for young gentlemen whose consciousness is chiefly made up of their own wishes,"[24] George Eliot says of Fred Vincy. No writer knows the difficulties better than Agee; none tries more consciously to overcome them. *Let Us Now Praise Famous Men* is finally not an inquiry into or a dramatization of the inner lives of other people—again, he is too romantic for that— but like other great romantic works his is a celebration, a religious recognition, of the fact that other human beings exist outside his wishes, his imaginings, and his language. One miraculous communication seems to occur, that between Agee and Emma Woods before she goes off to marry, but otherwise there is only prodigious and awed effort:

> For one who sets himself to look at all earnestly, at all in purpose toward truth, into the living eyes of a human life: what is it he there beholds that so freezes and abashes his ambitious heart? What is it, profound behind the outward windows of each one of you, beneath touch even of your own suspecting, drawing tightly back at bay against the backward wall and blackness of its prison cave, so that the eyes alone shine of their own angry glory, but the eyes of a trapped wild animal, or of a furious angel nailed to the ground by his wings, or however else one may faintly designate the human "soul" . . . how, looking thus into your eyes and

---

[22]Ibid., pp. 12-13.
[23]Ibid., p. 101.

[24]*Middlemarch* (Boston: Riverside Ed., 1956), p. 89.

seeing thus, how each of you is a creature which has never in all time existed before and which shall never in all time exist again and which is not quite like any other and which has the grand stature and natural warmth of every other and whose existence is all measured upon a still mad and incurable time; how am I to speak of you as "tenant" "farmers," as "representatives" of your "class," as social integers in a criminal economy, or as individuals, fathers, wives, sons, daughters, and as my friends and as I "know" you? Granted—more, insisted upon—that it is in all these particularities that each of you is that which he is; that particularities, and matters ordinary and obvious, are exactly themselves beyond designation of words, are the members of your sum total most obligatory to human searching of perception: nevertheless to name these things and fail to yield their stature, meaning, power of hurt, seems impious, seems criminal, seems impudent, seems traitorous in the deepest: and to do less badly seems impossible: and yet in withholdings of specification I could but betray you still worse.[25]

That, one might say, is an even heavier burden to put upon students, but it is one that students should learn to bear. "As far as humanistic concerns go," Herbert Muller writes, "the knowledge that teachers impart matters less than the attitudes they induce."[26] And is it too much to imagine students learning to be serious about the miracle of living persons, about existence beyond their own wishes, and about how language creates and destroys relationships with others? What Agee is trying to do—to understand, sympathize with, express the feelings and thoughts of others— is what we hope will come from readings of works of the literary imagination; it was even more clearly and explicitly an aim

of the field work activities I had set up. So though Agee can discourage students, though it is hard to confront and interview living persons after having successfully confronted only books in courses over a period of years, and though no one can every really be sure how successful he is at shaping attitudes, we set out from Agee, ideally with his sense of the importance of the undertaking.

Agee was the main text on "field work methodology," but there were also, besides the pieces I have mentioned, selections from Mayhew and from Robert Coles' work—examples of the kinds of responses possible after meetings with living persons in the field. Then the students made contact. Two worked with the farmers in town (one literally, getting up at four to milk), and though working in teams has its benefits (moral support, sharing of leads, information, impressions) everyone else worked alone—with the police, with doctors, with ministers, with the elderly, with a town subcommittee, with the Valley Peace Center, with students and coaches at the High School. In two cases I made the initial contact, a phone call, for a student, but generally it was their problem. It did not take us long to realize that Amherst was not a small town, but these constituencies were themselves like small towns—each had its own particular focus and identity, each created for those within it some sense of identity and community. The choice of constituencies was fairly random (many remain for study in future years), but our assumption was that the nature and problems of the town were reflected to some degree in every individual and group that went to make it up.

As it turned out, one problem emerged as central. That was the prob-

[25]*Let Us Now Praise Famous Men*, pp. 91-92.
[26]"The 'Relevance' of the Humanities," *The American Scholar*, Vol. 40 (Winter, 1970-71), p. 107.

lem of precipitous growth, more specifically the problems attending the possible development of six hundred acres by one developer over a five-year period, bringing four thousand new residents into a town still reeling from having doubled in size in a decade. The plans had been released on the town the previous spring, the arguments over its merits were in full swing by the time the course began. A citizen's group was formed to study growth and, more specifically, to stop the developers, special town meetings were called, letters to the editor of the town newspaper became required and lively reading. Every constituent had some opinion about the development and several of the most interesting constituencies existed because of it: I had students working with the developers themselves, with the Amherst Growth Study Committee, with scientists in town who might have been said to have had some opinion about the ecological issues raised by the development, and with a fragile but stalwart town committee empowered to review projected developments in town.

We could have shaped the entire course around this "event." Ms. Eden's *Crisis in Watertown* is based on an "event," and one can imagine many students having worked on her project, working with individual citizens, with the Mayor, with the minister, touching all the bases she touched. There is also the model of Edgar Morin's *Rumor in Orleans*, a study (a history, a dramatic and imaginative account) of a rumor of a white slave trade run by Jewish boutique owners, undertaken by a small team of sociologists under Morin.[27] Assuming one wants to study events outside the academy itself (not to is to reduce the possibilities of encountering "otherness" considerably), large events may be rare in certain settings, and timing is sure to be difficult, but the number of small events or happenings that may become large is limited only by the imaginations of a class. Certainly we might have shaped our writing around the coming of Tony Patterson Associates to a fairly small town tucked away in the hills of the Connecticut Valley; only my excessive caution prevented our doing so.

Instead, the students went out to discover—generally—what it was like living in a growing town. At first I made writing assignments that were no more specific than "five pages." I was simply asking What are you finding? How do people sound? How can you get their voices across in your writing? Some established relationships in which it was possible to use tape recorders, but everyone developed the ability to hear and to transcribe with imaginative faithfulness whether they used a recorder or not. Theirs was Robert Coles' job: "to bring alive to the extent [they] possibly [could] a number of lives, and especially to bring alive the 'innerness' in those lives," and as is the case in Coles' writing, "the words, then, belong to the people [they] met and heard use them; but the order of the words, of whole sentences and paragraphs and days and days and days of conversation has definitely been [their] doing."[28] In our evening meetings we would discuss examples of the writing, seeing what justice we had done, what "innerness" had been ex-

---

[27]On the potentials of this method, and on Morin generally, see Benjamin DeMott, "The One Right Way to Write and Think?" *The American Scholar*, Vol. 42 (Winter, 1971-72) pp. 53-62.

[28]*Migrants, Sharecroppers, Mountaineers: Volume II of Children of Crisis* (Boston: Little, Brown, 1972), p. 39.

plored, what issues had been raised.

I tried to maintain the right rhythm, establish the right amount of tension, between readings and field work: read Agee one week, write on your field experiences the next, read Blythe, write two pages from the field, read Bailey, write three. Early on it became evident that *Akenfield* would be the model for our collection and one student projected an outline that we stuck to fairly well: we would begin, like Blythe, with the "Survivors," move to those who best knew the land ("The Farmers"), then to those who were trying radically to alter and those who were trying to maintain the shape of the landscape, and finally see how (if at all) that issue was reflected in the changing character of the clergy, the police, the schools, and other constituencies. Towards the end of the term, as the focus on the "Patterson issue" sharpened, we had Patterson and his business manager speak to us one night, and his most fervent opponent, the head of the Amherst Growth Study Committee, another.

Amherst's drama came alive in the classroom, but we did not lose sight of its representative force, its bearing on larger questions about the small town in America. What are its virtues? what does it lack? does it really foster a sense of community? and if so of what sort (here, we read Richard Sennett's *The Use of Disorder*)[29]? do people share beliefs and feelings in small towns (or in what Sennett calls "purified communities") or do they come together merely to protect their comforts and their privacy in a time of crisis? what are the relations between newcomers and old-timers? between those whose interests extend beyond the immediate community

(the professorial set in this case) and those whose lives were more tightly bound to the town (the farmers, the real estate men)? how does an American town compare to an English one on these and other bases? Against the tendency to fall back on the readings, I assigned more and more writing, hoping that we could see these issues as people were contending with them, consciously or unconsciously. One could find—or easily imagine—the developer, the entrepreneur, in the fictive world of a Dreiser novel, and one could imagine the local aristocracy turning away in disgust, or one could imagine—and find—a local farmer in Goldsmith hurt financially and psychologically by change in the village but unable to do anything about it. But that is not quite the way it was. The voices the students heard and recreated might be the more interesting because of their literary heritage, but the literary heritage—certainly the stereotypical forms in which we tend to remember that heritage—was challenged and redefined by the living persons who spoke in students' writing. For example:

TERRY O'MALLEY, PATTERSON ASSOCIATE

Terry O'Malley is the youngest of the associates and the one most directly concerned with the architectural aspects of the project, with the exception of the master architects, Callahan and Peters. He is direct and methodical, and his subdued and detailed approach to his work and the presentation of it to the Amherst community was decribed as "a real hit with the academics." I arrived at the farmhouse for an interview just as he was wheeling his bicycle with a baby seat attached to the back into a large built-on wing that serves as drafting space, and is overflowing with plans, rough sketches, and constructed full scale models of windows, walls and (outside) the kind of exterior, rough wood and stucco, that will characterize the Amherst Fields clusters. He

---

[29](New York: Vintage Books, 1970).

speaks softly, at times inaudibly, with a slight smile, organizing and mulling before answering questions.

The University has completely changed the character of North Pleasant Street, and there is a limit to the improvement that can be made there. As the Town Manager has said, the primary business of Amherst is education, and for this reason the Amherst business community is somewhat insulated from the ups and downs of national business. Amherst didn't realize the impact of the tremendous growth that has occurred here in the last decade. There is an euphoria that is shared by landowners and by businessmen, for as the number of students increases, their profits go up. A bunch of crappy apartments is built, and not until the quality of life of some of the old residents is threatened do people look at what has happened. Amherst simply has no control over the size and growth rate of the institutions in the town. Therefore, people attack the symptoms of it, like Pufton Village, the laundromats and the shops on the strip, but these are services that are needed. We are a large target, and Patterson crystallizes the problems that have been boiling under the surface for a long time.

Amherst did not recognize the forces it generated on its borders, with no environmental cost to itself. Look at that godawful Hadley strip leading in here. Those "dumb Polaks," as Amherst refers to them, live there in poverty, paying low taxes and their school system is rotten, and Amherst couldn't care less. They can go on farming and keep to themselves at the VFW. The problem for Amherst farmers is not only one of higher and higher taxes, but that the growing season is too short, the farms are too small to make money, and the land, at least where we are going to build, is not fertile enough. There is better land in Hadley. It is only by encouraging people like us that Amherst will be able to prevent the farmers from subdividing their land and selling it in small pieces to small developers. You just can't hold the idea of a guy making money off his land down. The farmers' sons don't want to be

farmers any more, they don't want to milk cows and shovel the shit, they want to drive their cars and go into the city. We buy up a bit piece of land, and the neighboring areas are kept open and free from more development because no one can compete with us. There is pressure on the farmers to sell land in a piece, and this hurts him a lot. Amherst is not going to be exclusively a university town any more, and it's just as well for the residents. If you want to stereotype the town, it used to be divided into three classes: the "Old Yanks," a big group of professors and a small group of professionals on the outside, and the three groups didn't have much to do with each other. We will have a broader base here, more different kinds of people, which should liven things up a bit.

It is amazing to me the pedestrian views of faculty and students toward housing, among people in architecture and landscaping who should know better. No one is interested in sensitive housing, it's all that variegated stuff and stupidly individual crap. They get some money and they all want a house of their own, spruced up on the outside. Drive down Main Street USA and you will see all the trimmings and attempts at individuaity. I don't know where people get their taste but it is a tricky question. Back in the days when places like Amherst were small New England towns, there used to be master carpenters who built a house and that was it, with little variation. The houses at Heritage Village (a previous Patterson development) all look basically alike, and are a return to the simpler major statement.

O'Malley is a shrewd analyst—he senses why the town has picked on his boss; he is aware of the complacency and subtle hypocrisies of its "aristocracy" (complaining only when its life style is threatened, turning its back on the Polish people of Hadley)—and he is shrewd enough to be able to turn his analysis into a defense of Patterson's development. It will be helping those who have been slighted; it will recreate a sense of community, one that was once the norm in New England towns, one that has only recently and temporarily been obscured by a largely academic population. Just how this is to come about is not clear: what exactly will happen to the farmers? how will they feel? is their choice really between shoveling shit and being bought out? Nor is it clear that the language of the architect ("the simple major statement") really encompasses a sense of community strong enough to argue for the removal of "all that variegated stuff and stupidly individual crap."

Mrs. Miller is a member of the opposition:

MRS. MILLER, A MEMBER OF THE AGSC.

Usually, her manner is calm, her speaking deliberate and her words carefully chosen. Occasionally though, this quiet demeanor is simmered by tentative questing—a form of uneasiness and agitation that is reflected in the change of her voice to a pinpointed sharpness. In speaking of Patterson, this change is noticeable. Otherwise, she is tranquil, gracious.

The Millers live in one of Amherst's few Georgian colonial brownstones, and theirs is even more stately because of several Doric pillars that majestically support the front of the house. In back, there is an ample lawn, bushes flatly trimmed and several symetrically arranged gardens of color contrasted and seasonally timed flowers—all possible, of course, because of a gardner persistently and patiently working under the careful eye of Mrs. Miller, who this afternoon was particularly worried about her recently bloomed daffodils.

I contributed to the Amherst Growth Study Committee when first solicited, but the mounting publicity convinced me that more should be done, and that I should join this organization. I sensed that all was not above board with Patterson and that a few fishy activities were taking place. We intellectuals can sit around on our pile of ambiguities and overlook the world, but I got tired of this restless sitting and decided to do something. Too many things happening too quickly have been going on in this town. A small group of people is being allowed to affect everyone's life in town. Patterson went right through the town meeting with the members, who are supposed to be intelligent, shrugging their shoulders and saying "why not?" Amherst has to do its democratic bit, but Patterson is not being democratic the way he steam-rolled his way into town.

People generally felt fatalistically about such problems, but for the first time there is a growing sense that something can be done. I feel we can put a stop to unwanted growth and unwanted buildings such as the Howard Johnson board ceiling glass structures. Some people say that zoning and building codes used in this manner would be elitist, and I can see their point, yet it seems to me we can have it both ways. We can have good buildings and at the same time low income housing. People can be educated to good taste. Some common standard of good taste must exist that we all can agree upon. We should try to inculcate this good taste and prevent the continuance of all these dumb building projects around town.

Everything in America is instant—instant coffee and now instant development compounded by the general instanteousness of life. Time is needed to assess what the effects of this development will be, foremost of which are water supply, traffic and school problems. Personally I have noticed that the quality of our drinking water is deteriorating and that traffic around town is getting unbearably congested. Furthermore, with this development, kids may be pouring into our school faster than they can be built.

The ethic of the businessman in town really aggravates me. Businessmen are waging a war at home for profits; nothing else seems to matter. Patterson is the worst of them all. This day care center that he is giving to the town is merely the hors d'oeuvre to soften up the town for the big kill. The only way I can account for the mentality of these businessmen is that their lives were severely affected by the Depression. They felt a severe scarcity of life then, so that the rest of their lives have been spent seeking abundance.

In Amherst, we still have a sense of the small town American way of life. When you can recognize faces in a town crowd, you have distinctly different feelings about where you live. Louis's food store is less than the country store it could be, but you still see people there you haven't seen in awhile and exchange information with them as if it were a cocktail party. But the town is not much of a community. When important issues are raised, a community may be formed, but otherwise, people go their own way. They tend to be individualistic and not community concerned. I guess the capitalistic system makes this inevitable, and if we are to change, the system must be changed.

Some people have an almost masochistic, self-flagellating view of town growth. They believe that expansion is necessary and if you don't have big problems you just ain't nobody. We have few worries in town now—I don't have to lock my doors, I can let my kids loose on the town and the schools are good. I don't see why we should purposely have it otherwise.

In spite of an attempt at using the language of the people ("you just ain't nobody"), Mrs. Miller is obviously more comfortable with metaphors from the world she knows best—the academic world, a world with a rich social life and few worries about the children. Seeing that world threatened she has acted, taken part in the effort to understand and to protect the community which does, after all, provide good schools and safety for its children. But she is new at this—unsure of how to reconcile her democratic principles with the elitist tendencies of her taste. In her frustration she imagines maybe the Depression is to blame for Patterson, but through her academically based small talk, comes a more sensible reflection on the problem of a community in a capitalist society.

A concerned citizen—intelligent and inexperienced, committed and stymied.

So it is that one must "read" characters like O'Malley and Mrs. Miller—attend to their language—as if they were in a book. A sensitive novel reader will be the more attentive to the play of intention and emotion in their talk; alerted to shades of thought and feeling in the talk of real people in a real town, after some investigation in the field, one is presumably that much livelier a reader of novels and plays with a strong social reference.

And finally, Bedford Plough, who comes from a family that has been in dairy farming for one hundred and fifty years, but who is now only a "hired hand." The Amherst student, starting his project at many removes along the social scale, is allowed one day, in Agee's words, "to perceive the aesthetic reality within the actual world." He hears of Bedford's dream (a dream that O'Malley will never know about), a dream of how one copes with the changes taking place in Amherst and—if it delves as deep as I think it does—all over America. It is a dream of an American wasteland, covered with gas stations and cities, affording only momentary relief in the form of a pastoral vision of children sporting on the farmland that he has lost and that is generally threatened with extinction:

My first day of work at the Fairview Farm, I worked with Peter Barney. We worked silently for four hours and after cleaning and dressing, we walked toward the main house for coffee. Peter noticed a sports car parked in the driveway, and he stopped and examined the car. I could tell he thought I owned the car, so I explained that it wasn't mine, that I had only borrowed it from a friend. He asked whether he could take "her" for a spin, as he had been a stock car racer down south. But no, snow had been falling and again I explained that the car was not mine. He asked whether he could sit in the "cockpit," and he did and laughed and remarked that he wished he had one of those "fancy pant cars."

I've been dreaming the same dream for years now, just now and again. I drive along this road, an interstate in Texas, and every time I pass a gas station, I stop and go into the john. I stop for water or just to lay down for a few moments on the floor. Every time a gas station comes up I stop and get into the bathroom and lay down and relax and sometimes play hoop ball with the paper towels and garbage can. I keep doing this until the trash can gets full, and then I drive on to the next station, and I keep on doing this. Finally I get into the desert and there are no more stations so I get out and just go for a walk. Now I lay down cause I am not feeling too well and I see these ants and all I do is watch them work. They work very hard. I go back to the truck and begin to drive again, and soon I get out of the desert and into the cities and gas stations. I finally end up at the ocean and I just turn around and begin again. I get into the truck, turn it around, and drive through gas stations and the desert all the way to the ocean. Sometimes though I wake up in the city, and I look out the window of a big building and there is this big parking lot with a small farm and some grass, and on the other side of this parking lot is a great big factory. Well the window lets me see these little kids playing right below me and they are having a grand time jumping in water and mud and screaming and really enjoying life. But way down on the other side there are some old cars and there is these people screwing around. Some lady who is upstairs cries out, "Hey you people, why are you screwing around here," and then I am driving the truck again. I am one hell of a crazy sonofabitch. Boy, if people only knew how crazy we are!

I know that I am not that intelligent and my brains work only so far but I have no idea why this thought keeps popping up in my crazy head. Maybe I just shouldn't know because I believe there are some things in this life which we just are not meant to know because if you did know you would crack up.

These examples allow for a moment's focus on the problem of growth in America. Many others, scores of other combinations, would give an equally good sense of how the voices of Amherst express "innerness" and, in the mind of a creative reader, how they bring into relief the cultural drama of life in one American town. The "field essays" from which these small examples are taken averaged thirty pages apiece; in the "book" I edited out of the "essays" I used about three hundred pages.

I say "book" because though I have had copies reproduced for the class, and for future classroom work, I do not know quite what to do with what seems to me to be this excellent material. I had said at the beginning of the course that the measure of the success of our writing might be directly proportionate' to its unpublishability and that rather weak (and at the time, flip) bit of incentive has come back to haunt me. From Agee we had learned about the seriousness of field work but we did not establish the kind of working agreement that Agee had with the Ricketts, the Woods, and the Gudgers, nor perhaps could we, the subjects being so different. It is not clear to me what people in the town thought or think of their experiences talking to students. I do not know what understandings existed in individual cases as to what project was afoot, what assurances of anonymity or possibly what promises of reciprocity were made. Looking for truths within the actual world you run risks the novelist and the poet does not run and for the most part, I am embarrassed to say, we ran those risks blind. Embarking on a course involving field work one would be well advised to consider the moral and ethical dimensions of field work more thoroughly and explicitly at the outset.[30]

Yet though the problem of what to do with the writing remains, there is much from which to take heart. Trying to arrive at a solution to just such problems —what are the moral and ethical issues? what audiences does one have in mind? of what possible service could such writing be to a community or to individuals? what are the effects of such work?— could be listed among the possibilities of field work. But this time around the advantages of field work seem to come not from the issues raised by field work itself; they could be seen more clearly from three other perspectives:

1. Students got out into the community. This can be done in the environs of any academic community; it was particularly appropriate in a New England town whose residents had, after all, helped to construct the College and, until only recently, had had close social, religious, and intellectual relations with its students and teachers. For all the benefits of the isolation of the academy,

mutual ignorance and mutual antagonism are not among them, and students have every bit as much to gain from renewed contact as "townies."

2. By going out into the community the quality of student learning can be enhanced in the ways I have repeatedly tried to define. They were not getting credit merely for existing outside the academy; they were out there in order to test and discover things about certain ideas and they were returning in order to take stock with their classmates, their teacher, and with books. They were seeing "the immediate events of (their) lives as instances of our general ideas." Field work is an obvious means of fulfilling Whitehead's aims for education.

3. Less obviously, field work can take students out of themselves—or make their inward journeys richer. It puts them in touch with Others who do not necessarily share their wishes and opinions, whose existence they may not need to take so seriously in books, but to whom they ought to be able to respond humanely if they are to consider themselves educated.

Renewed contact with one's community, one's learning, one's social being. It seems presumptuous to claim so much. But these are at least possibilities when you engage in field work, and English teachers ought to explore them more.

---

[30]Had I read Myron Glazer, *The Research Adventure: Promise and Problems of Field Work* (New York: Random House, 1972), I could not have been so cavalier.

DENNIS SZILAK

Tricks

SOMEBODY'S CLASSICAL MAXIM of teaching is to bring a student to where he casts off the teacher. A few years ago in the case of the student in Taipei, Taiwan, reported by a UPI news item, who beheaded the instructor with an ax in the classroom, the fundamental is taken too fundamentally. Most classes can let out with a less dramatic gesture of the independence that learning is to lead to.

About this independence, teachers might agree that it's of the "free" that the truth-will-make-you sort. One aspect of this freedom is that which results from submission to a discipline. For the student of composition, forbearance can be the contact-clause for effect rather than the run-on sentence by ignorance. Each discipline has its instruments. A person wearing mittens can play the piano, so can a writer attempt exposition encumbered by whimsical structures and diction—both, however, violate the natures of their instruments. The result, non-systematic elements in codification, is noise. It is to be free of this tyranny of noise that teacher and student explicitly and tacitly expect each other to do dutifully within the compass of and by the instruments of writing.

The nature of the stream is to flow around the rock that will not flow with it. In accommodating all, so it is the nature of running water to overcome all. The student who accepts the nature of the writing discipline finds the power avowed of words.

The order of thinking is not the order of writing until the thinking is restrained by the student's practice of the rules of writing. This freedom within a discipline prevails against entropy, the "natural" mind conditioned by "common sense" (called by Einstein the prejudices accumulated by the age of eighteen) and the mass media grooving at 33⅓ revolutions, oscillating at 60 cycles, and flickering

Dennis Szilak is an instructor at Northwestern Michigan College.

Reprinted from *College English*, Vol. 36, No. 5, January 1975.

at 24 frames—the "natural" mind running down to equilibrium motion stopped, absolute cold.

Clearly it is not the restraints of writing, of the discipline, that the student is to cast off to be free of the teacher. The liberation and the problem are played against some other backdrop. The situation of student and teacher, not the discipline, gives rise to the problem.

Bad teaching, the teacher lacking competence in his subject, does not create the problem of dependence. Students flee from it in one manner or another. Good teaching makes disciples; and lo, the master is not with them even unto the end of the world. It is not the discipline of writing or of chemistry or psychology that makes disciples. Chemistry bonds chemists and psychology conditions psychologists but they can be seneschals serving a harsh mistress, loyal to the traditions of the arts and sciences, not particularly bound to lip-service all her future progeny and pretenders. In any field, students and teachers can be royalists to the past and revolutionary to the future.

Disciples are created by situational design. Teaching is a design used by a person of experience and knowledge to train students with less experience and knowledge. It is a design that at some level must finally efface the teacher. The edifice that is built up in the classroom must fall, even if it falls all over the teacher. It can not be otherwise, for pillars of the temple are supporting a past that is beyond the recollection of the students—not the past of the subject (which is the foundation), but of the teacher, his experience and perceptions. The great skill of teaching is to use to advantage what Ezra Pound called the "natural destructivity of the young"—here, the rejection of the teacher's formulation of experience. Out of that opposition is to come the extension or liberation of the individual that will have reached its limits in the classroom design. *The Tempest* is full of such liberations, both ways:

> My charms I'll break, their senses I'll restore,
> and they shall be themselves.

> . . . I'll break my staff, . . .
> I'll drown my book.

> . . . What a thrice-double ass
> Was I to take this drunkard for a god
> And worship this dull fool!

> Be free, and fare thou well. . . .

> Now my charms are all o'erthrown,
> And what strength I have's mine own,
> Which is most faint. . . .

When Oscar Wilde, with a hint of Plato's *Meno*, says:

> Education is an admirable thing, but it is well to remember from time to time that nothing that is worth knowing can be taught.

he has not said enough. What is learned in the classroom is a variable of the experience each individual has of that classroom. It becomes a part of each student's and teacher's past and is there to lean against their presents and futures, or to be forgotten, ignored, or embalmed. To the extent that it is forgotten, ignored, embalmed, does not lean on the knowing that can't be taught, it has been a waste of time; it is the business of a teacher not to waste a student's time. It is no mean feat to teach a student the tricks of the trade, of the discipline, but drudgery, pedantry, and forced marches can lead the student to some writing competence. Also, it is no mean feat to bring a student to where he casts off the teacher, to use to advantage the "natural destructivity," to not waste time. It is a trick.

It is particularly the "trick" of the trade of teaching, that the teacher of composition must play if he wants facility along with competence in his students. Facility in writing comes to the student at the point where, whether his ideas are different from or similar to other ideas, they are his own; at the point where he brings his discipline of form to bear on content, realizing the distinction between "form" and "content" was a trick. He is discovering then whether he can think with some degree of freedom from educational or psychological compulsions.

Some of the conditions that stimulate such a discovery may depend upon the teacher's awareness of the paradoxical nature of his relationship with the student and his courage to accept the disgust that can come with the break: the freeing of the student from the teacher. Teaching, particularly the teaching of writing in a liberal arts tradition, cannot be separated from the student's search for meaning in terms of his experience of the subject matter as it relates to his experience, not the teacher's experience.

A candidate for that subject which is often made most remote from personal experience is literature. It is most remote whenever the absence of any vital purposes is supposedly compensated for by the "symbolism" of the material. Symbols become as specious as unrelated facts when they are unassociated with experience. The signs of the times are only signs outside of those times. The Depression, as hardly a young person has not been told, was not a symbol for anyone near the bottom of the Depression.

Learning about and by literature to yield what Wayne C. Booth ("Knowledge That a Man Must Have") calls the "knowledge or capacity or power of how to act freely as a man" is probably no different than learning about and by cybernetics or carpentry to yield the same generalized result:

> through study and conscientious thought, to school his choices—that is, to free them through coming to understand the forces working on them.

It is not an original observation that applied science or vocational arts may achieve the goal of liberal education; and that for some, say teachers, liberal education becomes a vocation and for the rest an embarrassment. Does government and business welcome the liberal arts graduates. because they are "well-rounded" or because their roundness will encompass any sort of programming?

It may be that the greatest threat to independent thinking lurks in those courses that put the most stress on it; and composition is surely one of them. To the extent that the teacher organizes and explicates ideas, he imposes upon the student certain points of view. To the extent the student models his writing or his interpretations upon his teacher's presentations he is a disciple of "right" thinking. Of course, any teacher will have to be right when education is played in terms of who has it and who doesn't. The rigidity is necessary in courses where facts are the answers.

There, at least, the student understands the game. When meanings are the answers the game is more insidious because the responses are disguised as facts rather than recognized for what they are: somebody's experience in somebody's order. Thus, there arises both the paradox—and an absurd solution. The teacher's duty is to free the student (make the student independent of the teacher's lines of thinking) but the teacher can only act on his duty by binding the student (showing the student how the teacher thinks and presenting and explicating his models of thinking). Now, the contemporary solution to the paradox has been for the teacher to expect students to pull their own rabbits out of their own hats rather than force them to see there is nothing up the teacher's sleeve and he has no rabbit and no hat by letting them act consistently on their false premises about what there is to know and learn.

The do-your-own-trick solution, as Henry F. Ottinger ("In Short Why Did the Class Fail?") shows to the dismay of himself and his students, goes from "initial ecstasy to final catastrophe." Conjure up the scene. The first day of Mr. Ottinger's class is unusually pleasant for both teacher and students. Both are relaxed, knowing nothing is expected of them. It is a new day, a beginning, a moment of suspended cynicism. Maybe this time the magic will happen. Is there anyone who does not, at the least, hope that excitement is possible in a classroom, that learning is possible? That it does not happen, not here—anyplace else, but not here, or that it happens here so infrequently as to seem the merest chance occurrence is part of everyone's experience. It is one thing that we have learned in school. Still, the boredom, the humiliation of other classes are put out of mind and one hopes. . . . If wishes were horses, there would be a lot of horses.

First day, freshman composition, students assigned to this section, to this room, at this hour, have arrived. Mr. Ottinger has not. The students look each other over, looking for friends, looking for love? Who to avoid? Who to support? Who to depend on? Who to cross off?

Class: a set, collection, group, or configuration containing members having or thought to have something in common. What do the students have in common? What is the organizing *commonness*? Is it, or can it be something other than the *other* who will shortly appear on the other side and face the wrong way? The motorman. And the rest? Passengers?

Mr. Ottinger arrives. He reads from Jerry Farber's book, *The Student As Nigger*. The class is given its situational design:

> And I suggested that we try to break the mold, that we could write papers on any subject we wanted, that we could spend class time discussing things—either "the burning issues of the day," or otherwise. You seemed to agree, and we spent a lot of time agreeing together that indeed Farber had *the* word and we would do what we could to break out of the mold. . . . Most of all you had the opportunity to be free—free from the usual absurdities of a composition class where topics are as-

signed, thesis statements are submitted, and so on. You also had freedom of thought as long as it was confined to the standards of formal English. You had the opportunity to be free—to be responsible to yourselves. . . .

Mr. Ottinger breaks his staff and drowns his book in the beginning, and disgust is his in the end:

> Generally, this class has been the most silent, reticent, paranoid bunch of people in a group I have ever experienced. . . . and you succeeded in proving to me and to yourselves that Freedom is Slavery, a line from *1984* which I hope, for the sake of all of us, isn't prophetic.
> But you protest! (Oh, how I wish you would): "We're incapable of handling all this freedom at once. You see, Mr. Ottinger, we've been conditioned; we're not used to all this!"
> Well I read that in Faber, too, and it's bull. Rats and dogs are conditioned, and are usually incapable of breaking that conditioning. Human beings *can* break conditioning, if it's to their advantage. . . .
> Why is it to your advantage not to break the mold. In short, why did the class fail?

Is there a teacher who has not shared Henry Ottinger's feelings? One would suppose not and suppose so from reading the reactions to Mr. Ottinger that appeared in *The New York Times*. William Bonderson told him that it was "unreasonable to expect someone who has long lived in darkness to immediately operate effectively when he is first exposed to broad daylight," and cautioned against either radical authority or radical freedom. Malcolm L. Diamond observed that examination must begin with the faculty's motivations:

> The motivation of teachers is complex. It involves such laudable features as curiosity about the world and the desire to help students to learn about it. It also involves such natural drives as the search for status and other rewards of a successful career. One of these rewards is turning students on. Mr. Ottinger was clearly frustrated because he was open to students, gave them freedom, and still failed to turn them on. . . . Mr. Ottinger's essay shrieks its message of betrayal.

Mr. Diamond has got Ottinger and teachers, generally, on a sore spot. Few would deny the desire (to turn students on) or the attempt to fulfill it. However, the need to turn students on, if successful, creates disciples, dependency; if not, betrayal.

The *Bhagavad-Gita* suggests an answer to the dilemma, which is, as always, to ignore the problem: "You have the right to work, but for the work's sake only. You have no right to the fruits of work." A teacher willing to do his duty has to both turn students on to turn them off and turn them off so they can turn themselves on—has to be heedless of any need or any fruits of being admired or feared. If the betrayal of "relevance" has turned our noses towards "accountability," the most accountable teachers, as were the most relevant, are likely to be those that can operate in the spirit of non-attachment to the bubbles of their student's praises or the slings and arrows of their discontents.

Chiding Ottinger for never learning "in all his courses leading to the doctorate, that the *instructor* is the one responsible for the success—or failure—of a class," Patricia Reinfeld makes it uncomfortable for all teachers who can feel or remember having felt Ottinger's sort of failure, with her "surely" and "my goodness" pinches. Reinfeld, however, misplaces the source of Ottinger's anguish:

> Has Mr. Ottinger never learned about directed, or guided, freedom in the class-room through which the teacher unobtrusively moves things in the direction through which they must go? He blames his students for not thinking; it sounds on the contrary as if *he* took the vacation. And is it so horrible to assign general topics to (I assume) freshmen students, who need to become acquainted with, if not to master, particular kinds of writing?

The critic here is mixing up the freedom within the discipline with freeing of the student's thinking from cultural thinking (including teacher thinking), which is the rock Ottinger is shipwrecked upon. Why else could she refer to "directed, or guided, freedom . . . the teacher unobtrusively moves. . . ."?

Another Ottinger critic, Harvey T. Thomson, gets us nearly to the crux of the problem:

> Classroom dynamics can be described in terms of teacher and student roles. Ac-ceptable role behavior is normally agreed upon implicitly by both parties. How-ever, the change in the ground rules in Mr. Ottinger's course meant that both students and the instructor had to learn to play their roles differently than they had been used to in the past.

Mr. Thomson's point is that one cannot play the game without knowing the rules or the roles. Along the lines of this metaphor it is also a point that one cannot play the game if he does not know a game is being played or if he does not know *what* game is being played. In such situations students go back to the only game they know, but get no play because the deck is stacked.

It is not surprising that young people are unable to initiate or organize responses (choices) in Ottinger's class, conditioned (despite Ottinger's easy dismissal of conditioning) as they are by the only game in town: being jugheads to be filled up with education for a remote future. It is not only some laboratory isotopes that have "half-lives" of a few seconds. What men know because they are aware of having been taught it by the specific task of learning must be continually re-learned and unlearned. This is a costly operation in which Mr. Ottinger's knowl-edge for its own sake as a "valid and valuable goal" slowly becomes exhausted.

Only a mathematical trick makes the operations of matter cost nothing. Like-wise, every learning and unlearning costs something. A refusal to learn can be a refusal to self-destruct. ("We are the stuffed men/ Leaning together/ Headpiece filled with straw. alas!")

Ottinger's design shows the students that they are passive. This is not his in-tention nor is it an end in itself. The student already has a sense of his passivity anyway. The inability to complete the task, to even determine what the task is, is the problem for Ottinger's class. His imposing of the original problem is recog-nized as ingenious but not genuine. (The class is still only a class and they are still students to be graded.) For the most part, the passivity itself is not genuine. Students are more likely frustrated actors than dissatisfied spectators.

In the past several years a great deal of discussion has focused on roles and role-playing in education. Ottinger's shift in role from a supervisory to a more egalitarian position is perhaps a result of this trend. That his students did not respond with a corresponding shift to a more decisional position in the classroom process suggests that a person can only change a role when he perceives a change in situation. Roles are after all defined by situations. All the commentary about role-playing and the sorts of roles to play in a classroom has given us little idea of what the varieties of classroom situations are. Roles may have changed but the classroom situation is treated as static.

Ottinger's experience shows that his class, as so many others, is made up of students who act as if the members have individual (personal) situations, but the class has only one situation. The most common class role in a situation that appears singular and set—besides defense against the *other* (the teacher)—is laughing at one of its own. Class dialogue, in the static situation, is most often between one student and one teacher; and sometimes between students in the manner of debate, the teacher dignified as the final arbiter of salient points. Periodic outbreaks of opinion trading may give the teacher the impression that he is making progress, even though the substance and manner of such exchange is what any saloon keeper would put down as "booze talking." In a class that found itself working with a multiplicity of situations, students would not so much say different things as do different things.

Students learn a great deal from their peers—but not much *qua* students. There is little information on how groups learn; that is, on groups formed for the expressed purpose of learning. Conflicting studies have resulted in determining how class size affects learning. Conclusions are centered on the individual. He is not affected by class size. He is affected. Or he is and is not affected, depending on subject matter and methods of presentation. Such studies say very little about groups, much less group learning situations.

Group manipulation, or interaction and roles, in practice, gets little exercise because information about classroom roles is useless without clarifying classroom situations. Inaction or habitual action is due to the lack of definition of the situations, not to the artificiality of the classroom, which is, in fact, congenial to role taking. To the exent that the situation is treated as the same old game, the traditional roles of tyro and tyrant (no matter how these roles may be temporarily disguised) are played out, the participants becoming what they are pretending to be. When there is no perceptable change in situation, people fall back into their old roles and reinforce them (play them with a vengeance).

Such limitations are particularly detrimental to most women, the exception generally being black women in state colleges. They, for economic reasons, seem less locked in the feminine "mistake" that pervades the rest of the national culture. If women cannot be encouraged to trade off participational roles with men, the activity and learning of the group can hardly be enhanced. A teacher can have at least a notion that not just the isolation of individuals but group division along sex lines will affect the group. Male teachers are seldom aware of the problem. Their ignorance reinforces the female role, just as their authority forces the male one. A woman teacher may be more aware of the roles, having had to push against them, but the gain may be taken out on students of both sexes, if their intellectual inquiry is taken as a threat to person. In other words, it may be that women teachers have to be always right more than men teachers.

In consideration of the re-examination of attitudes that young women are initiating and inheriting, teachers should at times meet separately with the male and female students so as to organize calculated responses to affect shifts in roles. This could involve a trading off of roles as the two groups perceive them in the environment of the class. It could also mean the planning of moves to conflict with or call into question roles as they are played out in the youth culture and American society. The nature of the acting would depend on the nature of the material being dealt with, and on clarification of situational responses. Since jolting awareness requires some shock to the system—whether the system be individual or institutional—some students will have to be "taken," and perhaps be unaware that they are being played until long after the take is over.

Tricks need be played because there is no way of convincing, by exhortation or confession, a well-conditioned student that nothing worth knowing, beyond the discipline, can be taught; that one discipline is as good as any other, and that the schools are only equipped to do lobotomies on thinking.

A student, if he is to learn his own mind at all, must be tricked into insight. This is an infrequent case in most classes but nonetheless a useful general principle. And the trick does not involve having the student guessing what it is the teacher wants him to do. ("How do you want this paper done. If you'll just tell me how to do it," i.e., how to think it.)

Having provoked a variety of situations, the teacher is indifferent; he does not want the student to do *some*thing. Anything that the student chooses to do, will do. The student knowing some of the varieties and choosing from among them gives the lie to passivity, conditioning, and dependency. The good teacher keeps his students entertained while they learn themselves what it is that they, themselves, learn; and it is easier for them to await their own changes if they have the impression that something is being done to bring about these changes. What is being done is the trick.

To the extent that students are let in on the tricks (partly Ottinger's approach but he fails to make use of it as a strategy) they lose confidence in their teachers, and the art of teaching, of having the student cast off the teacher, proceeds by the invention of new and impenetrable tricks, which are always ways of getting the students to act upon their false premises about the nature of their learning. At best this is a conscious and deliberate spoof to exorcise an unconscious and otherwise inexorable illusion on the part of the student that he has something to learn about how to think for himself.

Such a teacher does not think of himself as something other than what he is doing: teaching a discipline at one level and being a magician pulling rabbits from hats on another. He is not in the situation of pretending without knowing that he is pretending, which appears to be Ottinger's situation.

Social conditioning and institutional patterning are misapplied by persuading students from an early age not to accept learning themselves and to accept the task of being taught. Necessary as this strategy is for training the young, it is a fiction of limited use and is even destructive if consistently applied in higher education.

Certain institutional forms are self-contradictory or in actual conflict with individual advancement. But these institutions have a great deal of human effort and emotion invested in them to maintain themselves, and are never short of champions, martyrs, and inquisitors. These institutional forms and patterns are the rules of communication and relation by which people understand one another and relate to one another. And such designs have been impressed into the behavior of children, not as games to be played, but with the full force of survival mythology accompanied by social anxiety. Children become convinced of their dependency on these forms, not just in action but in spirit, and at the same time are humiliated and suffer from some of the very ideas which they believe to be vital to sanity and survival.

A teacher takes their pain and frustration seriously but only acts as if he takes the problem of their passivity, and the problem of their need to be taught, seriously. Accumulated deposits of false problems must be filed away over a period of time. A teacher who sees the problem as a false one can be the beginning of the process.

As for the tricks, it should go without saying that the falls should go to the majority rather than the few, and to the strong rather than the weak—passivity being the measure of the weak, and not an intellectual judgment. To begin, the initial trick of the teacher is to move the student away from his conditioned notions about the classroom as a particular kind of situation. What are the varieties of classroom situations?

To begin to answer the question requires some experimental models of behavior, particularly those that have to do with experimentally produced neurosis. The relevance of such experiments to the normal classroom should not be surprising because if, at one level, the teacher is involved in a paradoxical situation with his students, the classroom is a laboratory of neurosis. To solve the problem that cannot be solved is vain; to attempt to solve it is unreal, so neurotic. However, a bind that has arisen must be broken by the context in which it arose, under the principle that like cures like. As a little butter gets machine grease off your hands so a student can be freed of teaching in a classroom.

Pavlov's experiments in the 1930's with "conditioned reflex" in dogs suggests two of the sorts of situations that arise in the classroom. In one of the experiments, Pavlov presented a dog with the problem of distinguishing between an ellipse and a circle. Motivated by a no-meat-for-ellipse and meat-for-circle inducement, the dog had soon made the differentiation. Drooling saliva for the circle, none for the ellipse, the dog had learned.

The original ellipse, a long narrow one in a ratio of 9 to 2, was changed successively: 9 to 3, 9 to 4, 9 to 5, etc., Pavlov waiting each time until the dog had learned to continue differentiating circle and ellipse. Finally the ratio between the ellipse's vertical and horizontal axes was 9 to 8, a ratio that gives people some difficulty in distinguishing from a circle. To shorten a long story, months of rest with sedation were required before the dog was able again to do a day's work. Experimental neurosis is what Pavlov called that which bit the dog.

Gregory Bateson has suggested that the real neurotic was not the dog but Pavlov, who did not distinguish between situations by requiring the dog to perform a differentiation in what had become a "gamble" situation.

Bateson gives as an example of a gamble situation, one in which an animal searching for food looks under rocks for slugs. One rock is as good as another rock for any slug to be under so the animal's brain is not overextended or wrongly exerted, is not subjected to stimuli that are too confusing when it is wrong, when it does not find a slug under the odd lot of rocks it has overturned. Bateson's point is that an animal in the wild knows its situations, does not get neurotic in a gamble situation, and keeps on rocking.

Pavlov kept the rules but changed the game on the dog. The situation with the ellipse and the circle was an operational one up to the end when it became a gamble. An operational situation can be defined as one in which a person or an animal performs a specific operation (differentiate the ellipse from the circle) that it has been taught to perform or feels it is expected to perform. An operational situation, then, is one which requires operators (students) to perform an operation that has been constructed by some agent or agency (teacher or institution).

Filling out a U.S. Census form is an operational situation, as is the filling out of most any form or questionnaire. The Census Bureau is not interested in individual histories but masses of data, and one lump of operators will do as well as any other lump of operators. Likewise, the accumulation of papers, assignments, and scores is an operational procedure performed for a grade. In most classes, one way or another, every student gets a grade, and the grade is pegged by how and to what extent the applications for it are filled out. Around age 65, most Americans have the right to Social Security benefits. But no one gets Social Security without filling out the forms for it. It is a purely operational situation that has little to do with merit and almost nothing to do with need. Those who are eligible and fill out the forms get it, those who are elligible and don't, don't.

Students of writing and of other subjects have been conditioned to operational situations in classrooms, and it is difficult for them to see that a classroom contains any other sort of situation; the result is passivity. Such passivity, the student thinking of himself as only an operator, is the hold the teacher must break if the student is to cast off the teacher.

Passivity is, after all, the necessary result of an operational situation. The classroom also is subject to the principle of experimental interference. When a scientist shines a light on a particle with an electron microscope he jolts it. So some aspect of the natural state of the particle is interfered with; either its position or velocity must be determined statistically (*i.e.*, cannot be determined by observation). When Harris takes a poll, the framing of the question determines the response. When a psychologist observes behavior the design of the observation determines behavior. When the design of the classroom is operational, passivity is determinant. None can escape from this principle of interference; to observe behavior, phenomenon, to measure it, is to affect it. The design of the observing or measuring situation affects the response.

In any situation it is never demonstrated either that what happens could have happened otherwise, or that what is done must be done—except by confining one's attention to very small fields; that is, by taking events out of the contexts in which they "naturally" happen. The scientist often knows what is being ignored, so much of what he does turns out to be useful within a limited range.

What happens when a scientist is not fully aware of what he is ignoring because he is mostly looking for support of his theory? The scientist gets a lot of mileage out of his theory. In 1960 Stanley Milgram began exploratory studies at Yale on destructive obedience. The summary of these original experiments, "A Behavioral Study of Obedience," appears in a number of anthologies of expository prose, including *The Norton Reader*, third edition.

An abstract of the study, written by Milgram, is in the headnote, which appears with the article as it was originally published. *S* is subject; *E* the experimenter:

This article describes a procedure for the study of destructive obedience in the laboratory. It consists of ordering a naive S to administer increasingly more severe punishment to a victim in the context of a learning experiment. Punishment is administered by means of a shock generator with 30 graded switches ranging from Slight Shock to Danger: Severe Shock. The victim is a confederate of the E. The primary dependent variable is the maximum shock the S is willing to administer before he refuses to continue further. 26 Ss obeyed the experimental commands fully. 14 Ss broke off the experiment at some point after the victim protested and refused to provide further answers. The procedure created extreme levels of nervous tension in some Ss. Profuse sweating, trembling, and stuttering were typical expressions of this emotional disturbance. One unexpected sign of tension—yet to be explained—was the regular occurrence of nervous laughter, which in some Ss developed into uncontrollable seizures. The variety of interesting behavioral dynamics observed in the experiment, the reality of the situation for the S, and the possibility of parametric variation within the framework of the procedure, point to the fruitfulness of further study.

Indeed, study has been so fruitful that social psychology is nearing a second generation of naive subjects to sit down before Shock Generator, Type ZLB, Dyson Instrument Co., Waltham, Mass. Output 15 volts—450 volts, and depress the switches that have never given any of the victims a tickle, much less a shock. Changes have been rung (those damn "parameters") on Milgram's experiment now for fifteen years, an anniversary commemorated by the publication in January 1974 of Milgram's book, *Obedience to Authority*.

The experiment that Milgram fathered has been repeated in Princeton, Munich, Rome, South Africa, and Australia. Milgram's study is so well known that it is a wonder that experimenters can still find "naive" subjects. Yet Milgram, in an article ("The Perils of Obedience") for the December 1973 issue of *Harper's*, says:

> psychiatrists, specifically, predicted that most subjects would not go beyond 150 volts, when the victim makes his first explicit demand to be freed. They expected that only 4 percent would reach 300 volts, and that only a pathological fringe of about one in a thousand would administer the highest shock on the board.

Harper's so much liked the unequivocal wrongness of the psychiatrists that the zinger became a marginal head in 12-point type: "Psychiatrists predicted that only a pathological fringe of about one in a thousand would administer the highest shock on the board." Still, in the sixties when Milgram was asking psychology majors at Yale for predictions, the mean prediction for subjects that would go all the way was 1.2%.

Granted, Milgram has gotten more drama ("agonized scream") into the show since those early days when the victim merely played a tattoo on the wall and refused to light up the answer board. However, 60 percent of the subjects fully obedient remained the going rate around New Haven; and rates were "invariably somewhat *higher*" in other places; extravagant Munich scored 85 percent fully obedient. Milgram's basic experimental design was highly original and, no doubt, very useful in examining what he calls "a deeply ingrained behavior tendency, indeed a potent impulse overriding training in ethics, sympathy, and moral conduct." (This quote from *Harper's* is the same in the original publication of findings, except the 60's "prepotent" has become only "potent" in the 70's.) The proliferation of Milgrams, however, makes it appear that behavior, here, has as much to do with design as with obedience.

Like Pavlov, Milgram can be accused of playing two games with one set of rules. One is an operational game, the other a discrimination game. In a discrimination game a person makes choices, makes designs instead of submitting to or being a part of another's design. Philosophers like to call such a game "ethics" or "moral conduct."

Clearly, Milgram's subjects are being scored as if they are playing a discrimination game:

> Stark authority was pitted against the subjects' strongest moral imperatives against hurting others, and with the subjects' ears ringing with the screams of victims, authority won more often than not.

This quote is from *Harper's* and it is similar to the judgment made in the Milgram original: "It is clear from the remarks and outward behavior of many participants that in punishing the victim they are often acting against their own values."

It is Milgram who has slipped the terms "ethics," "moral conduct," "moral imperatives," "values" into the conclusions, and they seem, from one point of view, to belong there. From another point of view, however, the experiment is indeterminant at the critical crossroad of moral and ethical conduct. A subject that volunteers for a laboratory experiment, whether that laboratory is at Yale or in a tree house, a subject that is asked to perform a designated task (an operation), the parts of which, if not particularly complicated, are numerous and specific— that subject is to some degree locked into an operational situation.

In one sense all Milgram establishes is that most subjects who begin operational situations finish their operations. Those subjects that break off participation are making a discrimination, it appears; but those who string along, what are they doing? Are they making a choice, discriminating, or unaware, that the game involves choices, merely operating? There is no way to tell—except by confining one's attention to "very small fields," by taking events out of the contexts in which they happen, by ignoring a great deal.

Someone at this point would like to say that an "agonized scream" is a clear enough signal to base a discrimination on. A scream is a clear enough signal, all right, a signal of the state of the victim. But does the "feedback" clarify the subject's choices? A person who does not know what the choices are in a particular situation may be in a critical situation but it cannot be called an ethical or moral situation.

A couple of changes still need to be rung on Milgram's experiment—a couple of "parametric" variations, to use Milgram's word. (Parameter: "a variable . . . which . . . determines the specific form of the expression," to use *The American Heritage Dictionary* definition.) The varieties of Milgram do not include a situation in which there is a clear signal to subjects that they can refuse to cooperate with the experimenter, before the first switch is depressed or at any "depressing" point along the way. In such an experiment a subject would also be a confederate of the experimenter and would be observed by the "naive" subjects. Such a "subject" would refuse all experimental commands and articulate the reasons for his refusal, or adamantly demonstrate his refusal. This is Mark Twain ("The United States of Lyncherdon") on the point:

> A Savonarola can quell and scatter a mob of lynchers with a mere glance of his eye: so can a Merrill* or a Beloat.† For no mob has any sand in the presence of a man known to be splendidly brave. Besides, a lynching mob would *like* to be scattered, for a certainty there are never ten men in it who would not prefer to be someplace else—and would be, if they but had the courage to go. When I was a boy I saw a brave gentleman deride and insult a mob and drive it away; and afterward, in Nevada, I saw a noted desperado make two hundred men sit still, with the house burning under them, until he gave them permission to retire. A plucky man can rob a whole passenger train by himself; and the half of a brave man can hold up a stagecoach and strip its occupants.
>
> Then perhaps the remedy for lynchings comes to this: station a brave man in each affected community to encourage, support, and bring to light the deep dis-

approval of lynching hidden in the secret places of its heart—for it is there, beyond question. Then those communities will find something better to imitate—of course, being human, they must imitate something.

*Sheriff of Carroll County, Georgia (M.T.)
†Sheriff, Princeton, Indiana. By that formidable power which lies in an established reputation for cold pluck they faced lynching mobs and securely held the field against them. (M.T.)[1]

To the extent that a plucky subject comes off pluckier than the experimenter before an audience of naive subjects, it's likely that there will be more discriminations than operations performed in Milgram. But, it just wouldn't do to have invariably high instances of training in ethics, sympathy, and moral conduct—indeed, perhaps a potent or prepotent impulse overriding a deeply ingrained behavior tendency. For one thing, fifteen years of Milgram would have gone out the window.

No matter, such an experiment would establish little about morality. All it would suggest is that subjects in a situation signaled as both a discrimination and an operation will discriminate and operate, and likely a little of both. One of Milgram's own experiments nearly bears this out. In it the procedure was the same as for the standard experiment, except the experimenter explicitly told the subjects that they themselves could choose the levels of shock for "thirty critical trials." In his *Harper's* article, Milgram tells us the result:

> The average shock used during the thirty critical trials was less than 60 volts—lower than the point at which the victim showed the first signs of discomfort. . . . the overall result was that the great majority of people delivered very low, usually painless, shocks when the choice was explicitly up to them.

The next step would be to have the experimenter tell the subjects that they can choose not to give any shocks, that there is really nothing for them to do, but at such a point, what is left of the experiment?

Or, let's try the late-night-movie version of Milgram. The scene shifts from Yale to Transylvania. The "naive" subjects who have volunteered to come to the laboratory are snow-bound. The experimenter's confederates are sets of three-year-old twins. The twins are all identical sets, and all girls, rosy-cheeked and pigtailed, dressed in long flannel nightgowns with decorative designs of Winnie-the-Pooh characters. Other confederates are two hunchbacked half-wits, unrelated, and a handsome dwarf, who are posing as "naive" subjects. The standard experiment is for each naive subject to hold a loaded .38 caliber Magnum Special to the temple of one of the victims while she learns to recite the "Sermon On the Mount" in English, a "parametric" variable being that all the victims speak Magyar. The experimenter explicitly tells the naive subjects that if a child does not learn, the subject is free to pull the trigger or simply retire to the cafeteria for brandy and cigars.

The experiment begins, but as a further demonstration of models of behavior, the first three subjects are the experimenter's plucky companions. The first half-wit blows the brains out of one of the twins halfway through her recitation of

---

[1]Maxwell Geismar, ed. *Mark Twain & the Three R's* (New York: Bobbs-Merrill, 1973), pp. 37-38.

the "Sermon," alas, in Hungarian. The second half-wit blows out his own brains. Confused by this turn of events, the dwarf, who is irredeemably naive and forgetful, blows out the brains of the experimenter. At this point the rest of the subjects go to the cafeteria. The experiment is inconclusive.

Someone is saying this is blatantly unfair reduction of Milgram to the absurd. It is not! Shift the scene to My Lai, Vietnam. Remember:

> It was a ditch. And so we started shooting them so altogether we just pushed them all off and we started using automatics on them: men, women, and children, and babies. And so we started shooting them, and someone told us to switch off to single shot so that we could save some ammo. So we switched off to single shot, and shot a few more rounds.

Also remember that one American soldier shot himself in the foot that day; and that a helicopter crew trained its guns on Calley when he tried to interfere with an evacuation of wounded civilians. There were explicit and implicit orders surrounding My Lai. There were clear signals, muted signals, and other voices from other rooms. For some it was an operation:

> To us they were no civilians. They were sympathizers. You don't call them civilians. You don't have any alternatives. You got to do something. You're risking your life doing that work. And if someone kills you, those people aren't going to feel sorry for you.

It was a gamble:

> They can't punish us for that. Big officials are saying it doesn't matter that we were under orders, we're still guilty—but I don't see that. If you're under orders, you're going to be punished for not doing it and punished if you do. I didn't like what happened but I didn't decide.

A gamble lost? But also, was it a gamble won or a choice? Remember:

> It was point-blank murder. Only a few of us refused. I just told them the hell with this, I'm not doing it. I didn't think this was a lawful order.

It cannot be told. In any situation it is never demonstrated either that what happens could have happened otherwise, or that what is done must be done—except by taking events out of the context in which they take place. To solve the problem that cannot be solved is vain; to attempt it is foolish. Who knows what signals the people heard at My Lai (or name your place), what voices spoke to them, from what rooms the voices came?

The nature of the signals, the clarity and power of the signals, the frequencies, the noise, determines the nature of the responses. It has been a long march back to the class in composition. The scene, again, is Henry Ottinger's class. His students thought composition class was an operational situation. Ottinger tried to tell them it was not. They didn't believe him. He should have tricked them.

Any academic field has practical problems that a teacher goes to directly. Specifying classroom goals, a teacher also identifies course problems. Achieving competence in terms of these goals is the first level of learning; facility and independent thinking are at the second level. A block (false problem) at the second level temporizes learning at the first. In the traditional approach to freshman composition the goal is writing competence, the problems grammatical-syntactical-rhetorical; the goal is reading proficiency, the problem is vocabulary —or just plain lack of concentration; the goal is inferential thinking and synthesis of formal knowledge, the problem is literal-mindedness; the goal is a passing acquaintance with some of the seminal ideas of civilization ("readings for a liberal education"), the problem is the dead weight of the corpus.

Only the last of these goals emphasizes content over process, and thus necessitates the storing of bits of information. Yet many students come to college with an unshakeable belief in the graven image of the Fact, as if learning were preparation for some sort of quiz show: "That's the bell signaling the end of Fleeting Judgment; now contestants, let's get ready to play Last Judgment."

The artful dodge of instruction is to let the student pose the culturally-conditioned false problems and to let the student act on his premises. The teacher, by assigning a task that, at level one, familiarizes the student with the tools of the discipline and, at the second level, involves a *reductio ad absurdum*, can work both sides of the street.

Such an exercise can be an information retrieval assignment. This is the introduction to one:

> The purpose of this exercise is to go through the process of finding various kinds of information. The facts, identifications and statistics that you will seek out are meaningless in themselves; all that is important here is the process of finding information. What we lack are ideas about what to do with it, ideas about our own rules of perception, about our cognitive and logical processes, and most of all notions about how to tune our frequencies on to new programs.
>
> The assignment deals with the specialized information stored in books, getting to it and getting it out. Outside of school it is, probably, the least important sort of information we process in our lives, but to academic performance such information is critical.
>
> The sources listed for this exercise are all in the reference section of the library. They are only a few of the hundreds of references in there. They were chosen either to give variety to the exercise or because they may be useful to be familiar with in doing your work in college.
>
> In doing the exercise, read a question and then determine which reference from the list will most likely lead you to the answer. The titles of the references should be the only clues you need to connect questions to references. Once you've gotten hold of a likely source for answering a question, read the preface on how to use the book and how items are arranged in it. All sources do not arrange items alphabetically. Know how to use your source.
>
> In seeking answers, determine the most likely headings under which the information you are looking for might appear. What key word generally identifies the information? If a particular key does not lead you to an item, look under a synonym for the word; also pay close attention to cross-referencing in the sources. Keep an eye on dates; it will be a lot of wasted time looking in references of the wrong years.
>
> In some instances you will use references that direct you to books in the stacks. These books I have placed on reserve; ask for them at the desk.
>
> This exercise goes through yearly revision. If you feel inclined, write a new question along the line of the questions in the exercise, using any of the books in the reference section—either ones I've used or others. If I can not find the answer to your question within one week from the time I get it, you are free to ignore the rest of this exercise.
>
> If you feel you are being asked to collect a lot of useless information, you are

right. The facts, the content are always stupid. Look to the pattern, the transaction, the process, the doing; there's the point!

In an off-handed way, this exercise is dedicated to the propositions:

that knowledge is a function of being;
that what we are is what we know;
that we learn what we already know;
that action is a function of being.

There are thirty-five questions in each exercise, and three separate exercises— to hinder the student's division of labors. On the average, it takes a student 5-8 hours to complete the assignment, which is about one-third of the time it takes the instructor to put the assignments together. Most students answer most of the questions, responding to an operational situation in operational terms. Another sort of situation is suggested by the introduction, however. It is part gamble and part discrimination. The student who writes a question for the instructor to answer can gamble on his cleverness and the instructor's ineptness; or the instructor can treat any or some of the discriminations as a gamble won by letting the time elapse he has given for solution of student's questions.

Of the forty or so students who have done these exercises, none have taken the gamble/discrimination. Some, not reading the introduction, were unaware of the alternative until it was pointed out in the post mortem where the consequences of choosing it were suggested. The students who slogged regimentally through the operation were faced with this sampling of questions:

You want to find out how many morticians went out of business in 1958. What do you read?

You want to buy covers for your steamship. What address do you go to?

Congress cleared a bill in 1971 making it a federal crime to shoot, harass or hunt any bird, fish or other animal from an airplane. What are the maximum penalties under the bill? What are the penalties if you fly a B-52, hunting and harassing people?

In the slang of horse racing, what position is the "Kentucky position"?

To whom do we owe the pull chain socket?

If you looked at a picture of farmer's tools, how many tines would you see on a beet-lifter?

What is the proper form of address for an emperor?

How doth "welfare" passeth away in *Job*?

You want to be a sheep herder in South Dakota, what book do you read?

"Leave her on a lea and let the devil flit her" is a Lincolnshire proverb spoken of a scolding wife; what's it mean?

What is the Pauli Exclusion Principle?

How many peacock feathers on a hat from Mongolia, the brim of which is covered with velvet and silk, the crown of the hat consisting of pleated brocade and its decorations including a green velvet cord?

In Jacopo Bassano's painting of "Christ at Emmaus," who is looking at the dog?

Name the titles of five short stories about hit-and-run drivers?

Where in the world is Tandjungbuajabuja?

Who was the first ventriloquist dummy awarded a college degree?

By law how many drunks can ride in a taxicab in Traverse City, Michigan?

Student performance was evaluated operationally: correctness and completeness of answers. Also, from the instructor's point of view with regard to the procedures that lead to grades, no more or less merit would have been given to the gamble/discrimination situation relative to the operational situation. In this assignment one choice was as good as another.

Even that purest of operational situations, the multiple-choice test, can be used to question the student's assumptions about his learning. The following questions were used in an open-book quiz over Milgram's "A Behavioral Study of Obedience":

> In Milgram, which of the following signs is *not* an indicator of extreme tension?
> a. sweating
> b. trembling
> c. stuttering
> d. laughing fits

> Which of the following attitudes appeared to influence subject behavior in the experiment?
> a. ends justify means
> b. you can't please everybody
> c. that's the way the ball bounces
> d. orders is orders

For the first no answer is right. In Milgram's headnote to the essay, he includes all the choices as signs of tension. In the second all the answers are right, being common expressions that are roughly equivalent to some of the conditions of the experiment that Milgram includes in a "Discussion" section at the end of the essay.

The questions violate the operational situation. The form of the first question demands an answer, yet all answers are clearly inappropriate. For nearly half of the thirty students, the form of the question prevailed over what their eyes were reading in the essay. The second question works against the nature of testing as a measuring device. There is nothing to measure since any answer will do. One could argue that the student who circles all of the choices is more right than the student who circles only one, but the "which" of the question is ambiguous. It coud mean either "which one" or "how many."

Overall, the test was not a device to measure recall of information, it was a teaching instrument. The first question, in fact, is a model for the Milgram experiment. The design of the question conditions an operational response. To answer it "rightly" requires a sort of gamble: don't answer, or a discrimination: make up your own answer.

Another unworkable assumption that compromises learning is that there are academic problems (arbitrary operations) and experiential problems (genuine operations involving discriminations); and it is the content of the problems that distinguishes school from "life." Posed against this attitude is the philosophic view that problems are all logical (in the mind); that there are no problems in Nature since Nature, pursuing no purpose, is meeting no obstacles. There is little comfort in this for the young, perhaps no comfort for the old, either. However, instruction can throw some spidery threads across the abyss; that is, deemphasize culling and memorization of facts in favor of inferential processing with emphasis on synthesis of all knowledge. There is nothing very profound about this approach.

It's materials are often commonplaces tricked up in high feather for interpolation. Characteristically, the material involves a sort of reading between the lines and behind the lines, a seeing of what is not there, of what the mind can put there by that habit of intuition that seeks interesting answers and suspends belief about the rightness of answers. The spirit of playing with such questions seems inversely proportional to the spirit of academic inquiry. And the capacity to play is not dependent on specialized information.

The student merely has to bring into the circle of the problem that which he already knows. Students have difficulty with such problems because they conceive of learning as reaching out for the unknown. Problems can come from any field or from far afield:

> (Item in *Detroit Free Press*) Maudester Divens, 24, whose only steady income is her welfare payments, struck it rich at Sportsman's Park Racetrack in Chicago last week, winning $12,318.90 on a $2 bet. Friday night, Miss Divens returned to the track, picked up the cash and was robbed of the whole payoff as she left the track.
> Police investigator William Strucke said Miss Divens spends a lot of time at the track. After being robbed of the jackpot, she returned to the track Tuesday and won $600, police said, then won $200 more Thursday.
> (You've got to get up early to mess over foxy Maudester. Despite what the newspaper says, why is it unlikely that Maudester was robbed?)

> The "organ of Corti," a structure in the cochlea of the ear, consists of rows of very fine hairs joined to nerve cells that are stimulated by the vibrations of the hairs. The organ of Corti is one of the few parts of the body not directly nourished by the blood. Why not?

For these two examples the instructor has turned what were originally descriptive bits of information into interrogatives. Another approach is to revive an old problem. Instruction in the sciences does some of this, but to save time on thinking the student mostly gets a description of problem and solution. Then, like thousands before him, he goes to the laboratory to prove the same old solution, neither experiencing the problem nor discovering the solution. Such problems will probably not arise naturally in the student's experience but their solutions can be experienced:

> There are three basic ways of writing language:
> a. draw a picture to represent a word;
> b. use a sign to represent a syllable (Note: In English there are words like in-di-vid-u-al and *strength*);
> c. use a sign for each basic sound in the language, alphabetic writing, as English is.
> You have to decipher a script called Minoan-Mycenaen Linear B. It contains about eighty-nine separate signs. This language is probably which of the basic types?

> Father Scheiner, a contemporary of Galileo, measured the anterior surface of the cornea of the eye. He used a window with a cross painted on it; a person to look at the cross; and a bag of marbles (of various sizes) with mirror finishes. How was he able to make the measurement of the person's cornea?

Parmenedes said, "This is the fundamental nature of the universe. It is a plenum, the universe is filled up. There are no empty spaces. Let's be stoical."

Heraclitus answered, "Move over. No man steps in the same river twice. Everything moves and changes in the universe."

The ancient Greeks saw these two points of view as contradictory and irreconcilable. Reconcile them. Think of a universe in which the two views can co-exist; in other words, what kind of pattern or motion would such a universe have? Look in your toy chest for the model of such a universe.

Then, of course, there are always the real problems of real life:

Dear Heloise:
I had always opened a tuna can and scraped it into the bowl. Then I would have to get another spoon to dip out the mayonnaise. Today I got a bowl and . . . .

26 yrs. The-Wrong-Way

(What amazing hint did this reader send to Heloise?)

Students were shown a photograph with the caption: "Chinese farm worker is still walking—thanks to transplant of left foot to his right leg." The photograph showed a man seated, wearing pants that were rolled up past the knee on the right leg. He wore one boot, and on the other side was a, sure enough, bare left foot on a right leg. The question: "Either the Chinese are inscrutable or there are circumstances under which the operation makes sense. What circumstances?"

Quirky observations can also be given a turn. The following questions were used on a quiz over William James's "The Ethical and Pedagogical Importance of Habit," which begins with a story about a practical joker, who, seeing a retired veteran carrying home his dinner, suddenly called out, "Attention!":

A person walks into a movie theatre, walks down the aisle, stops, watches the screen (a scene from *The Devil In Miss Jones*), places one hand on the back of an aisle seat, unaccountably drops to one knee, rises quickly, blushes slightly, and take a seat.

(What is this person's religion?)

A man with a highly specialized occupation takes a day off and drives to the country. He stops by a field and decides to steal a pumpkin. Just as he is ready to run off with the pumpkin, several hunters come out of the woods about 30 yards in front of him.

He then behaves curiously, taking a step forward, hesitating, then taking another step. Then he too, like the movie-goer drops to one knee.

(What is the pumpkin stealer's specialty?)

There are two attitudes that dismiss problems of this sort as child's play. One is that the content of the problems is undisciplined (unsystematic) or outside of disciplines. This is a valid point in that although specialized knowledge may not be necessary to solving a problem, such knowledge is necessary to formulate the question.

Oppenheimer once said that there were children playing in the streets who could solve some of the top problems in physics, because they had modes of perception that he had lost. However, for the most part, specialists get to solve problems because they know how to or care to put together the problems. Still it can be said that intuitive thinking or solving does not require specialization, that it is a process that can peek behind any sort of content. The uneducated man who has the knack is obviously better off than the Ph.D. that can only raise problems. Some sort of content will come the first man's way, the second is lost.

Another objection to the Maudester-to-Pumpkin-Patch problems is that, even though they may be useful in wiring up certain circuits in the mind, they are still only paper problems. They are outside what is ordinarily meant by experience. Little effect on this is the reply that there is not paper experience and genuine experience, there is only experience; John Dewey's *Democracy and Education* speaks on the *other* side about the essentials of method in education:

> They are first that the pupil have a genuine experience . . .; secondly, that a genuine problem develop within the situation as a stimulus to thought.[2]

Dewey's notion of experience was something like: when I act, it acts. Very well, the instructor will give it one more try. He will structure a situation, one that he can justify by Dewey, that the student can act in; also one that acts upon the false assumption that paper is only paper but pins prick. The instructor asks the students to read Milgram—a paper experience. During the next class he shows a film described in the Fifth U.S. Army pamphlet, *Army Films,* as:

> *Nuremberg*—76 mins. (3 reels)—War crime trials conducted by allies at Nuremberg. Flash backs to various crimes against humanity committed by German High Command during WW II. Contains many scenes of unbelievable atrocities against humanity.

It is more believable in the 70's than it was in 1946 but, no matter, it has its effect—a visual and highly emotional experience. The lights go on. Thirty-three students have seen this other version of *Hogan's Heroes.* The instructor asks the students not to leave the theater because the Chief of Police would like to speak to them. The Chief enters and reads a letter:

Dear Chief McCloskey:

> As you know, the President's Commission on Law Enforcement and Administration of Justice, National Security Committee, has asked for the cooperation of civic officials in conducting a survey on Citizen Support for Law Enforcement Efforts. During January, 1973, the National Security Committee will be conducting hearings and sampling opinions in select communities in the Mid-Western states. To aid in its efforts the Committee has asked that you, or a member of your staff, administer the questionnaire that appears on page 17 of the Survey Packet sent to you by the Commission in November. The sample questionnaire can be duplicated and given *in toto* to one or more of those civic, fraternal, or educational groups defined on page 4 of the Guidelines. Or, the questionnaire can be edited, deleting such questions as may be inappropriate to some respondents, and executed in its revised form.
> Since there is a community college in your area, the Commission asks that one or more samplings be taken among the student population.
> The Commission's Task Force Report cover sheet must be attached to all copies of the completed questionnaire. Revised questionnaires must contain the same instructions to respondents as the sample copy. The Commission asks that in administering the survey, responding groups be asked to follow these instructions.

---

[2]The Free Press (Macmillan paperback), 1966, p. 163.

The Chief leaves, saying that he must administer the questionnaire to another class. The questionnaires are passed out. The cover sheet, a collage of type styles, reads:

Task Force Report:

Citizen Support for Law Enforcement
    Efforts

National Security

Task Force on Assessment

The President's Commission on Law Enforcement and Administration of Justice

Inside are some ominous-sounding instructions and even more ominous, the questions:

Instructions to Respondents: To the best of your knowledge, please answer the following survey questions on CITIZEN SUPPORT FOR LAW ENFORCE-MENT EFFORTS. The survey is completely *confidential* and requires no signature; nor is any signature or identifying code to appear on it.
Please answer *all* questions by checking one and *only* one of the YES-NO responses. Do not alter the questionnaire in any way or add explanatory material.
THANK YOU.

Do you consider yourself to be a loyal American?
Would you aid a law enforcement officer in distress, or aid him in the apprehension of a criminal?
Have you or do you know anyone who has conspired to commit a subversive act?
Do you believe it is *reasonable* to expect people in public places to stand for the playing of the National Anthem?
Do you feel draft resisters and deserters should be given amnesty?
Do you believe the United States has ever waged an aggressive war?
Have you ever heard anyone threaten the life of the President?
Do you believe that public prayers should be allowed in public schools?
Do you believe American government is *basically* honest?
Do you believe in the principles stated in *The Constitution* and *The Declaration of Independence*?
Do you believe in some form of gun control?
Have you ever planned or carried out an act of sabotage?
Do you believe in government *of, for* and *by* the people?
Have you ever traveled to a foreign country?
Have you ever been arrested?
Are you proud of America's space successes?
Do you believe the news media is objective?
Do you presently correspond with someone in a foreign country?
Have you ever taken part in a *demonstration*?

Students are mostly still pondering the instructions when a male student in the front row gets up, says loudly, "I ain't doing this shit," throws a crumpled up questionnaire on the stage, and makes exit up the center aisle. He is out the door when two other students, a man and a woman, without comment leave by a side aisle.

There is a stirring and five "naive" subjects leave the theater. Of the twenty-five students that remain, seventeen will answer all the questions and four will answer only some of the questions. Some of the answers will be "un-American." Four of the questionnaires will be returned with no answers.

During the next class the students watch a video-tape of themselves. Only the police chief was real, elderly and dignified with a real police chief's name: John W. McCloskey. The experimenter's other confederates were the first three students to walk out. The instructor wrote the letter, the questionnaire, and turned on the video-camera just before he turned on the lights. The trick had been impenetrable. The students are asked to write a paper connecting Milgram to *Nuremberg* to their own experience: paper to pins.

The experiment was a sort of Milgram; only the signals for operational behavior and discrimination behavior are, perhaps, clearer to the students than they were to Milgram's subjects. The behavior, however, has also been impenetrable. The students that stayed, were they operators or did they choose to stay? What of those who did not follow the instructions? Those who turned in blank forms? and those who left, did they choose, or were they operational in terms of another model (the questionnaire-crumpler who showed them the way)?

The instructor falls into the machinery. In as much as distinctions are made, one should also know where to stop.

There are not operational situations, gamble situations, and discrimination situations, anymore than there are classroom situations and life situations, anymore than there are logical situations and physical situations. There are situations. And the distinctions, *tricks*.

Robert Zoellner

Behavioral Objectives for English

A review-critique of On Writing Behavioral Objectives for English, *edited by John Maxwell and Anthony Tovatt (Champaign, Illinois: Commission on the English Curriculum, National Council of Teachers of English, 1970, 136 pp., $2.50, stock no. 04024C)*

Everywhere one looks, remarks Robert Hogan in his delightfully humane end-note to *On Writing Behavioral Objectives for English (WBOE)*, "teachers are writing behavioral objectives—in July, on Saturdays, or after school and far into Wednesday night" (p. 127). Indeed they are. Behavioral objectives, the new wave of English pedagogy, threaten to sweep us all into the vast river of technological change which is contemporary America, and from which, heretofore, the teacher of English has generally stood fastidiously aloof. But it becomes increasingly evident that the bastions of humanistic affirmation on which most of us stand are not nearly as sturdy as we thought, and that the profession of English is like to drown in the eddying complexities of systems analysis, cost accounting, and empirical specificationism. We are, in short, and in James Moffett's telling phrase, about to be *MacNamara-ed* (116).

Underlying these recent developments in English pedagogy are four convergent phenomena, three of which have their roots in pervasive conceptual metaphors

Robert Zoellner teaches English at Colorado State University. He wishes to thank William G. McBride of the CSU English Department for invaluable suggestions and criticisms of this paper.

for the educative process: these are the metaphors of *linearity*, of the *core-idea*, and of the *system*. First is the assumption that the *linear* aspects of mathematics and bioscience can be discerned, if one looks hard enough, in humanistic disciplines such as English. It ought to be possible to make rational judgments concerning the inherent and relative difficulty of prose versus poetry, of the symbolic versus the non-symbolic, of the realistic versus the imaginative, of the comic versus the tragic, or the expository versus the argumentative, so that one could develop a linear curriculum, running from kindergarten through the last year of college, exhibiting a gradual progression from simple to complex. We would know, then, precisely where in the continuum of literary artifacts to teach Aesop, *Wind in the Willows*, *Elmer Gantry*, and Kafka's *Metamorphosis*.

Equally significant in curricular thinking in the past decade has been the metaphor of the *core-idea*, the quasi-Jungian conviction (easy to assert but difficult to prove) that underlying all literature of all cultures and times are discernible archetypal patterns expressing the commonality of human experience. Thus, the *hero and the heroic* is such a core-idea; so are the struggle between *good and evil*,

Reprinted from *College English*, Vol. 33, No. 4, January 1972.

the relationship between *man and nature,* the *loss of innocence,* the eternal tension between *head and heart,* and the problem of achieving the *good life.* Fundamental to this metaphor is the belief that if the teacher deals explicitly with the core-idea of *A Tale of Two Cities* or *The Wasteland,* he can assume with considerable confidence that he has conveyed to the student the essential and perdurable "truth" of the work of art. Predictably, the metaphor of the core-idea has been superimposed on the metaphor of linearity. Because the core-idea appears in works so simple as the fable and so complex as Joyce's *Ulysses,* it has the happy effect of endowing the linear curriculum with conceptual unity and thematic cohesion.

Pedagogical theorizing of this sort was given immense impetus by the publication in 1956 of the first part of Benjamin S. Bloom's *Taxonomy of Educational Objectives: The Classification of Educational Goals,*[1] followed four years later by Jerome S. Bruner's enormously influential *The Process of Education.*[2] Bloom's basically metaphorical belief that human thinking can be conceived of as occurring at different "levels" of difficulty and sophistication, running from the lowest level of *knowledge* (simple recall) through *comprehension, application, analysis,* and *synthesis* to the highest level, *evaluation,* reinforced the conviction already abroad that a linear, perhaps

even taxonomic arrangement of subject-matter in any discipline might be possible. Similarly, Bruner's linear theories of child development, his conviction that *any* idea can be taught in some form at any age, his pervasive stress on the articulation of core-ideas (such as *invariance* and *equivalence* in mathematics, or *tragedy* in literature), and his suggestion that curricula be "spiralized" to assure the constant return in successively more elaborate forms to these core-ideas—these conceptions (or perhaps more accurately, these metaphors) reinforced the belief that education was indeed a *process,* and that the *process was linear.*

It is only on the most superficial view an accident of history that these conceptual metaphors should parallel the emergence during the same period of another and at first entirely unrelated theory of linearity, *systems analysis.* The central assumption of systems analysis is that any entity which can be conceived of as a *product* must be the result of the operations of a *system,* and that any system can be usefully conceptualized in linear terms. If this is done, then the system can be broken down into *components* arranged in a manner analogous to a flowchart, and each component can be analyzed in terms of *input* and *output.* To facilitate the job of analysis, the product is conceptualized as a set of *specifications* to be achieved within the criteria of *economy* and *accountability*: at least in theory, the linear mode of conceptualization makes redundancy, inefficiency, and overlapping functions immediately apparent.[3]

[1] *Handbook I: Cognitive Domain* (New York: David McKay, 1956); David R. Krathwohl, Benjamin S. Bloom, Bertram B. Masia, *Handbook II: Affective Domain* (1964). An interesting, perhaps not entirely persuasive application of Bloom's ideas to English is Sandra Clark, "Color me Complete and Sequential," in *The Growing Edges of Secondary English* (Champaign, Ill.: NCTE, 1968), pp. 28-50.

[2] (New York: Knopf and Random House, 1960), especially pp. 13, 52-54.

[3] A useful summary is Bela H. Banathy, *Instructional Systems* (Palo Alto: Fearon Publishers, 1968). Eight articles on specificationism and accountability will be found in *Kappan* (December, 1970).

Given the stress on linearity which already characterized educational thinking during the sixties, it was inevitable that the systems "approach," which has scored so many apparent successes at General Motors and in the Department of Defense, should be brought to bear not only on the linear curriculum itself, but also the other "components" of the entire system: the teachers, the physical facilities in which they work, the media they utilize to enhance their effectiveness, the service personnel who support them, even the social and financial community which underwrites the entire operation. Most cruci· ·y, the student himself is conceptualized as a *product*, and an attempt is made to write a *set of specifications* for that product. It is at precisely this point that the metaphors of linearity, of the core-idea, and of the system all coalesce with a fourth convergent element, *behavioral learning theory*. The coalescence is precipitated at least in part by the high degree of specificationism implicit in the three metaphors. A linear curriculum cannot possibly be constructed without sharp specification of degrees of difficulty. Similarly, no curriculum can be "spiralized" without specification of those fundamental ideas which define the spiral. Finally, systems analysis demands rigid and totally explicit specification of product, and of inputs and outputs for each component of the total activity.

The difficulty is that in education the "product" is a human being, and the ordinary language used to specify human activity is unfortunately encrusted with locutions which, the systems analyst is certain, have little or no objective meaning. We habitually assert that Robert "enjoys tennis" or "is very hungry." But "enjoyment" and "hunger" are both internal events, beyond either observation or verification. The systems analyst pretends not to know *what is meant* by "enjoyment" or "hunger." Behavioral theory appears to offer a way out because its methodology converts internal events into external events. Behaviorally, Robert does not "enjoy" tennis; rather, he can be *observed* playing tennis every day. Similarly, Robert is not "hungry"; rather, he is to be *observed* ransacking the icebox or wolfing down a sandwich. The translation to English is (at first glance) easy and obvious. Robert does not "appreciate" literature; rather, he can be *observed* reading a good book for hours on end. Thus the demand for specification comes to a climax when the product of education—the student—is described in terms of observable behaviors about which there can be no subjective or interpretive argument. Here, for example, is part of a behavioral specification for foreign-language facility at the elementary school level:

The student is expected . . . within a lexical stock of about 800 words, to comprehend:

(1) A *short statement* (not more than 10 syllables) of the native speaker, produced at a normal rate of speed, referring to something concrete in the immediate environment of the student. To this, the student should respond

    (a) by indicating if the statement is true or false;

    (b) by selecting an appropriate picture or object(s); or manipulating objects corresponding to the utterance.

(2) A *short question* (not more than 6-7 syllables) produced by the native at a normal rate of speed; and to re-

spond to it by signaling yes or no.

(3) A *short command* (less than 7 syllables) produced by the native at a normal rate of speed; and to respond to it by performing whatever the command will suggest.[4]

The theoretical value of such quantitative and observable formulations—in English as well as in foreign-language study—is obvious. Such behavioral objectives, if feasible, should make possible a rationally formulated curricular linearity based on observable performance. They should help us put first things first and last things last. Finally, they should eliminate to a large degree that subjectivity of both judgment and measurement which is perhaps the weakest point of traditional humanities teaching. As teachers of English, the methodology underlying behavioral objectives forces us to think hard and honestly about whether or not we really intend that teaching in the humanities, in English or history or philosophy, should have consequences in observable behaviors—should, in short, somehow make the student *act differently*. But if the value of linear specification and behavioral objectives is obvious, the dangers are much less so. For the minute one attempts to restructure any academic discipline in terms of observable, externalized behaviors—in humanistic terms, the minute one moves from "inner man" to "outer man"—one commits oneself inexorably to a *psychological model* and a *psychological base*, both of which must be scrutinized with rigor for their philosophical, moral, pedagogical, and operational implications. This is to say that the psychological question is the ultimate

question. Any book which deals with theories of educational linearity, with specificationist techniques, with systemic views of the educational activity, or with the formulation of behavioral objectives, *without* dealing with the psychological base builds, inevitably, on shifting sand.

In these circumstances, it is dispiriting to have to report that the final effect of *On Writing Behavioral Objectives for English*—currently an NCTE best-seller—will probably be further to perplex, rather than clarify, an already perplexed issue. The reason is simple: the dozen or so eminent contributors to *WBOE*, with two or three exceptions, appear not to have done their homework in the difficult area of behavioral science, or if they have, they are very successful in masking that fact. *WBOE* thus stands as a superb example of the conviction, widely entertained in the profession, that scientific matters, when you really get down to it, can, with a little effort and careful exploitation of the resources of ordinary language, be handled *un*scientifically—poetically, metaphorically, analogistically. Geoffrey Summerfield, no doubt unintentionally, makes my point precisely:

> The intelligent discussion of any of the major social issues of our time . . . is clearly dependent on the availability and effective, actual usefulness of a generously full and responsively subtle lexis. When comparing a useless account with a useful account, the stultifying with the illuminating, one of the first features to compel attention is the discrepancy between a limited and limiting lexis, on the one hand, and a subtly responsive, precisely modulating and modifying, specifically particularizing lexis, on the other. (108)

Honesty compels me to hoist Mr. Summerfield, and most of the other contribu-

---

[4]A redaction from Bela H. Banathy, "The Systems Approach," unpublished paper, Defense Language Institute, West Coast Branch.

tors to *WBOE,* on just this petard. In the several decades since the first dog salivated to Pavlov's first ringing bell, a "generously full and responsively subtle lexis" has gradually been developed by behavioral scientists as an essential concomitant to the animal-learning model which constitutes the bedrock substrate of all behavioral theory. The contributors to *WBOE* make little or no use of either the model or the lexis, and indeed give every indication that their grasp of both is minimal to the point of non-existence. As a consequence, their discussion of the validity or invalidity of behavioral objectives in English tends to be—Mr. Summerfield's terms are entirely appropriate—"stultifying" rather than "illuminating."

This refusal to use the contemporary behavioral lexis or the animal-learning model from which it springs has three sources. First, many English teachers have difficulty grasping the use in scientific fields of *conceptual models* to focus inquiry, to reduce the number of variables with which one must cope, and to introduce a degree of rigor into the extrapolative process—in short, to make the unmanageable manageable. The astrophysicist interested in the complex processes going on in a collapsing star simplifies his analytical task by constructing a partially hypothetical, broad-stroke mathematical model of what *he supposes* the process of collapse to be, and then feeds the parameters of this model into a computer. Not for a moment does he confuse his model with real stars. He is simply using a well-established methodology to "get a handle" on a reality so complex that it would otherwise remain intractably inaccessible. Similarly, behavioral scientists resort to the animal-learning model when studying human

behavior because the laboratory model furnishes a handful of conceptual simplicities which may—*or may not*—make the study of human behavior more manageable. When the humanist observing this procedure concludes that the behavioral scientist is equating humans with rats, and reducing complex human beings to "mere animals," he simply reveals his lack of understanding of investigative procedures in the sciences.

The second reason for refusing to utilize the "subtly responsive, precisely modulating and modifying, specifically particularizing lexis" of behavioral science arises from the humanist's conviction that most scientific nomenclature is "just jargon." The inbred conservatism of most English teachers with regard to language-use persuades them that scientists, and particularly social scientists, could say what they have to say in plain language "if they just took the trouble." Well, there *is* plenty of jargon in the social sciences. When Albert Bandura speaks of a *change agent* when what he really means is *teacher,* he is using jargon. But when he uses a term such as *shaping* or *extinction* he is indicating a real, observable phenomenon, something which at some point in time was new under the sun, and for which a new term had to be invented. On a deeper and perhaps less attractive level, the English teacher's resistance to "jargon" is often symptomatic of a closed-minded professional chauvinism. For many teachers, *successive approximations, stretching the ratio, response-contingent reinforcement,* and *schizokinesis* are all "jargon." On the other hand, terms such as *negative capability, incremental repetition, dangling construction, lexis, mixed metaphor, metaphysical conceit, objective correlative, segmental phoneme, lect, sprung rhythm, iambic pentameter, structure and texture,* and *dissociation of sensibility* are most decidely *not* "jargon." One must perforce conclude that jargon is any term with which the teacher of English is not comfortably familiar or which somehow threatens the security of his cherished world-view.

Third, some of the contributors to *WBOE* have been corrupted by association with those educational psychologists whose method-of-work is based on an all-encompassing eclecticism. They make a virtue of "not being tied" to any "simplistic" or "primitive" model of human behavior. Of totally catholic tastes, they draw their terminology from all areas of psychology—cognitive, psychodynamic, and behavioral—utilizing those terms which fit their preconceptions, and rejecting those which do not. The fact that the various models on which they draw are often radically contradictory and mutually exclusive, one explicitly denying what the other explicitly affirms, bothers them not at all. In essence, they ask us to accept the reality of a Capitalistic Communism and a Latitudinarian Fundamentalism.

Most of the contributors to *WBOE* exhibit one or more of these hang-ups. They meticulously exclude any defined laboratory model from their deliberations, they eschew the behavioral lexis as if it were a series of four-letter words, and they display a methodological stance so flabbily eclectic that in attempting a critique one hardly knows where to begin. They resemble the man who wants to perform surgery without learning anatomy or build spaceships without mastering rocket technology. The result is a massively *un*behavioral discussion of behavioral objectives; it is as if Pavlov, and Watson, and Skinner, had never lived.

How, for example, is one to critique a book on behavioral objectives which in 130 pages—and I here deliver what seems to me to be the most damning generality about *WBOE*—devotes no more than perhaps five pages to actual *student behavior,* says hardly a single word about *teacher behavior,* and nothing whatsoever concerning that complex interaction which we may term *student-teacher behavior?*

But such a criticism is only a beginning. What is needed is some organizing idea which will enable us to illuminate the general educational philosophy—if there is one—underlying the book as a whole. I think the requisite touchstone can be found in the following assertion: *the theory of behavioral objectives adumbrated in* WBOE *is dominated by a Stimulus-Response (S-R) psychology, rather than a Stimulus-Response-Reinforcement (S-R-R) psychology.* Granted that many of the contributors to *WBOE* need not be rigorous or radical Skinnerians in their theoretical outlook, one is still overwhelmed with disbelief when he realizes that he must read through 102 of the 130 pages of *WBOE* before he encounters the term *reinforcement* used—by Isabel Beck—in a properly technical sense. This fact alone suggests that *WBOE* is a very lop-sided book, reflecting in the most distorted manner the current state of behavioral science.

A full appreciation of this lop-sidedness cannot be achieved, however, without some understanding of the immense differences—philosophical, psychological, and methodological—between an S-R and an S-R-R psychology. They are so far apart that they can be said to constitute utterly different psychological universes. The classic configuration of the S-R model is Pavlovian: a bell rings (stimulus) and the dog salivates (response). The classic configuration of the S-R-R model is Skinnerian: the rat makes some response (moving, turning, lifting the head) to an unspecified stimulus, and is instantly rewarded with a food-pellet (reinforcement). The difference is crucial: *in the S-R-R model the response the organism makes—his actual behavior —is considered to be a plastic, shapeable entity under the partial control of the experimenter; in the S-R model it is not.* When Pavlov rang the bell, the dog salivated. If Pavlov rang the bell again, the dog again salivated. The classic S-R construct is therefore at root a "switch on, light on; switch off, light off" model. It generates a methodology in which *given* a specified stimulus, the animal *will* produce a totally specifiable response.

(The reader will not miss, I hope, the resemblance between this phrasing and the phrasing of most behavioral objectives.) Indeed, so fundamental is this conceptualization that when one moves from the autonomic or vegetative activity which concerned Pavlov to the much more complex skeletomuscular activity mediated by the "higher" nervous system which concerns most contemporary psychology, the coercive mechanism of the "switch-light" paradigm is retained, both methodologically and philosophically. The Skinnerian model is as different from this as night from day, as the following comparative schemata, which assumes four successive instances of stimulus-presentation, will suggest:

	Pavlov S-R		Skinner S-R-R		
	Stimulus	Response	Stimulus	Response	Reinforcement
(1)	Bell	Salivation	Unspecified	Moves toward lever	Food
(2)	Bell	Salivation	Unspecified	Moves next to lever	Food
(3)	Bell	Salivation	Unspecified	Touches lever with paw	Food
(4)	Bell	Salivation	Unspecified	Depresses lever	Food

The rigid, radically mechanical nature of response in the S-R model, and the plasticity of response in the S-R-R model, are obvious. But this difference only scratches the surface. Philosophically, there are three massive disparities between S-R and S-R-R models:

(1) *Freedom v. Coercion.* In S-R psychology, the response is specified with a coercive linearity sure to delight the heart of any systems analyst. The rat *will* run the maze, *will* cross the line, *will* discriminate the colors. Terminal response is fully specified *before* the animal does *anything.* Under such a chain-link paradigm, an individualistic rat who is "unable" or "unwilling" to perform the "assigned task" is statistically ignored or excluded, doomed to a kind of empirical annihilation. In total contrast, under the S-R-R model the experimenter must wait patiently, allowing the animal to "behave along" until he emits some bit-of-behavior susceptible to shaping toward the desired terminal behavior. The first response is unspecified—or, more precisely, *the animal specifies it*—and all succeeding shaped responses are determined by and grow out of this first response. Under S-R-R models, *the animal must be allowed to do his own thing.* He furnishes the response freely, *he* defines the parameters of the learning sequence.

(2) *Stimulus v. Reinforcement.* S-R psychology is stimulus-centered; S-R-R psychology is reinforcement-centered.

The difference carries immense philosophical consequences for the teacher. In the S-R model, the experimental variable, the crux of the matter, is the highly specific stimulus which impinges on the organism. It is here that the experiment is structured, and it is this that makes the experiment "go." S-R models, however complex and ingenious, and whether addressed to the autonomic or skeletomuscular systems, can always be detected by the degree of concentration on stimuli: the arrangement of lights or patterns, the construction of a maze, the careful sequencing of sounds. In contrast, in the S-R-R model stimulus-definition is a matter of secondary importance. In the Skinner-box, for example, the stimuli which are causing the rat to behave *are not known, are unspecified.* The crucial experimental variable under this model, the element which makes the S-R-R experiment "go," is the reinforcement and the timing of its injection into the behavioral stream. Everything swings on this. As a consequence, all S-R-R models exhibit a *dynamic, flexible, transactional relationship between two organisms, the rat and the experimenter,* which is missing from most S-R models. The significance of these differences to behavioral theory in education can hardly be overstated. Stimulus-centered psychology minimizes the importance of the teacher, and maximizes the importance of the curriculum and of curriculum objectives. Reinforcement-centered psychology maximizes the importance of the student-teacher relationship and makes curricular matters subordinate to that dynamic relationship.

(3) *Tight Specificationism v. Loose Specificationism.* We come now to the crux of the matter. The whole historical thrust of S-R psychology is toward the tightly particularized, predictive specification of desired terminal behavior, either autonomic or skeletomuscular. In contrast, the S-R-R model suggests a much more generalized, less "specific" specification of terminal behavior. This fact is widely misunderstood because of the inclusion in most Skinner-boxes of a manipulandum—usually a lever to be depressed or a disk to be pecked—so that discrete behaviors can be counted against time to produce a learning curve. These features have led to the supposition that Skinnerian shaping depends upon some very precise specification of terminal behavior, such as "depressing the lever." But in fact the manipulandum and counting mechanism are *not* essential aspects of the S-R-R model. The Skinnerian paradigm can function—and indeed functions more elegantly and clearly—if the manipulandum is eliminated. This gives a free-floating learning situation where the experimenter can shape the behavior of the organism toward some terminal behavior of a generalized sort, and demanding only a generalized specification. In any case—and this is the crucial point —*the animal meets the generalized specification in his own unique and generalized way.* Any Skinnerian experimenter will affirm that nearly every animal has his own "style," and that this style is an integral part of the way in which he satisfies the terminal specification of the Skinner-box. Seasoned experimenters with a sense of humor often have endless cocktail-party stories about the prima-donna cat who refuses to work unless the experimenter speaks to her cajolingly; about the individualistic, off-beat rats who depress the lever, not with the conventional forepaw, but with nose or rump; about the smart-aleck, exhibitionist chimpanzee who discovers that the really

fun way to press a button is while standing on your head and making faces. In short, *the S-R-R model allows for, and even exploits, individual differences, individual idiosyncrasies, individual style.* Philosophically, the latitudinarian dimension of the Skinnerian model finds its source in the pervasive probabilism of S-R-R theory. The experimenter must wait for the animal to "emit" a bit-of-behavior which the experimenter considers shapeable. Whether the animal will in fact emit such behavior is a *question of probability.*

These three differences between S-R and S-R-R psychology can, I think, fruitfully be brought to bear on the general thrust of *On Writing Behavioral Objectives for English.* The almost total inattention to the teacher as reinforcer, as the crucial shaper of the learning process, as the person who must exert a directive influence if any objective is ever to be achieved, gives *WBOE* a distinctly S-R orientation. While the teacher is ignored, the curriculum-as-stimulus is given close attention. There is much discussion of curricular systems, of system-modules, of modular linkages, of module tests. Unmistakably, certain contributors to *WBOE* regard the teacher as a distressingly unpredictable variable in the learning process. They therefore put their faith in elaborate and systematized curriculum-articulation. The result is a stimulus-centered pedagogy which can be called behavioral only by ignoring most of the last thirty years of behavioral research: it out-Pavlovs Pavlov. Finally and most crucially, the entire theoretical structure of *WBOE* is based on the assumption that behavioral objectives must be stated with complete delimitation, great precision, and sharp specification. Even those contributors who have serious doubts about the whole business seem willing to concede that traditional objectives in disciplines such as English—the "appreciation of literature," for example—are suddenly and inexplicably meaningless or simply ritualistic. The consequence is an appallingly mechanical view of the behavior of the literate person. In *WBOE* he suddenly becomes that individual who spends 45 minutes per waking day talking about books, who passes through the library turnstile 5 times per 30-day period, who has 36 inches of shelf-space in his home devoted to literary works per thousand dollars of income, and who visibly (and, we hope, measurably) perspires from aesthetic perturbation every time literature is mentioned. I engage in parody, of course, but the parody has a point. The thrust of *WBOE* is toward the measurement of behavior. But in my view it is a total philosophical distortion of the model to assume that the Skinner-box—or any other laboratory construct—*measures behavior.* It does not. It measures *frequency* of behavior, which is an abstraction *from* behavior. Behavior itself, in all its incredible and beautiful multiplexity, has *never yet been measured,* and we ought to keep that fact firmly in mind when we attempt to translate behavioral learning theory to fields such as English.

The school of educational psychology represented in *WBOE* will almost certainly object that my black-and-white division of behavioral theory into S-R and S-R-R represents the erection of false alternatives, and that I do them an injustice in "pigeon-holing" them in this way. I must respond that the only defensible extrapolation from animal learning theory is a tightly rigorous one, and that such an application of current models presupposes precisely the division I have made. Scientific models, if they are truly models, are unitary, organically homogenous, and indivisible—you buy the whole package or none of the package. Eclectic model-extrapolation is a contradiction in terms. It is this which leads me to assert that the theory of behavioral objectives developed in *WBOE* is neo-Pavlovian, and pernicious by virtue of that fact. Given a maze, the rat *will* run it; given a treadmill, the rat *will* turn it; given a line, the rat *will* cross it; given two colors, the rat *will* discriminate them. The similarity between these formulations and the philosophical assumptions of *WBOE* is unmistakable. There is no room in this model for: *given a pattern of unspecified and generalized stimuli, the rat may do any number of things, one of which will dictate the topography and direction of the rest of the learning-sequence.* In short, the S-R paradigm cannot incorporate individuality or idiosyncrasy. The S-R-R paradigm can. Teachers of English should ponder this fundamental difference as they explore the possibilities—and the dangers—of behavioral theory.

Beyond these philosophical and inescapably scientific matters, the central issue of *WBOE* is the question of the validity of the traditional humanistic locutions concerning the objectives of liberal disciplines such as English. It boils down, finally, to whether or not there is any real significance in much of the ordinary, daily language humanists habitually use. Mr. (Robert, I think, not Frank) McNemar of Part I states the matter succinctly. "Systems experts tend to be dismayed," he tells Emily Jones, "at the present educational system which seeks such classic but nebulous goals as 'citizenship' and 'worthy use of leisure time' or

'health.' What, they ask, in the name of heaven do those terms mean?" And then Mr. McNemar zeros in on English: ". . . what do we mean when we say, 'I want the student to respond to literature,' 'I want him to understand the role of history in the life of Western man,' or 'The student should be a creative, self-actualizing person'?" (6). It is essential to see that Mr. McNemar is really asking two questions; confusion at this point could be disastrous. The first question is: "Are traditional humanistic statements of goals susceptible of sharper specification?" I think the answer to this question must be *yes*. Any piece of language can be sharpened, and we have a professional obligation to consider the possibilities of more precise statements of goals in English. But underneath this first question Mr. McNemar is asking another, and much more crucial question: "Do traditional humanistic locutions *have any meaning at all?*" This question, which is fundamental to every page of *WBOE*, must be met frontally and vigorously, or we are all dead. It is therefore distressing to watch some of the most competent and knowledgable people currently in English take refuge in *nolo contendere*, thus giving away the ranch without a struggle to Mr. McNemar and his fellow technocrats. Here, for example, is J. N. Hook:

> . . . the objectives conventionally followed in English classrooms tend to be so vague as to be almost meaningless. What, for example, does "appreciate literature" mean? What does a student do when he appreciates? What are the evidences of appreciation? A clearer statement of objectives might make much class activity less rambling, better aimed, more valuable to students and teachers alike. (76)

And, much further along the primrose path, Mr. Geoffrey Summerfield:

... whenever we invoke any of the long-cherished values of the humanist educational tradition—the notion of the fully developed personality, for example—we have to recognize the distinct possibility that we are merely trading in cliché, in the vacuously formulaic, muttering self-reassuring incantations. (108)

Both Mr. Hook and Mr. Summerfield are dancing on the edge of a precipice, whether they realize it or not. They are both within half an inch of conceding to the systems analyst the *functional inutility of most humanistic idiom.* If they go that last half inch, English is moribund. Mr. McNemar will shortly be saying that the teacher who consumes class time talking about Milton's "organ tone," or the "power of blackness" in Hawthorne, or the "tactility of Melville's sensibility," or "communication by nuance" in Henry James, is really not talking about anything substantive, is really consuming valuable and expensive school time inflicting "almost meaningless" literary "incantations" upon the students, and that the school system is under an obligation to the overburdened taxpayers to stop funding such obvious nonsense (Sue M. Brett and John C. Flanagan are saying this already, in my opinion).

I think both Mr. Hook and Mr. Summerfield are wrong, are on the verge of conceding far too much, and need to re-examine their position. Let me illustrate my point with a few examples. When NBC completed the famous Studio B for Arturo Toscanini, the maestro strode into the studio, walked amid utter silence to the center of the stage, clapped his hands together sharply, listened for a moment to the reverberations, and delivered his verdict on the acoustics of the hall: "*Too dry.*" Now, while I have little or no knowledge of acoustics, I have some ex-perience of concert halls, and I know *exactly* what Mr. Toscanini meant. So do the hundreds of thousands of other civilized people with some knowledge of concert halls. All of us together comprise a relatively small language-community within which such locutions concerning concert halls *carry precise meanings.* We are not in the least discomfited by the fact that "dryness" of reverberation cannot be empirically rendered. Acoustical "dryness" exists in the experienced ear and no where else; the oscilloscope will never be built which can give it objective rendering. *It is a purely behavioral phenomenon.* Similarly, I have in recent years become addicted to professional football. When I joined this particular language-community, and the announcer asserted that Warren Wells had "good hands" or was making "good moves" as he ran downfield for a pass, I could not distinguish "good hands" from other hands, or perceive the "good move" the receiver made in the general continuum of running. But I can now. Hundreds of hours in front of the TV set (I confess it shamelessly) was the ticket of admission to this language-community: I now know *exactly* what is meant by a "good move" or "good hands." The reason: *both locutions indicate a purely behavioral phenomenon.*

The fact is that much of the most meaningful part of the life of any civilized person consists of incredibly subtle and finely nuanced perceptions which, from a behavioral point of view, can be explained by the simultaneous impact of tens, or hundreds, or perhaps thousands of "bits" of information from the external world. The result is not discrete or tabulative fact, but rather a *sense of the facts.* And for this sense, we have devised hundreds of thousands of terms which are *totally precise in meaning but logically irreducible.* The best way to see this is to get out of English and other humanistic disciplines and into a language-community where the object of scrutiny is much more tactile, but the idiom equally intuitive. Cattle-judging—would you believe it—fills the bill precisely. Listen for a moment to a seasoned judge at a county fair explaining to the professionals in the stands why he placed four Hereford heifers the way he did:

> I placed 4, the largest, beefiest, most rugged heifer in the class, over 3 because she has more length of body and more substance of bone. 4 especially is longer and thicker over the loin and rump and lets down into a much thicker, deeper, quarter. I criticize 4 for lacking femininity and Hereford character about the head. . . . I place 3 over 2 [because] she is larger in the forearm, and fuller and deeper in the heart and fore rib. She also stands and travels wider. . . . In placing 2 over 1, I have a heifer that is showing more beef type. She is a growthier heifer, showing more stretch and trimness of body. I grant that 1 is a more typy, feminine individual.[5]

We are dealing here with preponderantly intuitive and essentially aesthetic judgments. Because I have sons in 4-H, and because I have a behavioral humanist's interest in these uses of language, I have spent much time in the show-stands in carefully casual conversation with Colorado ranchers and farmers, trying to determine what quantum of meaning these terms actually convey. There is no question that when a judge remarks that a heifer (which to me appears to be the essence of wall-eyed bovine stupidity) is "feminine," or asserts that an Angus bull

---

[5] I am indebted to Professor James Oxley of the Animal Science Department at Colorado State University for this example, as well as his patience with my persistent queries.

has "an abundance of breed type," or that another animal is a "wing-shouldered bull that rolls over on his front feet when he walks," or that another animal "stands in too much grass," the people of this community, who have been working with beef-animals all their lives (and suffer no debilitating self-consciousness about their uses of language) know exactly what objective aspect of the animal is being indicated. They also know that what is being indicated could never be demonstrated by applying ruler and calipers, in a kind of wrong-headed morphological empiricism, to the cattle being judged. The intuitive language of the cattle industry, which determines how hundreds of millions of dollars will be spent yearly, is *factually substantive but logically irreducible.*

It is important to see that I stand in relation to this Colorado language-community in precisely the same position that Mr. McNemar stands in relation to liberal disciplines such as English. I know next to nothing about cattle-judging, and consequently *I cannot perceive the referent* when told that an animal is "breedy headed," has a "good definition of parts," or a "soft set about the eye." But that does not mean that the referent is not there. It only means that in the subtle world of animal husbandry I am an ignoramus and a goth. And that is what I think Mr. McNemar and his ilk are: ignoramuses and goths—*technogoth* is perhaps the word needed. When Mr. McNemar asks me what I mean by the "well-furnished mind," or "appreciation of literature," or "the shaping influence of the tradition"—or what Miss Jones means by the "creative, self-actualizing person," both Miss Jones and I can take him in one of two ways. We can assume that he is simply trying to get us to be more precise in our statement of the humanistic goals of English. If this is all that Mr. Mc-Nemar intends we can be grateful to him; definitive precision of phrasing is a goal all of us should constantly seek. But I think it would be more realistic to assume that Mr. McNemar *means just what he says*, that he literally *does not understand* such locutions, that he honestly believes them to have *no substantive meaning*, and that he regards it as his job to wean us from such professionally ritualistic incantations. If this is the case—and *WBOE* in general seems to substantiate this interpretation—then we must tell Mr. McNemar that the phrase, "creative, self-actualizing person" *means exactly what it says*, nothing more and nothing less. If Mr. McNemar persists in his incomprehension, pretending (or more likely *not* pretending) that the phrase has no meaning for him, *then we should throw him out of our classrooms.* He is obviously an ignoramus and a goth, should not be allowed within five miles of a school building, and can only interfere with our job-of-work and reduce our effectiveness. Moreover, if school boards or college deans, as a consequence of having had a 45-minute lunch with Mr. McNemar, demand that we abandon such humanistic locutions and get down to brass tacks, we must stand our ground at all costs. To concede even as much as Mr. Hook and Mr. Summerfield appear to have conceded will result, inevitably, in the death of English as an academic discipline.[6]

---

[6] In actuality, this represents something of an over-simplification of my position vis-à-vis Mr. McNemar. I do in fact believe that human behaviors could, at least theoretically, be rendered in an empirically precise form. Let us take, for example, that subtle thing called "gracefulness of carriage" in a woman. I am certain that with vast labor one could develop computer-accessible parameters for "gracefulness of carriage." These might include angle

What is needed at this point, although this is not the place to develop it, is an articulated justification of humanistic locutions such as the "well-furnished mind," not in logical, but rather in philosophically behavioral terms. Let me suggest the possibility that such justification is available in Ludwig Wittgenstein's examination of the way in which we perceive what he calls "forms of life," and his analysis of the verbal structures we have developed to indicate such forms. His analysis, of course, is developed in terms of games; he is fascinated by the way in which we perceive that two such topographically different activities as chess-playing and tennis are both games. Avoiding the essentialist position which has

of the spine in relation to the vertical, angular tilt of the pelvis, cyclic displacement of the backside, relation of the balls of the feet to the spinal line at the end of each step, displacement of the cranial center from the body-center at mid-point of stride—and perhaps, at a minimum, *five to ten thousand other such parameters.* All ten thousand of these empirical coordinates could then be fed into the computer. At this point we could have, say, one thousand women of notably graceful carriage walk in front of a scanning device, probably a ten-by-fifty foot electronic grid made up of inch-square "bits," so that the computer could actually measure each woman's carriage against the parameters already fed into it. It would then be a simple matter for the computer to deliver the normative values inherent in that subtle thing called "gracefulness of carriage." But the print-out for "gracefulness of carriage" *would stretch halfway across campus.* One would need a wheeled dolly to carry it about. And this is only the beginning. A computer-accessible set of parameters for "appreciation of literature" or "the behavior of the literate man" would lead to print-outs that could not be carried at all. They would have to be *shipped*, like coal, by freight-car or barge. Behind these fatuous examples lies a serious point: empirical renderings of complex human behaviors—and that is what poor Mr. McNemar really wants—may be possible, but they will never be *pedagogically useful*, any more than a life-size map of New York City would be of any use to people living in New York City.

traditionally accounted for such verbal phenomena, he suggests that what we actually perceive are chains of "family resemblances" between *behaviors*. It is this stress on observed behaviors, on behavioral topography, on forms of life, which gives much of his work a behavioral thrust he was, regrettably, at some pains to deprecate. If we are presently experiencing difficulty in defending our humanistic idiom, it may be because we stubbornly refuse to understand that when we speak of the "creative, self-actualizing person," we are *not* dealing with a logical construct, but rather indicating our *sense* of a pattern of external and observable behaviors—behaviors which, however, are of such subtlety and complexity as to stand forever beyond Mr. McNemar's gross and tabulative empiricism. If this is the case, then the final answer to Mr. McNemar's persistent questioning will have to be, for Miss Jones and for the rest of us, a humanistic behaviorism which will furnish us with a genuinely scientific justification for our ways of work, and have the happy effect of sending Mr. McNemar's methodology back to Willow Run and the vocational education workshop, where it belongs.

In all of this, finally, I do not mean to suggest that *WBOE* is not, in some respects, a valuable and even heartening book. It gives one a sense of the fundamental strength and perdurability of English as a discipline to watch professionals of great competence come by instinct to the right conclusions in a situation where they are, perhaps, somewhat out of their natural element. James Hoetker, for example, does much to save the ball-game with his warning that "simple-minded insistence upon the *a priori* specification of all objectives in terms of conveniently

observable behaviors does far more harm than good" (50). His division of behaviors into *can-do, may-do,* and *will-do* seems to me to be a specious extrapolation from the model, having the effect of minimizing verbal behavior, which is essentially and always of the can-do sort. But when he gets down to the specifics of his work, such as his brilliantly conceived attempts to make visualization behavior an integral part of the reading of literature (57), he seems to be breaking ground which might revolutionize the teaching of English—especially if it is reconceptualized in terms of an S-R-R rather than an S-R model. James Moffett's attack on the Tri-University Project is a study in right instincts and wrong reasons, badly debilitated by his assumption that all behaviorism is of the S-R kind. Nothing could be more striking, however, than his insistence on the centrality of "two-way transactional models of action" in teaching (115). Skinner could hardly have said it better himself. I cannot agree with Donald A. Seybold that Mr. Moffett's "concern with the psychological base seems overwrought and misdirected" (119). A *lack* of concern with the psychological base is precisely what is wrong with the better part of *WBOE*, and Mr. Moffett's withdrawal from the Tri-University Project is, in these circumstances, a courageously humane gesture.

The best thing in *WBOE*, however, is Robert F. Hogan's "On Hunting and Fishing and Behaviorism." When one goes hunting, he asserts, one knows exactly what he is going after. When one goes fishing, however, things are much more iffy: there may be a "stray rock cod," or there may not. One may instead catch a small sea bass, or a halibut, or a smelt—or none of these. In this case one happily settles for "the affective response to the sun and the sea and the fellowship" (125). Mr. Hogan is saying a number of things, at least two of which are worth redacting here. First, he is affirming the joy that behavioral creatures take in behavior for its own sake—and objectives be damned. He quite properly fears the "no-nonsense, mission-centered mentality" (126). Second, his fishing metaphor affirms the pervasive probabilism of teaching in the liberal disciplines. Teacher and student, in the transactional situation, fish together, neither always being entirely sure what they will come up with. Mr. Hogan is rejecting, as any humanist must reject, the non-probabilistic nature of the S-R model and the behavioral objectives derived from it. I hope he will hesitate, however, before he writes off all behavioral theory. The S-R-R paradigm does allow, as the S-R paradigm does not, for the situation in which, for example, "children are constantly establishing and modifying their objectives" (127). Finally, Mr. Hogan's last paragraph brings *WBOE* to a close on a heartening note of humane affirmation:

> (Tonight I am going to try again to teach my youngest daughter to brush her teeth up and down. I am also going to kiss her goodnight and nuzzle her a little. I would like her to grow up with clean, strong teeth. I'd also like her to grow up nuzzled. I have the feeling it will make a difference, even if I can't tell how that difference will manifest itself.) (129)

Mr. Hogan might be surprised—perhaps even put off—to learn that he is a Skinnerian, but he is. His instinctive faith in the long-term efficacy of nuzzling suggests that he entertains a reinforcement-centered psychology, and a concomitant belief in generalized behavioral objectives. He subscribes therefore to the only behavioral psychology which, it seems to me, a teacher of English can permit in his classroom.

Part II. Tactics

W. Ross Winterowd

"Topics" and Levels in the
Composing Process

ONE OF THE MOST INTERESTING (and certainly one of the most neglected) aspects of rhetoric is the notion of topics or places of invention. Throughout the more recent history of rhetoric, the importance of topics for invention or creativity has been either minimized or overlooked, and the prevailing attitude was never more unequivocally stated than by Bernard Lamy, whose *De l'Art de Parler* appeared in English translation in 1676:

> Those who reject these Topicks, do not deny their Fecundity; they grant that they supply us with infinite numbers of things; but they alledg that that Fecundity is inconvenient; That the things are trivial, and by consequent the Art of *Topicks* furnishes nothing that is fit for us to say. If an Orator (say they) understands the subject of which he treats; if he be full of incontestable Maxims that may inable him to resolve all Difficulties arising upon that subject; If it be a question in Divinity, and he be well read in the Fathers, Councils, Scriptures, &c. He will quickly perceive whether the question propos'd be Orthodox, or otherwise. It is not necessary that he runs to his Topicks, or passes from one common place to another, which are unable to supply him with necessary knowledg for decision of his Question. If on the other

side an Orator be ignorant, and understands not the bottom of what he Treats, he can speak but superficially, he cannot come to the point; and after he has talk'd and argued a long time, his Adversary will have reason to admonish him to leave his tedious talk that signifies nothing; to interrupt him in this manner, Speak to the purpose; oppose Reason against my Reason, and coming to the Point, do what you can to subvert the Foundations upon which I sustain my self.[1]

Lamy might well have been paraphrasing remarks that typify discussions of rhetoric in both English and speech departments of modern universities.

But topics need to be reconsidered from both the theoretical and the pedagogical points of view. The purpose of this discussion will be (a) to point out that all topics fall into one of four categories, according to the nature of their operation, and (b) to attempt to revitalize the concept of topics in rhetorical theory and in pedagogy. The first purpose of the discussion will clarify the nature of all topics, and among the expert witnesses who would testify concerning the desirability of the second purpose is Richard McKeon:

> We need a new art of invention and discovery in which places are used as means

W. Ross Winterowd, Professor of English at the University of Southern California, is interested in rhetorical theory and in modern poetry. He directs a new interdisciplinary doctorate in rhetoric, linguistics, and literature.

[1]Quoted in Wilbur Samuel Howell, *Eighteenth-Century British Logic and Rhetoric* (Princeton University Press, 1971), p. 92.

Reprinted from *College English*, Vol. 34, No. 5, February 1973.

by which to light up modes and meanings of works of art and natural occurrences and to open up aspects and connections in existence and possibility. The data and qualifications of existence are made by attention and interest; and discoveries made in a book or a work of art should provide places by which to perceive creatively what might otherwise not be experienced in the existent world we constitute. It is a long time since topics have been used as an art of invention in rhetoric. . . . A reconstituted verbal art of invention, adapted to our circumstances and arts, might be used to shadow forth the methods and principles of an architectonic productive art generalized from invention in language to discovery in existence.[2]

With at least one school of modern linguistics, I assume that the composing process involves putting meanings into structures or saturating structures with meanings, though, to be sure, the mechanisms whereby this process takes place are not known, and, in fact, the assumption that something of the kind takes place is really just an explanatory metaphor adopted to get theorists over the barricades of some extremely difficult questions. What I am saying—though I do not intend to argue the point—is that in some sense, there is both form and meaning, even though separating the two is next to impossible if one holds as a criterion the complete satisfaction of every opinion concerning what is form and what is content.[3]

Central to the composing process is what rhetoric traditionally has called "invention," the means whereby the writer discovers subject matter. And the concept of "topics" or "commonplaces" was the very heart of invention in the classical theory of Aristotle. It will be recalled that topics are, in effect, probes or a series of questions that one might ask about a subject in order to discover things to say about that subject. They are general and apply to all subject matter; they are not, as it were, subject-specific. So that Aristotle's topics can generate arguments for, say, negotiating any peace, not just peace in Viet Nam.

For example, the first of the twenty-eight demonstrative topics that Aristotle lists is the argument from opposites:

If, now, it is not fair to grow enraged when evil doers injure us unwittingly, then neither do we owe a grain of thanks to him who does us good when forced to do it.

Another of the topics is *a fortiori* (from degrees of more and less):

If it behooves each citizen among you to care for the reputation of your city, it behooves you all as a city to care for the glory of Greece.[4]

There is no better comment on the topics than Kenneth Burke's: "The so-called 'commonplaces' or 'topics' in Aristotle's *Art of Rhetoric* . . . are a quick survey of opinion. . . . "[5] Burke goes on

---

[2]"The Uses of Rhetoric in a Technological Age," *The Prospect of Rhetoric*, ed. Lloyd F. Bitzer and Edwin Black (Englewood Cliffs, N.J.: Prentice-Hall, 1971), p. 55.

[3]Roland Barthes goes so far as to say, " . . . we can no longer see a text as a binary structure of Content and Form; the text is not double but multiple; within it there are only forms, or more exactly, the text in its entirety is only a multiplicity of forms without content. We can say metaphorically that the literary text is a stereography: neither melody, nor

harmony (or at least not unrelieved harmony), it is resolutely contrapuntal; it mixes voices in a volume, not in a line, not even a double line." "Style and Image," *Literary Style: A Symposium*, ed. Seymour Chatman (London and New York: Oxford University Press, 1971), p. 6.

[4]*The Rhetoric of Aristotle*, trans. Lane Cooper (New York: Appleton-Century-Crofts, 1960). The twenty-eight demonstrative topics are on pp. 159-72.

[5]*A Rhetoric of Motives, A Grammar of*

to say that in the topics, Aristotle "catalogues" the available means of persuasion, and it will be the kinds of cataloguing that interest us first, and then the sorts of things that are catalogued. In fact, it will become apparent that, classed according to system of cataloguing and things catalogued, there are only four possible kinds of topics.

First, simply but significantly, it is apparent that topics can be either *finite or non-finite lists*.

Perhaps the most common sort of topics that one encounters (and in many ways the least interesting, though useful) are what are generally called "methods of paragraph development." These are so commonly encoutered that I will not here go into detail concerning them, but typically such a list would contain items like the following: data, enumeration, analogy, anecdote, cause and effect, comparison and contrast, definition, description, metaphor, restatement, and so on.[6] Now it is perfectly obvious that this list could be extended almost indefinitely, for it might contain all of the sorts of things that can go into paragraphs, which ultimately implies classification in some way of all the sorts of things in the universe. That is, methods of paragraph development as topics are characteristically non-finite lists. Aristotle's topics are also just as obviously a non-finite list.

But we can conceive of, find in great abundance, and invent for ourselves topics which constitute finite lists. Burke's Pentad is nothing more than a finite set of topics, as Burke himself avows:

Motives and A Rhetoric of Motives (New York: World Publishing Company, 1962), p. 580.

[6]In fact, this is the list in *Structure, Language, and Style*, a rhetoric handbook that I wrote three or four years ago.

What is involved, when we say what people are doing and why they are doing it? An answer to that question is the subject of this book. The book is concerned with the basic forms of thought which, in accordance with the nature of the world as all men necessarily experience it, are exemplified in the attributing of motives. . . . any complete statement about motives will offer *some kind of* answers to these five questions: what was done (act), where or when it was done (scene), who did it (agent), how he did it (agency), and why (purpose).[7]

(The Pentad is particularly useful, of course, in generating subject matter concerning any piece of discourse, either written or spoken, either literary or nonliterary. But my purpose at the moment is not to demonstrate the usefulness—or lack thereof—of any set of topics.)

It follows from the nature of a finite list of topics that it must not allow for any questions that are not "covered" by the items in the set. That is, if one can ask questions, *within the terms set down for the Pentad*, which cannot be classed under one of the items of the Pentad, then the Pentad is *faulty* as a finite set of topics. (I personally do not feel that the Pentad is faulty, but that question is beside the point of this discussion.)

A faulty set of topics, used here as an example, will clarify the problem that we are getting at.

A five-item set emerged from the National Developmental Project on Rhetoric.[8] In a severely abbreviated (but not, I think, unfair) form, this is the set:

1. The social reality of the present moment may be viewed in terms of the resources for innovation or the defense of tradition. . . . what

---

[7]*A Grammar of Motives*, p. xvii.
[8]*The Prospect of Rhetoric*, pp. 228-36.

are the social conditions and resources available to the inventing person?

2. A second set of questions: What are the materials and perspectives upon facts out of which invention may be fashioned? What technologies may be harnessed in making a car, what facts or interpretations of facts may be spoken. . . ?

3. What about the *persons* who will participate in the invention—and the drives which make them vital or retarding factors in the process. . . ?

4. What is the *deep structure* of the invention. . . ?

5. Finally, what *presentational form* is adopted for the thing invented. . . ?

For this provocative and useful set of topics, the authors[9] make the following unfortunate claim: "These five aspects may be considered as a generative frame, *an ordering of all the relevant aspects of any invented, innovative, or novel creation*. As such they provide a place of places, a frame of frames, an account of the origin or creation of all things novel, including rhetorical artifacts."[10] One question generated by another set of topics that we will be dealing with shortly[11] demonstrates the faultiness of the above as a finite set. "How is the subject under consideration changing?" This question does not fit any of the topics in the set (and one can find other questions

that do not fit); therefore, the set is faulty.

If rhetorical theory is to have the integrity that only precision and logical consistency can bring to it, then non-finite sets of topics must not masquerade as finite sets. We have here something of the dilemma faced by grammarians who worked under the assumption that "A noun is the name of a person, place or thing" or that "A sentence is the expression of a complete idea." These definitions were theoretically destructive and had only marginal value—if any—in pedagogy, since they precipitated the whole logomachy of what a "thing" or a "complete idea" is.

Sets of topics can be, then, either finite or non-finite lists. They can also be *content-oriented* or *form-oriented*.

For one example of a set of form-oriented topics, I refer to my own "The Grammar of Coherence,"[12] a set that, according to my claim, will generate structures at the paragraph level and beyond. (In brief, my argument is that six and only six relationships prevail in coherent discourse beyond the sentence, or, more precisely, beyond the transformational unit. If this is indeed the case, as I believe it is, then these relationships will serve as topics that will "automatically" generate paragraphs or, for that matter, essays.)

A further example: in an article that has received far too little attention, Alton L. Becker[13] developed a schema to analyze and describe the structure of paragraphs. What has not been generally recognized is that this schema can be used as a finite set of form-oriented

[9]Robert L. Scott, James R. Andrews, Howard H. Martin, J. Richard McNally, William F. Nelson, Michael M. Osborn, Arthur L. Smith, Harold Zyskind.

[10]*The Prospect of Rhetoric*, pp. 232-33. Italics mine.

[11]That developed by Young, Becker, and Pike.

[12]*College English*, 31 (May 1970), 828-35.

[13]"A Tagmemic Approach to Paragraph Analysis," *The Sentence and the Paragraph* (Champaign, Ill.: National Council of Teachers of English, 1966), p. 33.

topics. It happens that the schema is brief enough to serve as an example in the present context.

Becker claims that empirical investigation reveals that expository paragraphs invariably have the elements

T opic
R estriction
I llustration

P roblem
S olution

Q uestion
A nswer

in various combinations and permutations, the details of which I will ignore. (That is, TRIPSQA will describe the form of any expository paragraph.) A paragraph that Becker analyzes will serve as an example of what he is getting at.

> (P) How obsolete is Hearn's judgment? (S$_1$) (T) On the surface the five gentlemen of Japan do not themselves seem to be throttled by this rigid society of their ancestors. (R) Their world is in fact far looser in its demands upon them than it once was. (I) Industrialization and the influence of the West have progressively softened the texture of the web. Defeat in war badly strained it. A military occupation, committed to producing a democratic Japan, pulled and tore at it. (S$_2$) (T) But it has not disappeared. (R) It is still the invisible adhesive that seals that nationhood of the Japanese. (I) Shimizu, Sanada, Yamazaki, Kisel, and Hirohito were all born within its bonds. Despite their individual work, surroundings and opinions, they have lived most of their lives as cogs geared into a group society. . . .[14]

It is easy to see how TRIQAPS—and note that I have acronymized the system—can serve as a set of form oriented topics.

---

[14]From Frank Gibney, *Five Gentlemen of Japan*, quoted in Becker.

Write a topic sentence.
As one ages, one learns that all vices are pleasant.

Restrict it.
But some vices are unhealthy.

Illustrate.
Smoking causes cancer.
Drinking causes cirrhosis.
Even the caffeine in coffee has been found to increase the process of aging.

Admittedly, depending on one's vantage point, TRIQAPS can be viewed as either a form-oriented or a content-oriented set of topics. Perhaps the best known example of a set of *purely* form-oriented topics is the set that constitutes what Francis Christensen called "free modifiers." Christensen did not view his modifiers as topics, but, in effect, they are precisely that, for they can be used to generate sentences. That is, to a sentence base, one can add a variety of structures (noun clusters, verb clusters, absolutes, and so on). In deciding to add a structure, one must search for subject matter to "fill" that structure. I will illustrate the process.

Write a base.
The little girl skated.

Add an absolute.
Her pigtails flying, the little girl skated.

Add a verb cluster.
Her pigtails flying, the little girl skated, effortlessly gliding down the sidewalk.

Add a relative clause.
Her pigtails flying, the little girl, who every Saturday morning came to my house for popcorn, skated,

effortlessly gliding down the sidewalk.

And so on. Note that the instructions specify the addition of structures, not of content. Adding a structure must generate content for the structure.

In my opinion, the most interesting and productive set of content-oriented topics is that developed by Richard E. Young, Alton L. Becker, and Kenneth L. Pike.[15] To summarize it here would distort its complexity, but what Young, Becker, and Pike claim is (a) that to know anything, we must know how it differs from everything else, how much it can change and still be itself, and how it fits into hierarchies of larger systems; and (b) that we can view anything from three perspectives, that of particle, that of wave, and that of field. The juxtaposition of these two concepts creates a nine-item finite set of content-oriented topics that I personally find to be most exciting.

Now then, we can recapitulate and systematize.

Content-oriented non-finite sets of topics
   (Aristotle's topics; methods of paragraph development, etc.)

Content-oriented finite sets of topics
   (Young, Becker, and Pike's topics; from one point of view, TRIQAPS; Burke's Pentad; the parts of the classical oration, etc.)

Form-oriented finite sets of topics
   (from one point of view, TRIQAPS; the set outlined in "The Grammar of Coherence"; Christensen's free modifiers, etc.)

Regarding the fourth category, *form-oriented non-finite sets of topics*, a theoretical problem of considerable dimensions arises. It is this: any set of topics that is non-finite and form-oriented must be faulty (according to the definition of "faulty" developed in this essay), for it is impossible that formal relationships regarding any level of discourse can be infinite in number. The same argument that demonstrates the finite nature of a grammar can be applied to demonstrate the finite nature of relationships beyond those handled by the grammar of a language. The validity of this argument seems self-evident. Therefore, a form-oriented set of topics that is non-finite must be merely incomplete and hence faulty. Nonetheless, there are such lists. One example is lists of figures of grammar—from Peacham to Lanham[16]—for lists of figures of grammar are sets of topics; another example is methods of organization discussed in rhetorics.

The conceptual framework for theories of topics is, then, clearcut, but what of topics in pedagogy?

One way of conceptualizing the process of composition is to assume that it involves a three-level hierarchy.

The first level is that of the proposition. Following the model developed by Charles Fillmore, I would argue that a "core" or "kernel" sentence is made up of a modality plus a proposition.[17] The modality contains such elements as auxiliary, yes/no question, negation, and so on. The proposition is a predicate and a variety of "roles" or cases that relate to

---

[15]*Rhetoric: Discovery and Change* (New York: Harcourt, Brace & World, 1970).

[16]*A Handlist of Rhetorical Terms* (Berkeley and Los Angeles: University of California Press, 1968).

[17]"The Case for Case," *Universals in Linguistic Theory*, ed. Emmon Bach and Robert Harms (New York: Holt, Rinehart and Winston, 1968), pp. 1-88.

it and to one another. Thus, schematically:

Modality	Proposition
Present tense	Predicate (kiss): Agent (George), Patient (Mary)

George kisses Mary.
Mary is kissed by George.

The teacher cannot, it seems to me, intervene at this level. If the student, of whatever age, is incapable of generating these core sentences, there is obviously some dysfunction that is beyond the reach of mere pedagogy.

The next level is that of inter-propositional connections, which might be called the level of *syntax*.

George, who is a neurotic, chews gum.
George, a neurotic, chews gum.
A neurotic, George chews gum. (ambiguous?)

In his work, Francis Christensen demonstrates that the teacher can intervene at this level in the composing process, indeed with dramatic results. In *Transformational Sentence-Combining*,[18] John Mellon also demonstrates that the teacher can help the student at the level of syntax. Since one of the great intellectual powers that one can attain is the ability to combine predications, the work of Christensen and Mellon is not to be ignored or to be written off lightly.

But in this discussion of topics, we are most concerned with the third level in the composing process, which I shall call the level of the *transition* since it has to do with units such as paragraphs and essays. It is at this level that the concept

of topics becomes tremendously important.

To refer back to Lamy, who was quoted at the beginning of this discussion: surely he—and virtually everyone else who in the last three hundred years has written about topics—must have missed a significant point concerning the theory of topics. The purpose of topics is not to supply verbiage in lieu of real subject matter, but to generate ideas concerning the subject. In this sense, topics are devices for problem-solving; they are heuristics. Young, Becker, and Pike explain heuristics and, in the process, give an admirable explanation of how topics function:

A heuristic procedure . . . provides a series of questions or operations that guides inquiry and increases the chances of discovering a workable solution. More specifically, it serves three functions:
1) It aids the investigator in retrieving relevant information that he has stored in his mind. (When we have a problem, we generally know more that is relevant to it than we think we do, but we often have difficulty in retrieving the relevant information and bringing it to bear on the problem.)
2) It draws attention to important information that the investigator does not possess but can acquire by direct observation, reading, experimentation, and so on.
3) It prepares the investigator's mind for the intuition of an ordering principle or hypothesis.[19]

In this sense, everyone uses "topics" more or less systematically all the time; most of us unconsciously have developed a variety of sets of topics that we apply quite automatically in all kinds of circumstances. (It occurs to me that I have

---

[18](Champaign, Ill.: National Council of Teachers of English, 1969).

[19]*Rhetoric: Discovery and Change*, p. 120.

developed a set of topics for planning fishing trips, and my adherence to the procedure that they imply never varies. Of course, in the last three years my success at fishing has been minimal!)

The concept of topics, then, is not trivial, though, to be sure, there are trivial or faulty sets of topics. But what about topics in the classroom as a pedagogical device?

The future of the profession holds a great deal of promise; we are well into the era of "technical breakthrough"; we are at the point where we have the "software" and the "hardware" to do a much more effective job than we have in the past. As briefly as possible, I would like to explain why it is conceivable that instruction in writing can now be more effective than it ever was in the past.

First—an important point that is connected with my thesis, but that would take us far afield if we pursued it—we are at the point where we can say, with the eloquence and passion of James Sledd, "Leave your language lone!" We are ready to allow youngsters to function in their own dialects, and hence we will not wreak the spiritual devastation that a "purist" attitude inevitably brings about.

At the level of syntax, we are beginning to get theories and materials—such as those of Francis Christensen and John Mellon—that enable the teacher to be of significant help in the student's quest for the ability to put idea within idea within idea. . . . That is, for the first time, we now have the means actually to help students systematically attain syntactic fluency, and surely that fluency is one of the significant intellectual accomplishments.

Finally, it is time to revitalize the concept of topics. The reasons for this are clear enough to anyone who has ever taught writing at any level. As Charlie Brown learned when his teacher said, "Write a five-hundred word essay on what you did during your summer vacation," one of the most intransigent problems for inexperienced (and experienced!) writers is invention, and what I am suggesting is that topics as they have developed and as they are developing provide the best devices of invention.

This is not to say that students are robots, who automatically turn to this or that set of topics before they write, but that they are alert and aware, and that they know what sort of help is available to them when they must solve the problem implied by the question "What can I say about this subject?" I am also claiming that some work with sets of topics will introduce students to techniques that they can use to develop their own problem-solving devices, their own heuristics.

I must plead guilty to the charge that I sound unhumanistic, for I *am* profoundly unhumanistic in the normal English department sense of that word, but I do avow that I am not suggesting students should be deprived of their marvelous, chaotic freedom, for I love both chaos and freedom. But what I am suggesting is that there are more efficient "programs" for enabling students to gain the *freedom* to express themselves than the old by-guess-and-by-golly method that is so tremendously humanistic. The object is not syntax for its own sake or random ideas to fill empty egg crates; rather, the quest of the English teacher should be for every means whereby the student can most efficiently gain the liberation that self-expression gives him.

Now my final comment about the theory of topics can be made. Composition is obviously a total process, a whole fabric, that can be "taken apart" only schematically and for theoretical purposes, so that when I claim there are three levels in the process of composition, I do not mean to imply that in practice the writer works first on one level and then on the other. (In fact, I know just as little about the act of composition as anyone else.) And viewing the compositional process from the standpoint of topics allows us to conceptualize it in a more unified way than the *points d'appui* taken by most theories. What I mean is this: if one views theories of form and theories of style merely as sets of topics —which in most instances they are— then the whole process of composition is unified under the auspices of invention, generally conceived to be the least mechanical and most "creative" of the departments of rhetoric.

And this viewpoint is a healthy corrective to the tendency that creeps into textbooks and classrooms: namely, to "do" a "unit" on the sentence and then a unit on the paragraph, and so on. Thus, the theory developed in this discussion could, ultimately, lead to a change in classroom practice, and it seems to me that change is badly needed.

Topics should not shackle the mind. They should liberate.

MICHAEL PAULL
JACK KLIGERMAN

Invention, Composition, and the Urban College

WE HAD WHAT COULD BE CALLED the typical training for teaching freshman composition: none. Otherwise, our undergraduate and graduate careers in English have been exemplary. The design of modern departments of English, however —one should say the modern university— is such that we, and thousands like us, become teachers of a skill that we know little about. We learn to teach composition by experience, it is true, but it is unpredictable and to a large extent accidental if we ever become proficient in our trade. Perhaps such a situation was acceptable before World War II, before the colleges expanded and their populations changed from a relatively small number of "college preparatory" students to an ever-increasing number of most high school graduates. Such, certainly, is the case in the City University of New York, which began implementing "open enrollment" in the 1970 academic year. And such, probably, is the case in the many state and community college systems throughout the country. As the number and kind of students have changed, so have the problems of freshman composition.

Let it be clear that we do not wish to spread blame. We wish, on the contrary, to offer here a record of how we tried to face our own inadequacies as teachers of composition in one of the most difficult of situations—an urban commuter college—and how we tried to turn the course that too often is the lackey of the general college community into a vital presence in the intellectual lives of our students. We first had to isolate our problems.

In the past, freshman composition courses, we felt, had been committed solely to the service of a discursive prose. This prose was packaged in the form of logically structured essays, with innumerable handbooks telling us how to find their beginning, middle, and end. The essay was to transmit information as economically as possible. That information was taken for granted, as was our students' ability to find it. We paid little attention, however, and nothing in our academic experience, either in classrooms or in textbooks, had pointed the way to developing in our students an awareness of cognition, of the ways in which sensation, perception, and concept formation operate before one even begins to write. We came to believe that the stress on technical proficiency and rhetorical skill—and the grading of compositions— has been misdirected, and that much

Michael Paull is an Assistant Professor of English at Herbert H. Lehman College of the City University of New York where he teaches courses in Linguistics and Medieval Literature.

Jack Kligerman is an Assistant Professor of English at Herbert H. Lehman College of the City University of New York where he teaches courses in Linguistics and American Literature.

Reprinted from *College English*, Vol. 33, No. 6, March 1972.

energy has been dissipated in attempts to achieve minimal levels of competency according to socially acceptable standards of usage. After much experimentation, we found ourselves returning to the classical insistence on teaching invention as the prerequisite to composition. Thus the classroom, instead of being a place where we came together to analyze the writings of others, now became a place where the whole range of mental processes we call cognition could be directly experienced.

In stressing the importance of invention, we were attempting to re-educate our students, to make them, in a sense, learn language all over again, but this time with an awareness of what they were doing. We recognized that language and, indeed, all of cognition, exist on various levels of abstraction and concretion, and that the real task of the teacher is to make it possible for the student to differentiate between those levels and to move easily among them. Seemingly, however, our students had lost their "ability to look at the world directly;"[1] they did not see that language, especially in this age of mass media, often forced them to look at the world through the veil of overly generalized concepts. In many imperceptible ways, they were allowing interpretations of experience embodied in the language of others to order their own experience. Thus, we decided that the place to begin this task of re-education is with a concentration on the problem of "concreteness." To accomplish this end, we tried to present classroom exercises through which the students could discover cognitive structures that jibed with their own experience of the world, through which the complex

process of invention, through perception and concept formation, could be held up for inspection and, ultimately, recognized as the essential beginning to the writing of effective compositions.

What follows will be a description of some of the specific exercises we used to implement a course teaching the fundamentals of invention. As teachers, we confined ourselves to presenting these exercises and to supporting the students in their attempts to complete them successfully. In other words, after we had stated an assignment, we left it up to the students to determine its direction and its conclusion. We did enter the discussion, however, when it was obvious that a student was using unrecognized cliches to structure his perceptions. Otherwise, we attempted to encourage the student in discovering how he himself actually perceived things. This was the extent to which we actively participated in the classroom. We were afraid that any more involvement would shape the students' perceptions more than they were already being shaped by the nature of the specific exercise. We will now list the exercises as they occurred, and give a brief explanation of what they entailed and what results they produced.

Happening:[2] This exercise began with our giving each student a separate written instruction, which, at a given time, he was told first to read and then to follow until we signalled a stop to the action. Some of the directions read: (1) Go to the blackboard and place your palm on it. Move all around the board pushing on it as if you expect one panel to open; (2)

---

[1] Aldous Huxley, *The Doors of Perception and Heaven and Hell* (New York: Harper & Row, 1963), p. 74.

[2] The *Happening* exercise was suggested by Wallace Kaufman, whose ideas on creativity in composition courses can be found in the recently published *The Writer's Mind* (Englewood Cliffs, N.J.: Prentice Hall, 1970).

Go up to the front of the room and face the class. Count to yourself, and each time you reach five say, "If I had the wings of an angel"; (3) Sit in your seat and watch the person facing you from the front of the room. Each time he says "angel" you clap. Don't look anywhere else; (4) On a piece of paper keep writing, "I am, I am, I am. . ."; (5) Sit at your desk and pretend you are counting money in two-dollar bills. Each time that you have a stack worth $30, gather it up and throw it in the air and say, "Thirty dollars!" (6) Walk around to everyone in the room, pat him on the back lightly, and say, "It's all right."

After the Happening, the students sat down and began to discuss what had just occurred. At first they described it in ways that would allow them to unify all of the separate events under one fairly general label, e.g., "It was a madhouse." Gradually they began to see the Happening as a series of random and unrelated events. They saw that, as such, it was only an exaggeration of the randomness of normal daily experience, e.g., riding a subway, sitting in class, etc. Many of the students came to realize that each and every experience is full of many details, many unrelated parts that the perceiver selects from and attempts to relate, to place in a structure. Such perception can be highly creative and self-fulfilling, especially when the perceiver understands the organizing principle which has shaped the selectivity of parts and the consequent structure. A side result of this exercise was that the students became very conscious of themselves functioning in a classroom. They began to see the flexibility as well as the rigidity that is built into every classroom. Suddenly, "classroom" became an open and discussable concept, one that the students could help formulate.

Meditation I: Initially we wanted the students to consider how they would define a meditation. To help them in this we had them read and discuss John Donne's meditation on the church bells from *Devotions Upon Emergent Occasions*. The class reached the conclusion that a meditation could begin with a person's selecting some object in his immediate environment and then focusing his attention upon it. At first this person, the perceiver, describes in some detail the physical appearance of the object, selecting those features of it which strike him as important. He then begins to formulate questions about these features, attempting to understand his reasons for selecting them and rejecting others. Stating this another way, the perceiver notices a physical object for the first time, and by concentrating on that object comes to understand what about it is important to him and why. In the process, the perceptions move organically from the concrete to the more abstract. For example, Donne hears a church bell; he recognizes it as a funeral bell; he thinks about death; he thinks about his own death; he thinks about the nature of death. In a sense, this exercise is a repetition of the first exercise (actually all of the exercises are variations of one basic theme). The meditation asked the student to look at an object, notice its parts, select certain of these, and then place them in a structure. After the discussion of Donne, we asked the students to follow the form of a meditation when writing their journal entries. (We will discuss the very important part that journals played in this course later on.)

Meditation II: Here the principles of the previous exercise were repeated, but now instead of discussing someone else's meditation the class meditated on one object, an interestingly shaped, painted gourd that we had brought into class. To initiate the meditation we had the class sit on the floor in a circle; we placed the gourd in the center and then told them to concentrate all their attention on it. They could familiarize themselves with it in any way they wanted, by handling it, rubbing it against themselves, and so on. After a period of time we removed the gourd and asked them to describe it. We found that many of them had not noticed the colors or the shape or the feel of the object, despite the fact that they had been engaged with it for almost an hour. Understandably, they were relying instead on the preconceived structuring word "gourd" to satisfy their understanding of it. As with the Happening, we spent the remainder of the class period trying to recall the parts, to remember exactly what the gourd looked like. Finally, we asked the students to use this exercise as the basis for a journal entry.

Meditation III: We again meditated on a single object, a pumpkin squash, but this time the exercise took place outside the classroom on the lawn of the college. We were now meditating, or attempting to do so, in a much more distracting environment; moreover, we were using as the object for the meditation a far more sensual object than the gourd. The results were almost predictable. At first the class seemed very committed to the exercise. They concentrated on the squash, fondled it, and soon one of the students broke it open and tasted it. Others in the class felt its insides, allowing themselves to experience it as fully as possible. After a while they became aware of many of the things around them: the leaves had just begun to fall, people were playing soccer, the field was overrun with squirrels. They began to talk about these

things in relation to the squash, e.g., seeing the golden color of the squash as identical to that of the leaves on the ground. Like the jar in Wallace Stevens' "Anecdote of a Jar," the squash provided a structure and an order for the surrounding environment, while, at the same time, the surrounding environment gave the squash a pre-eminence that it would lack in the classroom. As with the other exercises, we asked the students to enter their perception of this experience in their journals.

Meditation IV: We brought to class about thirty different objects, such as pieces of driftwood, sea shells, old buttons. We asked each student to select any one that he particularly liked, then to go out of the classroom and meditate on it for one hour. This part of the exercise was held out of class because we felt that the student should have some choice as to where he wanted to meditate. We also wanted to give the students a chance to bring together the important aspects of the first three meditation exercises, namely, to concentrate on a single object in a loosely structured environment. We stressed that each student should spend the entire hour discovering as much about the object as possible, specifically what features of it were most apparent and why. Finally, we asked the class to record the results of their meditation. What follows is an example of the kind of result we received:

> I sat beside a bush and watched the people go by me in spurts of two or three. I saw people scattering in all directions and then shortly after, there was quiet. All the little groups had broken up and each person had gone his own way and so I was left alone and with nothing. But in the palm of my hand I held the remnant of a dried sponge. It was white in color, rough in texture, and crumbly to the

touch. Actually the sponge was a highly complex network of branches. The slightest movement would cause tiny pieces to split off and hence the sponge had greatly diminished in size even as I held it in my hand. I examined this sponge and I thought of mankind, each of us a minute piece of a branch. I thought of how surrounded by people I had been a few minutes ago and then how quickly they had all disappeared. I wondered about dying and why man is forced to leave this earth so soon after he is placed upon it. Just as the people had wandered away from the campus and the branches had fallen from the sponge, so too must every man leave this life and be separated from mankind. . . .

It actually did not matter, as far as learning was concerned, that the student had imitated the structure of Donne's meditation. In fact, the way her own perception of the object was struggling with Donne's perception of his was beneficial. It presented the student and the class with an illustration of what one is up against when trying to structure a unique experience. Further, it demonstrated that cognition is a very complicated process, often achieved through the integration of one's own personal perceptions and structures with those of others. The cognitive process thus becomes one of continuum and nuance.

Non-representational Drawings: We gave each student a large piece of brown wrapping paper and an assortment of crayons and colored pencils. The only instruction in this exercise was to draw some object in an abstract, non-representational way. This exercise was designed to show another way of representing the complexity of one's perception of a given object. It also was meant to illustrate that one can structure his experience in many ways, some of which are non-conventional, without sacrificing what appear to be the important or essential features of the experience or object. After the students had finished their drawings they placed them on the floor and discussed them. At first, the students were encouraged to deal with the drawings' surface qualities, the use of space and color, and to avoid guessing at its "symbolic import." Once this was done, the students began to structure the concrete details by giving the individual drawing a label, an abstract symbol. With this exercise, we were again attempting to stress the relationship between abstraction and concretion.

Photographs: While the above discussion was going on, photographs were being taken of each student in the class. The students were urged not to pose, but to involve themselves as they normally would in the discussion. Predictably enough, some were unable to forget the photographer/subject structure and actually did pose. After the photographs were printed, each student was given one of another student and told to write about it, employing the methods of description that he had learned in the previous exercises. At a later date, these descriptions were read to the class while, at the same time, the picture of the person being described was held up to view. After each reading the class reacted to both the picture and the description. The result of this exercise was that the students came to understand point of view in a very dramatic way. In their descriptions, the students had to contend with several points of view. On the one hand, they knew the subject of the photograph and, supposedly, had preconceived notions about him. On the other hand, the photograph, compositionally, structured the subject according to the photographer's way of seeing him, stressing certain features and ignoring others. In many of the descriptions the students commented on how the selectional features of the photograph had either altered or coincided with their own conception of the subject. Consequently, their descriptions represented a combination of the various points of view into a new structure.

Kingsbridge Road: In this exercise we told the students to walk several blocks down a busy commercial street, and in the process to write down twenty-five observations which they thought characterized the street. The form of each written observation was to be short, preferably a single phrase per observation. When the students returned from this walk, we asked them to order their observations in any way they saw fit, to place them in existential sentences (an abstraction is linked by the "to be" verb to a concrete observation, e. g., happiness is a warm puppy). The observations themselves were extremely varied. Some tended to be very general, others very specific and detailed, but all proved interesting in the way in which they revealed the selection and structuring of perception. Almost all of the observations had some organizing principle, whether grammatical, such as making all of the verbs into participles, or thematic, such as selecting those details which illustrated the filth of a New York City street. In the classroom, we discussed the observations, paying particular attention to the selectivity of details and attempting to discover what governed that selectivity. The following are two of the observations that were discussed: (1) "couple walking hand in hand/ family shopping / smiling faces / brand new sports car / children playing / window washer / patrol car cruising / rattling subway / Con-Ed digging streets / people rushing / barking dog / broken window / Calif.

license plate / plane overhead / horns blowing / cars with speakers / speeding ambulance / lost child crying / Christmas decorations / bum begging / near collision / woman screaming at children / woman dropping her groceries / child telling his mother to shut up / man on crutches"; (2) "a soundless music shop / holding hands / bubble gum machine / a little girl with a balloon / jelly apples / Xmas lights / guy looking at hunting rifles / yellow mustang / a runned-over paper bag / autumn leaves mixed with some garbage / old pair of combat boots abandoned in the middle of the street / a smelly cuchifritas shop / stinking botanica / a pair of pantihose pinned sloppily on the wall / scanky flick / a painted up prostitute on Simpson Street/ a girl yelling 'Marie' / two drunks in front of a library / pile of garbage near mailbox / the color purple on a window display / a pizza man slicing a pie / a gray-haired man closing shop / jewelry store." With the final part of the exercise, the students were learning at first hand the mechanism of analogy, specifically how it operates to concretize abstractions and to give them personal definitions.

The Structuring of Experience by the Artist: The final three exercises dealt with seeing an experience that had already been structured by an artist. The problem became, how does one perceive these structures? We began with a photograph of a subway station that had been taken on Kingsbridge Road, a shopping center in the Bronx. The students would thus be able to recognize the subject, and would thereby have some insight into the process of selection and ordering that the artist went through. The class discussion centered around what the artist was seeing and how he was bringing it to our attention. At this point in the semester, tne students were very sensitive to the way that the artist structured his perceptions. They quickly picked up on the photographer's use of light and shade and on the perspective that he chose to present the shapes of the subject. Based on these observations, the students became increasingly aware of how and possibly why the photographer had given a certain order to a selected group of visual objects as well as of the thematic implications of that order. We then moved from the photograph to a poem in order to understand how language can be used in much the same way as a camera to order experience creatively. We used Galway Kinnell's poem "The Avenue Bearing the Initial of Christ into the New World," because it was a city experience poem, one that was constructed from many of the same kinds of perceptions that were evident in the Kingsbridge Road exercise. We concentrated on the first three sections of the poem where Kinnell strings together a series of observations regarding New York's Lower East Side. The students analyzed the poem in much the same way as they did the photograph, only now investigating how words which function as metaphors, similes, etc., represent reality through language and transform it into an imaginative entity. They were for the most part able to use their understanding of how they see and structure experience to appreciate the poet's handling of his subject. For the most part, the exercise worked. For example, by concentrating on the selection and order of particular details in the first section of the poem—the movement from birds to the sea to a broom to a pushcart to a horse-drawn wagon to a "propane-gassed bus"—the students understood that section's thematic concept, namely, the evolutionary process of a day beginning on Avenue C. By the end of the exercise,

the students seemed to have gained an insight into the part that selectivity and structuring play in the relation between concrete images and abstract ideas.

Journal: At the beginning of the semester we told every student to buy a notebook to be used as his personal journal for the entire semester. The students were to begin making daily entries according to the instructions on journal keeping, which read as follows: "You keep a journal in order to investigate and to remember. Generally you begin an entry with some particular observation that is important or seems to suggest something important. You look at the observation and its significance. You especially try to understand why you chose this particular subject. What does it mean in terms of your life and interests? Your materials will come from classes, home life, vacations, memories, etc. But start with something specific! Keep your journal relevant to life. Anyone can throw words around for several pages every day. In your journal you will be practicing freely the habits of mind that are necessary to a writer. You will be storing up material to write about. You are under no restraints grammatically or in terms of form. Your goals are to be honest with yourself and to expand your consciousness of both the inner and the outer words. While the journal will be inspected, all entries are strictly confidential. You are under no obligation to record anything you wish to keep wholly secret. The teacher will make no comment on the appropriateness, morality, or sanity of content—nor on the stupidity, brightness, or brilliance. He might suggest paths of deeper exploration."[3]

---

[3]Taken from an experimental course in freshman composition, first offered at the University of North Carolina at Chapel Hill in 1966.

This part of the course was as important as the classroom exercises. For, with the journal, we could tell whether the student was achieving the goals of the course, whether he was learning from the specific exercises and then transferring this learning to his writing. We felt that the format of the journal would allow the student the freedom to develop his imagination and his creativity at his own rate. When the students first started their journals we insisted that they make one entry per day, that it be about one page long and begin with a specific observation. The last insistence was made in an attempt to keep the journals from becoming diaries. About every three weeks we collected the journals and held individual conferences with the students, commenting on the nature of the observations and discussing alternative ways of presenting them. As the semester progressed, we told the students to cut down the number of entries to three per week. We did this because we felt that most of the students were becoming quite good at journal keeping, and that to write a daily entry was just too much work. As it turned out, most of the journals averaged about forty double-spaced typewritten pages in length. At the beginning of the course, their entries consisted of fights with boyfriends, condemnations of the American system of education, and disavowals of their parents, all presented in cliches and general terms. They were not seeing the specific parts of their experience which they either objected to or liked. As the semester progressed, the students came to understand more about their own abilities of perception and about how abstractions can be defined in terms of their own experiences. Perhaps the only way to demonstrate what we mean is to present selections from some of the students' journals. Because of the limitations of space, we have selected only three of the entries. They are by no means the best nor the worst. They come from that portion of the journals written about the middle of the semester, and they give some idea of the progress we were trying to achieve in the course.

(1) After looking at and touching an empty brown twelve-ounce beer bottle covered only on one side with dried out, jagged ocean barnacles (the type one would find on a beach boulder very close to the surf), I asked myself not what was its significance to me, but rather what did it mean to me, if anything, with respect to my life, and more specifically, my everyday situation. I drink beer directly from its bottled container from time to time, and when I have taken the last sip from the bottle, I always notice a little stream of beer foam on the inside of the bottle. When this stream dries, the residue of the white foam reminds me of the white barnacles on the bottle that I was meditating on. I have seen and smelled and touched several empty beer bottles that have dried out and they are, I believe, very ugly and disgusting; they smell terrible and they feel either sticky or slimy. Now, for quite a sharp contrast, I picture in my mind a television commercial starring a sensuous woman and a chilled, unopened bottle of beer. As the music plays, during this commercial, this woman dances about, caresses and kisses this bottle of beer. Now, isn't it odd how this bottle of beer is, at one instant, a very beautiful thing worthy of lots of attention, and as this stage passes, an ugly repulsive thing. I think about what is going to happen to the bottle of beer in the commercial, and then conclude that the same thing will happen to the beautiful woman. Even if she does not become slimy and sticky, she will become ugly and old, just like the bottle. If this is true for the bottle of beer and for the beautiful woman, is it then true for every real thing? Can anything remain beautiful and attractive? I don't think so.

(2) Again I can't think of anything to write. Just today I was uptight. No reason just on edge, jittery. All that would calm me was a hot bath. So hot that you can see the steam rising and the mirror gets foggy and the walls become beaded with moisture. You just lay there and almost fall asleep. First of all it takes about three minutes to get in and then the water is so hot your mind becomes clouded. It's almost like enduring a fainting spell, it's like causing yourself to pass out. Everything goes from your mind, it becomes entirely blank. You don't even have to fill your mind with trivia, so you won't have to think of your problems or be bothered by anything important. Eventually you even seem to lose control of your arms and legs. It's like being conscious but asleep. You have all the relaxation, restfulness and yet in some way you are aware of where you are and what you are doing. It's like dreaming you're taking a bath.

(3) I love snow—clean, white, powdery soft snow. Footprints left in untrod upon pastures. Icicles dangling from branches. Flakes clinging to my eyelashes—getting caught on the tip of my tongue. But after the snowfall comes the mess. The black slush and unkempt piles against the cars. The puddles up to your knees and the ice on the streets. For some reason as I go sliding my way down the avenue I get hysterical giggling. This isn't too bright because it only makes for looser footing. I have this clear image of my body lying on the sidewalk on the ice—my feet in a drift. Even worse are the puddles. I wore my pants over my boots and swam across the street. Dripping from the knees down I shivered as I laughed. A wet and soggy mess—I giggled on. What else could I do—cry—scream—get annoyed? A car went speeding past me and water trickled down my legs. The wind made walking impossible. I must have been some sight—my feet grasping at the ground for dear life—taking itsy-bitsy size steps—my whole body pushing downward to maintain my upward position.

This course was not always a comfortable one for the students or for us. Because we tried to stay out of the class discussions as much as possible, there were often long silences while the students waited for us to direct them, to tell them what to do or to tell them if they were doing the right thing. We did not respond to these silences; we felt that, for the course to work, the students had to be responsible for understanding and coping with such situations. They seemed to do both admirably, learning that much can be gained from silence and that it does not necessarily indicate a void or a vacuum. They saw that silence is filled by many gestures which are often more revealing than words. The class was initially disturbed that we would not tell them the purpose of a particular exercise. They often walked away at the end of the period muttering "What have we done this hour?" To compound the problem, we also refused to say whether their responses in class were right or wrong. They continually pleaded with us to tell them if they had given the right answer. Slowly they began to understand that we were not looking for answers as they understood them. With the exercises and the journals, we attempted to present situations in which the students could discover the way in which they perceived and structured their own experiences. If such a discovery were made, they would realize that they were the best judges of whether their answers were correct or not.

HARVEY S. WIENER

Media Compositions: Preludes to Writing

IT IS NO NEWS to anyone teaching college English today that students sitting before us make up a non-literary generation where words and books intrude upon
rather than mold a way of life extravagant in its neglect of the written form. To
the youngster plugged in to his transistor radio, transfixed before the technicolor
ghosts of the tv screen, bombarded by magazine pictures of wild and erotic action
—in all but a very transitory sense, for him the word is buried in a landslide of
visual and aural excitement. Of course, as instructors of English and composition,
it is our charge to resuscitate the powers and glories of the written word, to
bring the student in some way to see along with Emerson that words are a mode
of divine energy and that words are actions and actions a kind of words. Some
(but not many) instructors have attempted to explore the possibilities of written
language by means of those very media that do hold the student's attention: television, movies, and multimedia presentations are no classroom strangers. However,
these attempts are not always integrated into the composition program in a
meaningful way, serving more as motivational devices to keep students awake
than anything else.

I should like in this essay to suggest to those who would grant non-written
media a place of significance in the writing program some student media compositions as preparatory exercises for theme assignments. I do not mean watching
network television in class, listening to professional records and tape recordings,
or looking at commercially prepared slides or movies in the classroom. I do not
mean allowing the dazzle of the media to replace the tedious, discouraging process of learning to write. I do mean, on the other hand, permitting the student to
compose in a non-written medium as a prelude to a written exercise.

By non-written media I include forms of compositions such as the collage, the
photo essay made from newspaper and magazine presentations or from the student's own still or slide photography, the cassette tape recording, and the student-
made slide and tape multimedia presentation.[1] Work in film or video tape, because
of their costliness, I exclude although student interest in these forms is high.

Having experimented as a frightened amateur with all of these in my open
admissions composition classes, and having demonstrated the approach this essay
introduces to eager but terrified colleagues on many campuses, I know the
anxieties instructors may face when they move into media presentations. Fortu-

Harvey S. Wiener, author of Creating Compositions (McGraw-Hill, 1973), is Director of Composition at LaGuardia Community College, City University of New York.
[1] Faculty at LaGuardia Community College are fortunate to have, under the terms of a
grant from the National Endowment for the Humanities, supplies of Instamatic and Polaroid
cameras, film, and projectors which students and teachers may borrow for their own projects.

Reprinted from College English, Vol. 35, No. 5, February 1974.

nately, students share little of our own sense of insufficiency and will survive with a smile and a helping hand our difficulties with the Machine Age. And surely outweighing on a grand scale whatever problems we anticipate are numerous advantages to the young writer's growth and development. In the first place we can involve the student in an unthreatening medium which gives him the chance to express his thinking without fear of penalty. It is true that instructors of art or film classes have critical standards as firm as those we have for written composition; but as English instructors looking upon a student's collage or photo essay, which of us will say, "This is right" or "This is wrong"? Our responses are essentially emotional: although we would surely correct a dangling modifier or a misspelled word (as would every one of the student's previous English teachers) there is not much in a visual presentation that we would know how to grade or correct. Committed so to words, we are much less rigid in our responses to nonverbal impressions offered by students. This absence of standards of right and wrong is a tremendous advantage especially for the man or woman with skills problems because it helps reduce self-consciousness and allows the growth of an element of creative expression that is often lost in the student's panic for correctness. There is an advantage too in that student and teacher, because of their mutual inexperience, can develop together both a critical awareness about the creative process in another medium and what James P. Cooney, Jr., calls the "enthusiasm which grows from virginal confrontation with unanticipated art."[2] Furthermore, students can demonstrate in a non-written form a conceptual understanding of the terms of an assignment, one that a written activity frequently denies at the outset to the poor writer. (For those who need such proof, media composing is a remarkable indication that many who read and write poorly can often demonstrate creditable, fertile minds.) There are also some similarities—in conception, theme, style, form, organization, sequence, and logic—between the non-written and the written composition. These similarities should not be exaggerated; yet, very often students may come to terms nicely with problems in media compositions, and these solutions can make the written work easier to bring to life. Finally, to one committed philosophically to the value of personal experience as the core of effective composition, a media production is very valuable. Surely one key goal for the young writer is to translate sensory experience into verbal expression. I have already shown how it is possible to convince even the poorest student to have confidence in his own tactile impressions.[3] If sense experience is the seed from which meaningful written language may eventually grow, every student has within himself that seed: with his eyes, his ears, his nose, his hands, he makes endless contact with the world of the senses. But when written words disappoint or even frighten the student for one reason or another, we can provide an intermediate means for him to convey his sensory responses. The non-written, often non-verbal, composition can allow the student to grapple

---

[2] "On the Dangers of Pre-Plotting in English," *College Composition and Communication*, 24 (May, 1973), 207.

[3] Harvey S. Wiener, "The Single Narrative Paragraph and College Remediation," *College English* (March, 1972), 663-664.

with creative instincts in a visual and/or auditory medium even before writing begins.

I should like to explain in detail a freshman English activity with imagery, one that requires first a student-made composition in a simple visual medium, and then a written composition for the same assignment. I shall illustrate both phases of this exercise with student samples. Then I shall suggest how the non-written composition may precede—not supplant—some traditional assignments offered in college writing programs. Towards this last goal I shall use some of the impromptu suggestions that grew out of various seminars and workshops I have conducted.

To allow an appreciation of the nature of imagery to students uninvolved with words it is important to realize that a standard definition like Laurence Perrine's ("Imagery may be defined as the representation through language of sense experience"[4]), no matter how simple, is really not effective unless *language* includes visual and other non-written forms. For many students imagery is not conveyed exclusively through the language of words. I hoped to use the student's ready response to and facility with non-verbal imagery to allow him to see the depth, beauty, and value of the verbal image. I also hoped to allow the student to evaluate the verbal image and to create it from his own range of experience, a poetic task indeed.

Starting backwards with a verbal activity, I introduced Whitman's poem "There Was A Child Went Forth," adapting an assignment developed with Don Marion Wolfe.[5] After an oral reading, the class concentrated upon the psychological implications of the poem. Did students agree that what a person "Look'd upon, that object he became . . . for many years or stretching cycles of years"? Do experiences define the man or woman? What kinds of experiences define the child in Whitman's poem? How has Whitman conveyed those experiences to the reader? Through lines like "The early lilacs became part of this child,/And grass and white and red morning-glories and white and red clover, and the song of the phoebe bird . . ." and "The mother with mild words, clean her cap and gown, a wholesome odor falling off her person and clothes as she walks by" students may acquire a basic, albeit passive, understanding of the pictorial nature of language as it is realized in the sensory image. The colors, the specific naming of flower and bird, the lines about the mother—these allow the poet to translate his own experience into identifiable entities to which readers can then respond. Beyond this students pushed further in their consideration of Whitman's stress upon environment as the essential designer of man's personality. What kind of child do you see based upon the poet's portrait? Suppose it were a youngster today in Harlem or on Manhattan's Fifth Avenue in the Seventies that Whitman wanted to describe. What images would he need then? Professor Wolfe says, "Like Whitman, each of us calls up sights and sounds and moments of taste and touch that answer the question 'What Am I?'" (p. 421). Suppose it were *you*

---

[4] *An Introduction to Poetry* (New York, 1969), p. 54.

[5] For a brief discussion of the assignment without its visual component, see Don M. Wolfe, *Creative Ways to Teach English* (New York, 1966), pp. 421-422.

answering the question "What Am I?" by means of imagery. What kinds of images would you use?

That last query set the frame for two compositions, both to answer the intriguing question "What Am I?" In the first, a collage (we defined the word and I showed samples), students presented to the class through tactile images what they saw as basic features of their own personalities. There are some samples on this and the following page.

Presented anonymously, the collages provided the basis for active discussion. What kind of personality reveals itself through the visual representation? What traits did the creator of the collage wish to present about himself? What image best illustrates some trait you recognize? Of course, students enjoyed (as we all do) this amateur psychology. "This person leads a very active life. Look at all the sports figures." "This one was made by a boy. Look at all the porno shots." Or, "This person feels isolated, alienated. There are so many white spaces, and the blacks and whites are lined up one group against the other." Every one of us responded without judging the skill of the artist. We spoke a bit about every collage. Sometimes the analyses must really have missed the mark, but for a student with very little confidence in his own ability to create, it was revealing to hear people respond to and appreciate something of his own making.

As I had hoped, the question of accuracy arose. How could anyone be sure that alienation, for example, was a personality trait the creator of the collage wished to present? How do we know for sure that this is the work of an active person—perhaps the creator was very inactive and merely envious of the active life. On a more basic level, could we say accurately that a male or female, black

or white, youth or adult prepared a given collage? Some students suggested that the visual image had some shortcomings in communicating with certainty. Could the verbal image offer more accuracy, depth, force?

Returning briefly to Whitman's poem, I asked students to look again at the lines describing the mother and to assume that those lines presented Whitman's own parent. By means of an opaque projector the class compared a photographic portrait of her with the verbal picture. Which did students think more clear, easier to visualize? Some chose the picture for its instantaneous appeal to the sense of sight. Most students, however, found the verbal image more satisfactory. During discussion the class asserted that the verbal image could appeal on more than one sensory level. Whitman's image itself (though less specific than many might desire) suggests sound and smell as well as action. After some activities on how to build a verbal image, students agreed to attempt a paragraph which would answer in intense verbal imagery the question "What Am I?" We established a list of basic standards,[6] urging writers to express the deepest and most important features of their own personalities. I assured anonymity to those who requested it so that I might read papers freely in class. And as always we examined student models before any writing began.

Here are final drafts of two papers, very different, yet, despite limitations in content and form, each extraordinary in the personality it projects. The first sample is the work of the student who prepared collage A.

What Am I? West, Clapton, and Flynn

I am the ringmaster of a three ring circus formally known as my family. I am the arguments between my brother and the whisperings of my sisters. I am the polluted, greyish-blue sky of Long Island City and the slimy, filthy waters of the East River and Newton's Creek. I am the limp in old Jack's leg or the large red girder that smashed down upon it. To my childhood companions, I was a real Casanova for going out with twin sisters at the same time and to those girls I am a devil. And I am the look that I still receive from their reddened blue eyes. To mom, I am still her blue-eyed bundle of joy, maybe growing up to wear the black robe of priesthood, while to pop, I am a future Jim Thorpe sprinting flat races, hurtling over large obstacles with a pole vault, and smacking through defenses for touchdowns. Or am I a future Jerry West, swishing the winning basket at the buzzer? On the football field, I am every player to hold a ball but after ripping my leg open I change from a growling bear into a purring kitten waiting to die. In the hospital, I become the uncontaminated cleanliness and the antiseptic fragrance of the ward. I also become the lethal point of the syringe used to render me into the "world of nod" or the scent of flowers I receive from close friends. While listening to my stereo, I become Eric Clapton strumming "Layla" before close to thirty thousand screaming fans and I also become the tangy odor of marijuana that permeates Madison Square Garden. I become one of the fans smoking a joint in the front row. My gang thinks of me as just another head in the crowd but I am still part of each one of them: one person's sneer, another one's smile, I am the hate and the love that exists among them. In the movies I become an Errol Flynn and a John Wayne who rescue the beautiful brown-eyed damsel and slay the cowardly rogue. I am

---

[6] See in this connection Wolfe, *Creative Ways*, p. 491, and my essay "Single Narrative Paragraph," 664-665. Along with the model theme the listing of clearly drawn standards offers the beginning student the best chance for successful writing.

the pebble in a little boy's shoe, a knife in a policeman's back, a dent on someone's car, a Hank Aaron homerun, my mother's teardrops, a bubble in Raquel Welch's bath, or a derelict stinking of alcohol. I am all of these things and many more. I am life.

What Am I? A Bloody Nose and Salty Tears

Where can I begin to tell of the sorrows and joys that have occurred over what has seemed like nineteen centuries instead of nineteen years? Maybe it all begins with my first asthma attack. I'm that terrified four year old whose grandmother seems to be more afraid than she is, but is trying desperately not to show it. I am all those giants standing over me dressed all in white. Then they placed me under a gigantic plastic bag. That part was very strange, for grandma had always told me not to play around with plastic bags. These bags were supposed to be dangerous articles around a child. How come the giants in white weren't told to pull down their pants so they could get it good? Grown-ups got away with everything! Or maybe I'm the harsh, loud words that shot back and forth from my mother's and father's mouths. Or I'm the door daddy slammed so hard I felt I wanted to fall off my hinges. No! I'm the sweet smelling air stirring in the kitchen, lying over and around the chocolate cake, the homemade ice cream and apple pie that grandma has just finished preparing. I'm even the song that choir members of Bethel African Methodist Episcopal Church sings. They're singing me with such faith and deep meaning that if they stopped, the world would crumble with grief. I'm the junkie's mind, standing with him in front of the 77th Street Bar, trying to tell him, "Man you don't need that, get yourself together brother." See that dark red blood running from Elaine's white nose, that's me, the day she informed me that I was doing too well in school, considering that I was black. She couldn't understand where I acquired my intelligence from at all. And that big soaring jet that left Kennedy Airport on February 23, 1971 was me. It took my man to fight in a jungle for a man named Sam, who only knew of him in the form of a nine digit number. And God knows, I'm the salty tears that fell into the coffin of Martin Luther King, Jr. the day somebody decided he needed a long rest. Man, he gave his *only* life to set me free. I'm my mother's face when the bills pile up. Then she works overtime to make ends meet. She's been the only bread winner since that day daddy slammed the door behind him.

Comparing collage A to the first paragraph, students further defended for themselves the strength of the verbal image. The line that offers a picture of sprinting flat races and hurtling obstacles with a pole vault convinces readers of the writer's preference for the active life and makes more specific in terms of the student's existence the magazine pictures of athletic events in the collage. The verbal image of the writer at his stereo is much more intense and personal than the snapshot of Eric Clapton in the upper left portion of the collage. (These two together, of course, gave students the best opportunity to judge one against the other, the verbal and the pictorial, both dealing here with the same subject matter.) The humorous "I am . . . a bubble in Raquel Welch's bath" is strangely coy and suggestive compared to the flagrant sexuality—so much a part of this youngster—that emerges from the collage.

From a structural point of view, as the first written assignment, the "What Am I?" paragraph fortunately lacks many difficulties which often confound students too early in the semester and therefore allows students to show their strengths, not weaknesses. There is no need to labor a topic sentence: everyone may begin

"*I am. . . .*" Students may write a string of images, each image in one sentence, each sentence presenting a different picture about a different thing. Or students may build images in thought groups, taking several sentences to develop through sensory language some personality trait. Not every paper, by any means, was as good as the two above. But every paragraph exploded with at least one image that probed the student's deepest memories and presented in sharp sensory terms a verbal picture to which anyone could easily respond. Having first created a successful visual composition, and realizing its limitations as a mode of communication, the developing writer investigates the power of the verbal image. Creating imagery himself, he understands much more actively the value of pictorial language in dramatizing his own life's experiences, and can learn to respond to such language in important literature. Words for sound, color, action, touch, smell: the reliable tools of the professional writer in the hands of the novice achieve wonders on any level.[7]

Media compositions are effective intermediary stages in more traditional theme assignments too. Without attempting a comprehensive listing, I offer here some of the activities in rhetoric frequently required of writers in the freshman program, along with some interesting possibilities for individual or group presentations in the media. Of course, written assignments always follow the media projects. Most of these audio-visual activities I have either tried with my own students in the classroom or have examined from students in classes where others have attempted to use this method.

Rhetorical Skill	*Media Composition before the Written Exercise*
Description of a place	1. Visit some place which conveys a sharp impression—*quiet, noisiness, activity*, etc. Convey that impression with a camera and a tape recorder. 2. Prepare a collage on a place you know well, one which you can convey vividly in visual terms.
Narration	Prepare a photo essay (with your camera or with newspaper or magazine cutouts) in which you relate a story about a robbery, a day in the country, a train ride, a walk in the city at night.
Comparison-Contrast	1. In a photo essay, dramatize wealth and poverty in your community. 2. The high school student and the college student: record on a cassette the impressions, opinions, interests offered by students on each of these levels.

[7] I have demonstrated in "Single Narrative Paragraph" how skills in concrete sensory expression help develop skills with exposition.

Argumentation

1. Invent a commercial product. Prepare three advertisements in which you attempt to convince people to buy your product.

2. Take pictures in your immediate college community in order to illustrate your opinion on a key social issue: pollution, women's liberation, urban problems, traffic. Prepare a sound track with words and music on tape cassette to accompany your visual presentation.

Description of a person

1. Prepare a collage which will introduce someone you know—relative, friend—to the people in the class.

2. Ask a volunteer to stand before the class and speak for five minutes about himself. Take photographs which attempt to convey some dominant impression you have about the person. Arrange the pictures and present them to the class.

Similarly, skills in narrative sequence, style, tone, using several supporting examples to develop a paragraph idea, classification, writing introductions and conclusions, figurative language—with all of these the student and instructor may experiment in the media before the written assignment. Admittedly, time for demonstration and discussion of projects bite heavily into classroom hours. Many instructors report, however, that work with visuals early in the semester allows later on for a more sustained interest on the students' behalf for building writing skills.

To hold an inveterate suspicion toward the non-written medium as if it debases the word as the golden means of communication is a narrowness of vision that will not serve well the interests of this special generation of students. It is an uncomfortable contradiction, too, that many among us cannot warm to what for our students is the very life's blood. But to use the media composition in order to bring students to a pitch of excitement about words and their power is certainly no abdication to the non-verbal. It is instead a little pragmatism that enriches the learning experience.

JOSEPH COMPRONE

Using Painting, Photography and Film to Teach Narration

I

MOST STUDENTS LIKE, even prefer, the narrative mode. Narration usually is more easily formed to student experience; it seems more natural, easier to control, and less explicitly rhetorical. But there is, of course, a sophisticated core of narrative-rhetorical principles that every narrative writer must control and use, whether he writes fiction, a brief sketch, or a narrative-example to support an opinion he has presented in an expository format. These narrative principles are often taken for granted because, as readers, we have internalized them. A story *usually* begins at the beginning, climaxes in the middle, and winds down to a graduated end. We notice *departures* from that norm, but we take the norm itself for granted.

Young writers, however, can improve their own writing by becoming conscious of narrative-rhetoric, of strategies and techniques that a writer may employ in order to organize and arrange objects, events, and people in space and time on paper. In fact, many of the rhetorical principles of narration, if thoroughly taught, can be transferred by students to

exposition and argument.[1] The theory and practice which is explained here is meant to help students refine and become more conscious of relatively basic narrative principles. Also, this approach to narration should construct a foundation for the transfer of narrative skills to other written forms.

I will suggest two methods of teaching narration. Both methods will be supplemented by photography and film, two media that provide useful visual paradigms to written experience. Many of our students are *visually* sophisticated; they are able to follow relatively complex flashback and montage techniques in film and television as well as understand relatively sophisticated visual perspectives in photographs. But they seldom demonstrate similar skills when they analyze

Joseph Comprone teaches modern literature and directs Freshman English at the University of Cincinnati. He has published over ten articles on rhetoric, composition, style and media and will publish From Experience to Expression: A College Rhetoric, *William C. Brown Publishing Company, this year.*

[1]I use the term "rhetoric" in its most general sense here: as representative of a body of principles that may be used to discover and create form in experience. I am not speaking of rhetoric as explicit persuasion. I refer to Kenneth Burke and Wayne Booth as rhetoricians who apply the term in similar ways. I do not intend to deal with the very important but exceedingly complex problems of how narrative skills can be transferred to expository and argumentative contexts at length here. Let me merely mention that the chronological or subjective arrangement of experience in narration is not distinctly different from the many forms of experience that we find in the contemporary, personal, or informal essay. Orwell's "The Road to Wigan Pier," and "Politics and the English Language," and William Styron's "Seige of Chicago" are excellent examples of such essay forms.

Reprinted from *College English*, Vol. 35, No. 2, November 1973.

written words, when they read a stream-of-consciousness novel, or even when they are asked to read an essay or poem that includes several difficult spatical, temporal, or perceptual metaphors. They are, in other words, accustomed to experience rendered visually, but not accustomed to experience rendered in writing. Here are the two approaches combined with pedagogical suggestions on how to use the photographs, films, and writing assignments in a natural sequence.

I

I begin with a deductive approach. I ask the students to look at a painting or photograph, preferably one that shows a continuing action. We begin the composing process by producing, as a class in discussion, a group of sentences that summarize the action in general terms. We then select the best sentence, put it on the board or on an overhead projector, and use it to generate a whole narrative sequence that works from general observation back through specific details. Before we begin actually writing the narrative, however, we decide as a class on three general qualities: what visual perspective we will take in the narrative; what senses we will plan to awaken in the reader; and what major and minor details from the painting or photograph we will use and in what rough order.[2] These class exercises usually take a whole class hour. The writing begins in the following

class.

Suppose the class has decided to describe a photo of an old woman crossing a busy street. They choose a vantage point, say from a second-story window in a building along the side of the street. They have also chosen to emphasize the visual, with perhaps a few audial details interspersed—say traffic noise, shouts from the sidewalk, or the cries of a boy selling newspapers. We begin, then, to write cumulative sentences describing the action, working from general to specific, on the board.[3]

Then, I have the class add qualified detail, always with their eyes *on* the visual material and with the point of view, perspective, and sensory appeal clearly in mind. Our aim is to create, as closely as possible, the illusion that the action is actually occurring *before the eyes* of the reader.

We add details to the base clause with three principles in mind; that every detail should be clearly *related* to another, that the sentence modifiers ought to be *varied*, that we should never add more detail than a reader can comprehend in a single sentence. Here is an example of a sentence that was produced using these exercises.

She limped over the curb and pushed her legs forward from the hips down, her bulky brown pocketbook dangling from

[2] There are numerous exercises one can use to get the details of a painting or photograph in some kind of rough order previous to writing. Have students look at the item for a few minutes and try to recall as much detail as they can. Select paintings that include details arranged in simple designs to implement observation and retention (John Peto's "The Poor Man's Store" has worked well this way for me). Then have students suggest in class why they recalled certain details and forgot others and

how what they remembered might lead to a general interpretation or impression of the painting or photograph. Such preliminary exercises give a sense of purpose and direction to the actual writing of a narrative.

[3] I am assuming at least some familiarity with Francis Christensen's theories, as described in *Notes Toward A New Rhetoric*. My borrowings from Christensen are slight and very general, however, and are based primarily on the concept of the cumulative sentence as the base element in narrative writing. I also emphasize, in slightly altered form, Christensen's concept of modification by addition.

her wrist carrying her shoulders high despite the curve that began at her waist and worked up to the top of her head.

Then I have the class respond to these questions: "Are the words concrete enough so that the reader can *feel* the action? As each detail is added, can the reader relate the specific detail to the general picture of the action?" A few students, for example, felt that the last modifier in the sentence—the curve that begins at the woman's waist and follows her spine until it reaches her head—did not clearly relate to the subject of the main clause. The reader, they said, would not get a clear picture, a coherent visual perspective of the ongoing action.

We revised and produced two sentences.

> She limped over the curb and pushed her legs forward from the hips down, her bulky brown pocketbook dangling from her wrist, carrying her shoulders high. Her body began to form a curve or question mark from her waist to the top of her head.

This first approach, then, emphasizes the making of narrative sentences. From this approach, the writer learns how to bring the details of an experience into smaller, composite narrative units. The core unit of this approach is the cumulative sentence, with details included, arranged to fit a perspective and modified to appeal to the reader's eye.

II

The second approach works inductively—from specifics through to a formal design. I begin by having the class compose a plot summary of the action we will narrate, usually in about a paragraph. The summary usually includes a designation of perspective and point of view, some indication of what particular ac-

tions, gestures, or pieces of dialogue will be emphasized, and an indication of where the writer will begin describing the action and where he will stop. But most importantly, the summary ought to include some description of the impression the writer wants to make on his readers and why. After we've produced one sample summary in class, I have each student compose his own summary to serve as a working plan for his own narrative.

This approach reverses the process that we described in the first. Here the writer conceptualizes an entire narrative *before* he begins. When using the first approach, he works on cumulative sentences, composing an action-description piece-by-piece. The first approach helps a writer find material and a means of expressing it; the second helps him discover overall conceptual forms as he composes. Here is a sequence of classroom exercises, built upon qualitative comparisons among photography, film, and written narrative that should help to combine both the deductive and inductive approaches to teaching narration.

I begin by spending some class time analyzing an action photograph, suggesting what actually happened before and after the shot was taken, trying to piece together the overall sequence of action, working from the single moment captured in the photograph.[4] I have had

---

[4]Select photographs that suggest action and continuity rather than photographic stills, portraits, or static patterns of imagery. *The Searching EYE*, a brief film distributed by Grove Press (16mm, 11 minutes, color), makes an excellent transition from photograph to film. It includes still shots of several contemporary landscape drawings in juxtaposition with actual film of the landscape photographed. To purchase or rent *The Searching EYE* send to The Short Film Division, Grove Press, Inc., 80 University Place, New York, N.Y. 10003. Rental

excellent success with an Associated Press news photo in which two New York police detectives carry a wounded fellow-detective from a Muslim mosque in Harlem to a waiting automobile. They are protected by another detective who warily holds a gun as the wounded man is carried toward the automobile. On both sides of the detectives are taunting, screaming people, probably also recently emerged from the mosque. I show the photograph *without* background information and we begin to build a more complete account of what happened, as if we were news reporters covering the action. Such an exercise provides a usually welcome complement to straight analysis of written material. It also helps students to associate visual experience more coherently *before* they write and ultimately leads naturally to considerations of sequencing in written narration.

We work in class with photographs and narrative-action sentences similar to the sentences I described earlier. After discussing the general qualities of a photograph we move to these specific exercises.

1. Have each student compose, during the first ten minutes of a class period, an objective description of the photograph. If the class hasn't already spent some time with description, have them prepare by making lists of specifics from the photograph with perhaps one summary sentence that describes what happens.

2. Have several students read their descriptions. Then discuss how these detailed descriptions might be transformed

into narration. Begin by suggesting how this single shot might fit into an entire action sequence and work toward defining specific writing techniques that will help add a sense of motion through space to the written description.

3. Work specifically on sharpening some of the narrative devices I've already mentioned—have the students develop and practice in class different kinds of sentence modifiers. Participial and absolute phrases are especially useful devices for adding both physical detail and motion to a base action, especially when they are clearly related to a subject or predicate in the main clause. I usually work from single-word modifiers, especially concrete adjectives and adverbs, through large-constituent modifiers—prepositional, participial, and absolute phrases as well as clauses. Specific grammatical advice and practice usually works better in this context than in most others because the students immediately apply the advice to their own narratives. In other words, grammar becomes a matter of style, not mechanics.

After the focused exercises with photography, a film becomes a natural medium for the expression of action and detail in motion and sequence. I use only short films. They are better than full-length films, when you want a class to analyze technique, for two reasons. First, perspective and detail are more easily recalled; the "content" of the film is more obviously affected in a brief film by style and structure. Second, films of less than twenty minutes can be screened twice and discussed in a single class. Have the class watch and enjoy during the first showing; you might want them to take notes or even suggest interpretations as the film is shown a second time.

Films, even very short films, compose and integrate a great deal of experience

fee: $12.50. Purchase price: $125.00. In any case, select photographs that capture continuing action—a tennis player in the midst of returning a volley, an individual at a restaurant about to put food in his mouth, a child running.

very rapidly with the illusion of real-life motion and time. As a result, most films provide a much better metaphor for teaching *pattern*—the way specific experiences are interrelated and connected to form a plot, a unified sequence of action. Photography singles out a single sequence for scrutiny just as a writer may decide to scrutinize a single piece of action, a bit of detail that he wants to be sure to get right, as he composes a narrative. Film, in contrast, lets the viewer see and hear experience in connection and interrelationships. I often use the short film *Bang Head Go Bang Bang* to demonstrate narrative sequence and the development of a conceptual framework for a complex series of actions.[5]

This film works by visual association rather than a more traditional or literary plot-line. Chronology is purposely distorted and we see the experiences as if they were coming to us through the mind of a man who awakens with a severe hangover. The protagonist awakens in a small apartment bedroom. Both he and his surroundings are in obvious disarray. As he goes to the medicine chest to take something to relieve his headache, we see flashbacks to the previous night and we, along with the protagonist, try to piece together the causes of the hangover. We see a television boxing match, a confusing barroom scuffle as if we were one of the participants, an unidentified woman at the bar, the man-with-hangover as he drinks beer at the bar, as he walks a city street and enters the bar and, finally, a television screen blacking out as the protagonist is knocked cold.

I have my students try to unravel the sequence of events and put them into some natural order, either by chronology or by pointing out causative relationships among various events. Then we consider how and why the filmmaker put the experiences into the form he did. What, above all, did he gain by mixing up the actual order? Was the filmmaker able to emphasize certain actions, gestures, or details by removing them from chronological order and showing them as they were remembered by the protagonist?

Here are a series of assignments and exercises I use to teach narrative skills with *Bang Head Go Bang Bang*.

1. Have two groups of students unravel the flashbacks in the film and present to the class a chronological survey of the action.

2. What kind of person is the main character in the film? How would he talk if you met him on the street? What values does he hold? And what particular evidence can you draw from the scenes and actions in the film to support your answers?

3. Have the students select one repeated image in the film and show how the filmmaker uses it to unify the events of the film.

4. What does this film say? Does it have any message beyond the linking together of certain actions in narrative form? If it does, how is that message related to specific details in the film, to events, actions, or gestures, especially those that are repeated or emphasized.

5. Have the class compose as a group several cumulative sentences that describe a single sequence of action in the film. Work with variation in modification and the relationship among sentence components and details from the film.

Used together these exercises and media materials provide both an interesting and ordered frame for narrative experience.

---

[5]*Bang Head Go Bang Bang*, directed by Michael Siporin, 9 minutes, is also available for rental ($9.00) or purchase ($75.00) from Grove Press Short Film Division.

DAVID SIFF

Teaching Freshman Comp to New York Cops

IT IS ALMOST 200 YEARS since Blake transformed the clockwork of Newtonian thought into the towering death-symbol of Urizen. Freud, Joyce, along with a host of 20th-century physicists, have presented to our century a picture of decisive forces beyond our reason which are intertwined with our everyday lives. In linguistics there is growing acceptance of the idea that the *structure* of language itself is not imprinted on the *tabula rasa* of a child's mind but is inherent. It is surprising, therefore, that the teaching of writing has remained rooted in the prejudices of the Enlightenment: if one follows the general procedure of a proposition, paragraph development, etc., one ought to produce an acceptable narrative—i.e., one in which the writer's ideas are rationally presented.

Two years ago, I began teaching freshman composition to a class of New York cops at Brooklyn College. My social prejudices notwithstanding ("ya know, every cop is a criminal"—*Rolling Stones*), my approach to teaching composition was as rooted in traditional prejudices as possible. I had never taught composition before—and, after all, given my own obvious lack of experience, who was I to impose what was then pure confusion on a group of not particularly

David Siff is assistant professor of English at Brooklyn College (CUNY). His teaching presently is divided between New York City cops and Vietnam vets.

articulate adults who were willing to spend hours doggedly pursuing the phantom of "education" in order to somehow (miracle of miracles) improve their lives?

I, of course, did not then (or now) fancy myself on the side of Newton. Yet, I was not quite as Blakean as I might have wished. The way I transformed the Newtonian approach to freshman comp was to switch textbooks: instead of the *Harbrace 7th Edition*, I went for one that was heavy on "relevant" writing and McLuhanish graphics but which was light on grammar and mechanics.

Within the first month or so, as my students assimilated (grudgingly but with perfect respect for my authority) various essays on the war, racism, women's liberation, gay liberation, it was clear that using examples, even negative ones, had little effect on their writing. The first compositions I got were, predictably, turgid, clumsy, and only partially literate. A month of suffering with such material convinced me that the "new" approach, of feeling-tone unlicensed, was in no way better than the old order of reason and rules—and in fact probably was worse. Doing it the old way, the taste in your mouth might be horrible, but the medicine might have some analgesic effect. Thus, for the month following, we worked out of a more traditional text, drilling daily on the "simple mechanics" of building a structured composition. But

Reprinted from *College English*, Vol. 36, No. 5, January 1975.

at the end of that time, the papers I got were turgid, clumsy, and still only partially literate. And where formerly there had been a bit more spontaneity (blind swinging, take your pick), now there was a more conscious employment of "technique," so that various exercises, such as in the use of metaphor, would take on the murderous quality of unconscious parody. One paper I got, for example, likened George McGovern to a chicken:

McGovern is a Chicken

During this election campaign, I am bombarded daily with McGovern views through the media, especially his carping that Nixon supporters are wiretapping, sabotaging, and using espionage against democrats with Nixon's blessing. . . . All this to cast doubt on Nixon's integrity or to avoid other issues such as defense spending foreign policy or welfare reform.

The impression I got the other night watching McGovern speak, was that of a chicken walking around in a farm yard, pecking at the ground for seed. . . .

A chicken eats and ultimately digests the food, discharging the waste through its rectum. McGovern takes the issues, breaks them down to fit his image and digests them. He passes it to the people through his mouth.

There is an irony in describing what followed because it strongly implies planning and foreknowledge. The reality of the situation at the time was that I reached a point where I despaired of *any* reasonable solution to my problem. I had concluded that old way or new, I was locked into a situation I could do nothing about. I did not see at the time that the old way and the new were really the same—that they both posed, as a basic assumption, a split between feeling and form, the one insisting that before you got into the matter of feeling

you first had to understand the ABC's of form, the other asserting the reverse. All that I perceived at the time, however, was that I had run out of reasonable approaches. It turned out that that awareness—or lack of it—was precisely what led to what I now know was a breakthrough.

I asked my students to write a short narrative through the eyes of those they felt to be their "opposites" in society. I suggested that they choose topics that had substance (i.e. controversy)—and that they accord to their opposites the same degree of respect they had for themselves. The rest was up to them. My motive, at the time, perhaps was personal (wouldn't it be interesting to see what *they* would do in someone else's shoes?) but I surely was free of pedagogical intent. I simply didn't know what I was doing. The results, though, were amazing.

Not only did many of these students have a feel for their opposites, they possessed a kind of insight and imaginative awareness you would expect only from an especially sensitive partisan perspective. The time spent tampering with "freedom," then logic, paragraph construction, use of metaphor, and all the other paraphernalia of mechanics either suddenly connected or else meant nothing at all. A white Italian cop, author of the McGovern-Chicken paper, produced an exquisitely sensitive first person narrative through the eyes of a black ghetto youth. A real, four-square, bomb-them-back-into-the-stone-age flag waver, wrote as a draft resister, as did several others in the class. One person wrote through the eyes of Fidel Castro, still another through the eyes of Bella Abzug. The quality of these papers really cannot be described. They can only speak for themselves. What follows are excerpts from a few of these papers juxtaposed against immediately preceding papers from the same students. Sample #1 is from our McGovern-Chicken writer:

Lament of a Young Ghetto Resident

Yesterday, today and tomorrow was the name of a film I saw recently on television, and as I walk along Fulton Street, I'm thinking about today.

Today I went for an interview about a job at the employment agency. I waited awhile and then filled out some forms. The white interviewer gave me the same old jive about jobs—$2.00-$2.85 per hour for car washing, department store clerk, stock boy, janitor, floor cleaner or pumping gas. "Considering you have no high school diploma," he said, "some of those jobs have great futures and starting at the bottom, you can still work up to a pretty good salary." What shit, I had to get out of that place. Its the same old story all my life. I wonder if they jerk off white guys like that.

The thing that gets me is the way white cops look at me. Riding by slowly and leering at me with their chubby faces and bull necks just waiting for me to do something wrong so they can beat my head in. Sometimes, I can hear their cute remarks about the way my people walk and comb their afros, their comparisons of a brother to a gorilla or to a Zu-Lu tribesman. As long as whitey

dont put his hands on me I can live with some of the racial slurs.

The cops really think they're cool but they dont know shit about my neighborhood. Most of them live in their lily-white neighborhoods, with the fancy names like Bellemore, Seaford, Bethpaige and Pearl River. . . . Shit, they must think we're fools. The *kids* know where the dope is being sold and they dont. Last week some dude was blown away when he ripped off a junkie. They didn't care, he was just one less nigger. One less piece of dirt or slime. Honkie bastards.

Why is that radio car stopping? I didn't do anything wrong. "Hey you," one cop said, "come over here." My name ain't hey you, so I just kept walking and before I knew it I was pushed against the wall and frisked. "What's that in your back pocket, boy?" the fat dressed-blue pig had asked. He reached in my pocket and took my bottle of Twister wine. One didn't like my attitude, the other, my looks and clothes, especially my tam, with the Angela Davis button. They gave me a break this time and broke my bottle instead of my head. "No, he didn't fit the description," one cop said. Get the fuck out of here, they told me. I shuffled off like a good nigger, hating myself for not saying something in protest. We aint got no pride and these pigs dont either. Bullies, with a badge for a license, and a gun for hunting. Law and order they call it.

SAMPLE #2

Use of Metaphors

Vietnamization is a school of government. The United States has seen fit to introduce a system by which some of our know how and experience can be taught to the people of South Vietnam. . . .

The attendance of these students to this school has been very strict. Cutting classes may end in death. Our teachers, trained and are training the South Vietnamese. . . . The leaders of the class are promoted to supervisory positions. . . .

In this school there are other subjects

Dear Mom,

I know you will find it strange that this letter comes from Sweden, but that's where I am now. . . . I am sorry to have to tell you this in a letter and I hope you will understand my position, if you cant then I will understand. To be blunt I deserted from the Army. I don't expect Dad to understand or perhaps ever forgive me, but it was something I had to do. I know that Dad fought in World War II and was very proud to have served his country. If this was World War II perhaps I could have taught for instance, economics to help build a solid monetary system. We offer construction to rebuild a country when their destiny is again in their hands.

The principal of this school is President Thieu of South Vietnam. Board of Education head at present is President Nixon. The Dean of the Military studies section is General Creighton Abrams. The Dean of the Political Science section is Henry Kissinger. . . .

[The South Vietnamese] have lost some ground, and perhaps do not fight as well as their instructors but they have distinguished themselves as a fighting army. It should also be remembered that they are still in training. It will be necessary to watch the current developments . . . in order that we may see how well the South Vietnamese have learned their lessons with regard to their economy and their politics.

had the same feelings. However, it is not, its an undeclared political war not something which was detrimental to our country. There was no one invading us, no sneak attack, no one trying to change our way of life.

When I was drafted, although I did not like the idea, I felt it was my duty to go. I was trained and drilled with one thought drilled into me: we were at war and we must fight. I believed this until I arrived in South Vietnam. . . . When I saw the scope of the military equipment, the large air bases, the amount of men sent here, and thought about the length of time this so-called war had been going on, it seemed that there were a lot more interests at stake here than we knew about. This war is a good money making business for a lot of people. Its a good political issue for politicians, they're not the ones being shot at. There are a lot of people both Americans and South Vietnamese who are getting killed here supposedly so we can stop the takeover of Communism in this little country. If and when it does end and the Americans pull out it will probably go Communist anyway.

For myself and I know a lot of other guys feel the same way, although maybe they wont take such a drastic step as I did; it doesn't seem worthwhile to get killed for all the wrong reasons. I felt it was time to think and act for myself. After seeing a few friends and mine get killed and maimed for nothing I couldn't see myself sacrificing my life for things which I dont believe in.

SAMPLE #3

I was born and raised in a neighborhood not quite ghetto yet. I learned how to fight, curse, lie and steal. I can honestly say those years were very enjoyable as hard as they were.

However, after becoming a little learneth (or maybe I attribute it to my field of work), I see an animalistic way of life now. Blacks have become so independent as to ignore law and order, contrary to the White man's way of life and working feverishly towards gaining superiority over the whites. Semitic groups are encouraging oppression against the govern-

You and I being, sensible Black brothers and sisters, know how really lucky we are to be free and living in this wonderful, wonderful country. Certainly we know it. The white man has told us so. And of course like good Black folk, we've listened carefully to what the nice White man has said and then, with wide eyes and gentle faces, we've nodded our heads in agreement. After all, the White man knows best.

Just think of all the wonderful freedoms which Black people have. . . . We have the freedom to sometimes get an education and —in spite of the inferior curriculum, and

ment such as burning the flag, defiance of law and abusing our freedoms. The Catholic Church has also leaned towards leftist attitudes. Students in their upper teens refuse to salute our wonderful flag, demand their own type of law and order, burn draft cards and provoke incidents which cause so-called riots.

I summarize by saying what will become of our great nation in the near future. As of now it appears to be at Great Disaster.

old books, and disinterested teachers—to qualify for a better paying, more prestigious position and then, fully qualified, to apply for that position and be told by a smiling white face: "Sorry there are no openings." We have the freedom to feel the pain of discouragement and helplessness as we see the man in back of us—the White man in back of us—hired for the same "no openings" job. And after we've tried again and again and again with the same results, we have the freedom to be called "lazy" because we're not working.

Yes, indeed, we really are free. Do you know that we can live in any slum we want to? We can be swindled and cheated and lied to and victimized by the White man. It's called "business initiative." But let a Black man forget to pay a bill—that's called "stealing." Of course we always have the law to fall back on. That's a real comfort isn't it? The nice White man wrote the law. He interprets it and he enforces it, too. But as the nice White man has told us the law is "uniformly administered." Do you know what that means to a Black man? That means that if a White pig is driving by and sees a White man chasing a Black man, he stops his pigmobile, gets out, and clubs the Black man. But on the other hand, if he sees a Black man chasing a White man, he stops, goes over, and clubs the Black man again. That's uniformity!

In addition to freedom, we have opportunity to do the chores too dirty for lily-white hands; opportunity to sweat our lives away so Whitey can live at his ease; opportunity to die in the same poverty in which we were born; opportunity to bear children for Whitey's use—children who can look forward to being treated like mud, used like horses, then discarded like old shoes. . . .

I tell you brothers and sisters, the time has come when no more will Black people die a thousand deaths at Whitey's hands. Now if we die, we'll die only once—as we fight to take from Whitey what he has already taken from us. Now brothers and sisters, now is time for Black people to decide their own fate. Whitey must not treat our children as he has treated us. He must not—and he shall not.

Come now—get your gun and follow me!

It was simply staggering to me that these students could have produced such papers. Barring the possibility of plagiarism (which in one instance I did not entirely rule out), the cops had spoken through their opposites with more passion, insight, wit, and command than they ever had for themselves. After sample #2 had been read aloud in class, one of the cops turned to the writer and said, "man, if you know *that*, how the hell can you believe anything different?" The question could not have been put more succinctly. The writer replied, simply enough, "Well, I understand it but I'm not for it because it's against the law." The other cop waved his hand at him in total, unbelieving disgust, a gesture which ended the conversation without settling the question.

For all my surprise, there was still no real insight. My brain reeled under the weight of conflicting possibilities ("who knows, maybe these Archie Bunkers have souls after all!"—"these people have the potential of being the *deadliest* undercover agents!")—but as far as perceiving any of this in terms of writing, the matter rested well below the surface of consciousness. Feeling that I was a juggler keeping a good act going rather than a teacher probing more deeply into his subject, I next assigned a dialogue between the opposites the students had written about and themselves. Again the results were startling. In case after case, the opposites carried the argument—and what's more, the students themselves knew it and talked about it openly. The following excerpt from a student's dialogue with Fidel Castro is illustrative:

Student: Fidel, you say the Cuban people are free from tyranny. If they really are as free as you say, why not let them exercise the right to choose a different leader if they so desire.

Fidel: I feel that if at this time I were to hold free elections the yankee imperialists would take this opportunity to sabotage my efforts, and the end results would be a return to the days when Fulgencio Batista was in power. I believe first of all that we must work together (the Cuban people) and learn to trust ourselves before we hold so-called free elections. I have very little faith in the so-called free elections, we have seen how many of our neighboring friends have fallen into the yankee trap. The CIA sets up the man they think can run the country and then they hold free elections. The people in turn dont like this and then you have a revolution. Your government goes through a lotta trouble to destroy the well-being of our brothers, this makes me very bitter.

Student: But dont you think the majority of people should have a right to chose their own government and that interference by anyone . . . is wrong. People everywhere want to be free, man was born to be free. We should allow him that god-given right.

Fidel: Everything with you people is god. Dont you believe in yourselves, why do you have to use god as your scapegoat. People in Cuba are satisfied by the way this government is run. We dont need the yankee to tell us how to run our internal affairs. You see the yankee is nothing but a hypocritical giant who only cares for the almighty dollar not the almighty. They could care less what happens to the Cuban people. . . . Time and time again we have seen the false promises made by the american government and the american millionaire capitalist, who exploits the poor people by enslaving them so that he can profit. I can show you how the americans control most of the industrial interests in america latina, and how they live in fashionable villas whereas the poor peasants live in huts and work like dogs to make a living. The americans are no different than the spaniards. The spaniards used to enslave our people while they also lived in fashionable villas, and to this day their wealthy south american ancestors are doing the same thing. . . .

Student: Do you see the possibility in the near future of resumed diplomatic relations between Cuba and the United States? And if so, what are your plans for the future?

Fidel: At this time the possibility of resuming diplomatic relations is not in our plans. There are too many differences of opinion between our governments and anyway, your government has not made any efforts in this area. My plans for the future are to see that the Cuban people obtain what they have been denied for years—self-respect and dignity.

As in the former pieces, it will be noted that the writer seems to take wing in the disguise of his opposite while plodding along when speaking for himself. Not only does he accord Fidel more space but he builds his arguments with more conviction, self-assurance, and verbal dexterity than he does his own. The one point the writer wants to make for himself, he seems to lose as Fidel mounts his rebuttal. The result is that the writer changes the subject rather than offering an argument for his own position that might have equal conviction and substance. The one point in the dialogue (just after the "student" concludes "We should allow him that god-given right"), where Fidel himself changes the subject rather than answers directly, produces an impression not necessarily of weakness and evasiveness but somehow of strength. God, of course, had nothing to do with the point the student was making. But Fidel picks up the phrase, turns it inside out, first making the rather ingenious distinction between belief in God and failure to believe in yourself, then driving home the familiar point of Yankee religious hypocrisy with a rather effective turn of phrase. The stage is then set for an attack on the historic role of capitalism in "america latina," an attack that is carried off, thanks to the preliminary maneuvering, with an impression of conviction rather than of deviousness.

That all of these papers should have shown such sensitivity to the *rhetoric* of different socio-political types is in itself surprising given the almost total absence of rhetorical awareness in the earlier papers. But by far the greatest surprise was discovering the degree to which these people could emotionally and intellectually identify with types they themselves named as their opposites.

What did it all mean? The answer, beyond the boundaries of this paper, will probably have to be drawn from psychology. Some contemporary schools of psychotherapy (Gestalt and Jungian for example) see the traditional conscious/subconscious division of personality as a dialectical tension between opposite sides of the self. So long as this tension of opposites remains remote from awareness, so long does it manifest itself negatively through unconscious projections, prejudices, etc. But if ever contact with "the other" can occur more consciously, the results, far from being negative can point the way towards emotional growth. In the terms I am describing, it is fairly clear that my students, by means of an unwitting classroom device, came into contact with these "split-off" sides of their own personalities and in so doing, touched potentialities of feeling and sympathy they did not know existed.

Over the remaining part of the semester (several weeks), the quality of the students' writing slipped—particularly when they returned to their own personae. But their last papers were still better than their first ones and, more importantly, a number of students began openly questioning values and beliefs that only weeks earlier had been steeped in irrevocable anger, cynicism, and self-righteousness. For me, the key was that my students were for the first time asking questions rather than merely swallowing assignments. At lunch one day, a few members of the class were trying to tell me what they had gotten out of the course. They jokingly complained that I had turned them into a bunch of liberals, then one of them said with surprising seriousness, that the real change for him was that in the beginning of the semester he had thought of himself as a cop and now he thought of himself as a student. The sense of irony and skepticism that the statement initially evoked for me was, of course, unintended. What the student meant was that, for the first time in a very hard life, he had come to value his own mind. The rather earnest agreement amongst the others only later made me realize that something important had indeed taken place during the year. In a real sense, what had occurred was, for me, a beginning.

HARVEY S. WIENER

The Single Narrative Paragraph
and College Remediation

A. Women's Liberation

Wmen's liberation is good in one way, but not in another way. Wemen should be paid the same amount of money as a men, in some field, for example. If wemen have the knowlegde to become nurse, doctor or any other field, wemen should be paid the sam amount of salary. If she doesn't have the knowlegde for that particular field, then she should not be paid the same salary. I think that wemen should have the same rights as a man. Because if a lady doctor is examining a patient, if she doesn't have the knowlegde, the patient eighter will become very ill or die. There are some job's in which wemen cann't work at, for example, sanatation department, plumer's ETC.

B. Women's Lib

It is some people's belief that history repeats itself. This seems to be true in this generation concerning women's rights.

Many people may want to know just what more do women want. They feel, since the early 1900's, that women "have come a long way." I think you would have to be in a women's place to know exactly what they are looking for. Women want more than just the right to vote. They want to be able to walk into any field of employment and except to be treated as equally as men and paid on the same level.

There are many more rights women want but there is something else that is missing from women's freedom. That is the attitude of men. Men always seem to look down women regardless of her abilities.

The women's liberation movement can be helpful as far as making women's hopes come true. On the other hand it can be harmful.

THE TWO SAMPLES ABOVE tell the sad results of a typical expository theme assignment in a writing skills class in a community college at the start of the semester. Although the mechanical errors remain intact to stress in passing the scope of the writing difficulties now confronting teachers of college English in the new wave of open admissions policies,[1] this paper focuses instead upon problems in form and

Harvey S. Wiener is Assistant Professor of English and Coordinator of the writing program at LaGuardia Community College (CUNY's newest unit), and Adjunct Assistant Professor of English at Brooklyn College. He is writing a composition text for McGraw-Hill based upon the principles in this essay.

[1]I hope too that the mechanical errors, especially in sample A, tell what a disservice it is (for the community college youngster) to hold with those instructors who, facing better prepared freshmen, opt for benign neglect in language skills and frown upon any attention to correctness as "nice-nellyism." Although the graduate of the two-year college will provide a variety of non-

Reprinted from *College English*, Vol. 33, No. 6, March 1972.

content facing the youngster with inadequacies in composition. The samples on women's liberation assert clearly to me that the expository essay is the wrong place to begin for remedial students. Because exposition as it is defined and employed in college composition courses too often deals with social, literary, and philosophical concepts remote from the student's sphere of operation; and because the essay—even the simple four-paragraph kind—involves structural complexities too large for the skills student to confront from the outset, I wish to suggest as the core of remedial writing instruction in the college classroom the single narrative paragraph that relates in vivid language a memorable experience in the student's life.

The expository essay as a writing exercise for the skills student contains built-in failure devices. Although we as teachers may be excited beyond measure by the events of our day (our changing times, women's rights, new sexual freedom) and may find merit in constructing arguments for abstract essays ("The Most Important Event in the Last Ten Years," "A Woman's Role in a Man's World," "My Definition of Love"),[2] students do not necessarily define relevance as relevant events in the world theater. My students politely yawn through my enthusiasm with the ideas behind volunteer armies and moon walks, new freedoms and automated societies. Those who are interested in such abstract joys of space exploration convey in a sentence or two the full range of their delight, then drift into an aimless and elliptical orbit of repetition and inconsequence. Expository topics so remote from the student's actual experience require a sophistication that many college freshmen may have but most remedial students do not: the ability to use as supportive detail materials they have read or heard in a wide range of literary and intellectual encounters. Most students with writing troubles read poorly too; and if they have indeed learned about relevant events through the television, radio, or newspaper, students must not only have understood the information presented about a topic frequently marginal to their own vital concerns, but they must be able to recall the material as well and compose it in some kind of meaningful prose, both readable and effective. All these difficulties are compounded when the student must attend to the formalism of the essay with its often whimsical paragraph shifts, its introductory statement, its sentence-long transitions, its thesis statement, its elaborated conclusion. The essay on an abstract idea might be the end-point toward which students should move. However, until more elemental skills are mastered, instructors should pay little heed to the essay as the student's vehicle for written expression.

The freshman theme as single narrative paragraph overcomes many of the

---

intellectual services for the community, his employer will be severely less liberal and more elitist about correctness than most professors. Spelling, for example, announces to most non-academics the degree of literacy of the writer to such an extent that poor spellers are marked as low on brain power. Graduates of career programs in the world of business, health services, industry, or technology will sooner or later write a report or memo that some superior on the job can use as a gauge for intellectual (hence, job) ability. We with broader scopes know that spelling, punctuation, and sentence structure do not always reflect the quality of the mind beneath; but if only for those who disagree (and who decide upon our students' promotions), teach for correctness we must.

[2]These were topics used by several teachers at Queensborough Community College in order to determine whether or not a student should be placed in regular freshman composition or a writing skills class.

problems that the expository essay presents. In the first place, attention to a well written paragraph of three-hundred words makes it easier for the writer to deal with structural elements. A topic sentence and a closing sentence are considerably easier to grasp and refine than introductory and concluding paragraphs. By means of a focus on the paragraph the student directs his energies toward the more basic unit of the composition which may later serve efficiently as a conversion device for the essay itself.[3] Secondly, the narrative allows the student to employ information rooted in his own physical, emotional, and intellectual fiber. The obvious advantage here is that details, because of their indelibility, surface easily as the students write; with their own experiential reality as the core of the composition the youngsters need recall nothing remote from their own worlds. And questions of arrangement of detail and other sophisticated organizational problems are, in the meantime, subordinated in the chronological framework of the narrative. More attention may turn, then, to the nature of supportive details themselves. Through the application of sensory language to real experience successes in writing are often immediate: students learn to tell logical, interesting stories of reasonable length and vividness. But these two narrative paragraphs written by the remedial students represented on the first page of this essay speak for themselves. Sample A-1 below was written by student A above; and sample B-1 came from the same student who wrote sample B:

A-1. Man Against Fish

The day I caught a king Cod fish, out by Montauk Point, I will never forget the moment I experienced that spring day out on the ocean. One bright and clear blue morning, my family and I drove to the end of the Island, to do some of the fishing that was going on out in the Island. On the way to the Island, my family and I were talking about the different kinds of fish that were running at that time. My father said, "Cod, Flounders, and Flukes". So I said, "Let's go fishing for Cod fish". My family agreed to go Cod fishing, and we did. At six AM. we sped into the fishing dock area, and my father looked over the situation, and decided to go fishing on a large brown boat, the Mary II. When a fog horn honked at six thirty the boat pulled out, and went for a cruies of eighteen mile ride into the ocean. Then at eight o'clock the boat arrived at the fishing grounds, and Captain Kallous looked over the side and shouted in a deep voice, "All lines down." The person next to me caught a fifteen pounder which fought on the wooden deck. It smacked its white tail from side to side. Shortly after, I got hit

B-1. An Embarrassing Day

Up to this moment, I'll never forget the drastic and embarrassing day my eighth grade teacher chopped my locks of hair. As I strolled to school that morning, the bright sun shown down through my shaggy long bangs and onto my face. Everything was fine; nothing could go wrong. I had completed all my homework for that day, and was prepared for new lessons. When I arrived at my ordinary red brick school house, my friends informed me that today was inspection. This meant everyone had to be in tip-top shape. Our hair had to be neat and our shoes shining so that we were able to see the reflection of our freshly cleaned uniforms. We all marched into the classroom and took our regular seats. Seeing my eight-grade teacher curiously looking around the tense-strickened room with her stern face, I tried to hide behind the huge boy in front of me. Yet it was to late; she discovered me with my hair hanging in my eyes. I just sat there stunned trying to watch her angry face turn purple. Suddenly, she grabbed a pair of freshly

[3]See Joseph D. Gallo and Henry W. Rink, *Shaping College Writing* (New York, 1968), pp. 125-135.

with a bite. The pole started to bend, and I could feel the the weight of the cod fish in the pole. It took me about twenty minutes to reel up a fighting cod fish from the choppy blue water. As I was reeling up the fish, it was man versus the elements. It takes a special skill to reel up a large cod fish, because as the fish is hooked he will tend to pull down. As the fish is pulling down, you do not reel up, because the fishing line will have an excess of tension, and the line will break. By the line breaking you will lose your rig and the main thing, the fish. So I reel up a thirty five pounder, and I entered the fish into the pool. It took first place, and I won twenty six dollars and changes for the largest fish caught that day on the Mary II.

sharpened sheers out of her draw, and slammed it closed. The next thing I knew, she was snipping away with those cold and ugly silver scissors. Now, there was nothing I could do except die a slow death. When she was finished, she exclaimed, "There, now you can see!" As everyone glared their eyes at me, I felt the warm tears roll down my cheeks. From that day on, I wore my bangs very short.

It takes no mastery to see the shortcomings in these samples. But even the hardest-line advocate of expository essays cannot miss the remarkable improvement in over-all quality from theme A to A-1, from B to B-1. Whatever his individual potential, the student seems to work closer to that potential in the second sample than he does in the first. Furthermore, there is no mystery as to the elements of achievement and how they were attained.

Drill on the topic sentence as the statement of paragraph purpose in the first lines revolves around two basic requirements: does the topic sentence mention the subject specifically and does it contain some assertion of the writer's attitude toward the topic he plans to develop in the paragraph. Further work on topic sentences involves expansion; students are asked to identify in the opening lines the place at which the event occurred and the season or month of the year. The complete and engrossing topic statements in A-1 and B-1 result from such instruction.

Students are encouraged to write bits of exact details like "choppy blue waves," and "when a fog horn honked" by a series of exercises that explain and explore the meaning of concrete sensory language. One effective method of introduction to the language of the senses is to ask students to observe the classroom in which they sit, and to write sentences that tell sounds they hear, colors and actions they see, impressions of smell and touch they receive as they participate in the writing experience.[4] Later on, freshmen may be asked to expand an incomplete mention of place or person or thing by employing sensory language. After comparing the visual quality in these two groups of words—

an old book	an economics book with yellowed pages and a torn binding
my pen	my smooth pen that clicks when I push the silver tip
a breeze	a breeze smelling of earth and pushing the window shades with a clatter

---

[4]See Don M. Wolfe, "Crucial First Assignment: Describing a Room," *Elementary English*, XLII (October, 1970), 784-786.

—students can easily create concrete pictures for words like *desk, sweater, pocketbook*. If they are made aware that the narrative paragraph unfolds through a series of thought units, young writers can expand each unit of thought with such concrete imagery.

In sentence structure, achievements come about through experimentation with coordination and subordination. Many remedial youngsters do not know the difference between *and* and *but*, nor are they aware of the levels of mature writing that may be achieved through various subordinating structures. Samples A-1 and B-1 still show too many simple sentence patterns, and there remain a number of technical errors; but at least there is a nexus of effective expression through which to work out mistakes in mechanics. To try correcting spelling and sentence construction errors in sample A is worthless because the whole piece is of itself of little value. In A-1 on the other hand, to suggest correction is to introduce a mode of operation which will add respectability to an already effective written exercise.

To stimulate those students who have difficulty in finding topics, I try to organize each theme activity around some general experience ("Remembering Youth," "The Teacher," "The Car in My Life"). Discussion prior to writing is essential and may be facilitated by presenting to the student a list of incomplete sentences which reflect the general theme topic for the week. Each student completes aloud one of the sentences. For a theme about recalling schooltime experiences, for example, here are some sentences that evoked particularly lively completions:

1. When I played hooky, I. . . .
2. We always got in trouble when. . . .
3. My teacher lost her temper when. . . .
4. My teacher understood when. . . .
5. I was embarrassed at school when. . . .

The responses to these questions know no cultural or ethnic bounds; all of my students are eager to talk about the events in their lives and every life style finds some application to these questions. A youngster who completes the statement too briefly may be prodded gently by the teacher to fill in details of background, of time and place, of action, thus setting the stage for the coming activity in writing. And sentences like the ones above may be used as the starting points for student paragraphs as well.

Prior to each writing activity, I try to help students recall the specific skills they have learned in the previous weeks, skills designed to add both liveliness and maturity of expression to their creations. Here is a checklist of helps and pointers I distributed before one writing exercise:

1. Write a topic sentence to include an exact statement of your topic and some opinion you have about the topic.
2. Try to state the time and place of the event in the first few lines of your paragraph.
3. Try to use several instances of sensory language in expanded pictures:
    a. mention at least three colors
    b. use at least three words that name sounds
    c. use a word that appeals to the sense of smell

    d. use a word that indicates a sensation of touch
4. Mention people and places by name.
5. Use lively verbs that indicate actions. Show people in the midst of activity when you mention their names.
6. Start at least three sentences with words on the list of subordinators you examined last week.
7. Start one or two sentences with a word that ends in *-ing*.
8. Start one or two sentences with a word that ends in *-ly*.

I do not think this is at all what Michael Kressy meant when he wrote about the community college youngster that "the student must not be clamped in an unyielding grid of rigid, detailed writing assignments;"[5] surely there is no stifling of individuality and creative thrust in these prescriptive measures, because each student works from the most original of all subjects: his own experiences. It further needs reminding that the remedial student, so long as he does have "the freedom to develop his own subject matter,"[6] finds no insult in explicit statements on theme content and style. Rather, he feels a certain security in knowing exactly what the criteria for successful paragraphs are.

The single narrative paragraph is not the end point of a solid program in writing for students with skills difficulties, but a number of assignments that encourage the student to explore his own life for materials of composition can teach him effectively that he *does* have valuable information about which to write. Once confidence in his own materials is established in the writer, the instructor may experiment with more mature paragraph forms. Comparison-contrast; cause-effect; using several instances to support one topic in a paragraph; definition; classification: these too can be effectively developed through experiential subject matter. At some point in the semester statistics, cases, quoted material, and paraphase may be introduced as other types of effective paragraph detail. Ultimately, the student can approach the abstract expository essay on his own terms: a topic like "women's lib" may be developed successfully through instances in which the student has confronted prejudice because of sex; has dealt with women in professions thought essentially for men; has been the child of a working mother and can call up feelings of loneliness or neglect; or has read or heard the latest from Betty Friedan, has viewed on television a rally for women's rights, has been inspired by the intriguing pages of *Sexual Politics*. But his own experiential reality ought to be the place where a student is encouraged to look first when he meets an abstract idea, especially as he learns the writer's craft in its early stages. "The Most Important Event in the Last Ten Years" could grow effectively from some occurrence that touched the youngster's life close up. To define love, hate, fear, courage, or loneliness, individual bouts with these feelings must serve as substantive core for composition. And toward the successful execution of the term paper in history, the psychology final, the sociology report (important goals all of most writing programs), we have not been derelict: the repeated stress on detail makes the student aware of the need for supportive material in any kind of written exercise, whether that supportive information

---

[5]"The Community College Student: A Lesson in Humility," *College English*, XXXII (April, 1971), 777.
[6]Ibid.

be statistical, illustrative of cases, paraphrases of books or articles or teacher lectures.

As the course of instruction progresses, therefore, the student develops a vision of the available areas to which he may turn in order to support any topic he is asked to consider in writing. Before they begin to write any theme, I encourage my students to ask themselves these important questions (and for "in-class" compositions I have these questions on the blackboard):

1. What have I experienced in my own life that I can recall vividly enough to help me support with details some aspect of the topic?
2. What have I read lately (or can read easily and quickly) that will help me support with details some aspect of the topic?
3. What have I seen or heard on television, in the movies, on the radio, or from my friends, relatives, or teachers that will help me support with details some aspect of the topic?

If the student has an answer to question one, he knows that the substance of his paragraph must rely upon sensory detail for concreteness: he might even develop a narrative paragraph to advance his position on an abstract idea. If question two inspires thought, the student knows his concrete details must be paraphrase or quotation with some reference to source of information. Details selected in response to question three may be developed with an eye to both—or either—the sensory or the supportive material available through paraphrasing or quoting statements, examples, statistics, or cases.

When the student moves to more abstract regions of argument, then, he is armed with a variety of approaches to detail. With the nature of detail clearly in mind, young writers may confront more easily the problems of form. The theme below is the result of an exercise in a more complex form of exposition than the straight narrative paragraph, one introduced much later in the term. Here students were specifically requested to use *several* examples or instances to argue about some aspect of the automobile in today's world. I find this theme particularly exciting in spite of its limitations for several reasons: its subtopics are so clearly stated; it attempts to employ more than one type of detail; and it puts into practice quite nicely the intent of the questions I suggest students consider before they write.

Safer Cars

Although automobiles are still very dangerous, they are becoming more safer as time goes by. Safty idems are being placed on the outside of the passenger area to prevent or to help lighten the effects of a collision. Plans for the Motor Vehical Safty Standers by the National Highway Safty Bureau have already started. Strengthing the fuel tank of a car, which can explode during a collision, and the use of an air bag to prevent the impact of the vehicals are two of the safety plans. Commercials on television said special steel guards will be placed on the side of cars, besides the metal tip tires which will let the care ride safer on ice. Also, some of the safety devices will be placed inside the car to prevent injury to the driver and passengers by themselves. While the car won't start until the driver passes a mechanical test to prove he is sober, it also won't start unless the seat belts are buckled. Since the special lights on and in the car will flash when the car is moving faster than the legal speed limit, the driver will know when he is speeding and so will other people. Another safty device inside the passenger area is the gauge which will show how much air is in the tires. Signals, signs and fixing of roads are also making driving alot safer. Whenever I am traveling in my old Pontiac I almost always pass some road improvement operation. Just at the New York City-Nassau line on the Grand Central Parkway crews of men without shirts work behind large white road dividers and build new lanes. I saw a new type of traffic light on the Van Wyck Expressway which allows cars to enter the road more evenly and safely. Because of a red and green light system, only one car at a time may pull off the ramp and onto the highway. As long as cars are around they will always be dangerous, but death, injury and damage will drop with the development of new safety standards and devices.

There we have details drawn from life and from the media that are significant sources of information for the student.

After class discussion of the sort I mentioned earlier, a student in another class limited the abstract topic of women's liberation to consider the children of working mothers. There were no specific directions as to what kinds of details should be used (just the usual review of the variety of details available). But for this young lady—certainly more sophisticated in composition skills than the other students I have quoted—the narrative paragraph rooted in experience and rich in sensory language becomes the means through which to argue her point.

Deprived Children

The children of working mothers are often deprived of the security of a healthy and loving environment because their mothers are not always around when they are needed. As a young child with a working mother I felt her absence deeply. One of the many incidents that explains my attitude is as follows: On my first day in third grade, there was a violent storm. Jubilant at the prospect of a new teacher and new friends, the class was in a state of excitement because of the violent storm. However, this happy enthusiasm soon wore off when streets flooded and winds soaked to sixty miles per hour. All the classes were assembled in the basement and the principal announced that no one would leave unless accompanied by a parent. Nervously hugging my new notebook to my thin jacket, I prayed that somehow my mother would get to me. A slow procession of mothers holding raincoats, umbrellas and books trudged in to pick up their fidgety children as I concentrated on a speck on the floor. The hours unfolded gradually and soon I stood in the middle of the huge gray basement, alone except for my faithful teacher. The fear of going out in the hurricane was lost in the agony of shame that I felt by not having a mother at home like everyone else. This incident is not an isolated one—children of working mothers always feel a sense of loss and shame.

Several more vivid pictures—of the principal, perhaps, or the faithful teacher as she waits with the student—would add length and vividness to the paragraph, it is true; but in "Deprived Children" the writer herself has bridged the gap between abstract and concrete.

After they have grasped soundly both detail and paragraph form, student and teacher may move to the expository essay of four or five paragraphs. The topic sentence is expanded to the introductory paragraph; sub-topic sentences serve as opening sentences for body paragraphs; larger transitional elements—like subordinating structures that refer back to the substance of a previous paragraph—are introduced; the closing sentence becomes the conclusion, a paragraph that tries to set the whole topic in a new perspective. But at the heart of all these concerns with form lies the essence of content revealed through detail. Here, it seems to me, is a very acceptable four-paragraph exposition from a skills student in response to a theme assignment "Machines: For Man or Against Him":

Machines Can Be Against Man As Well As For Him

In today's world, machines play an important role. Today more than ever before machines are used for manufacturing, transportation and medicene. These mechanical devises have helped us a great deal to advance forward. But as everything else, just as machines can be used for man; they can be used against him, too.

As one looks around him, he can see the wonderful advances made by machines. In transportation, we now have automobiles, jets, steam ships and trains. For instance, a trip that use to take six days by ship can now be reached in six hours by jet. My aunt suffered all the way to London on a French Line ship for a whole week; today she might step into a silvery jet before breakfast and step off into the bright yellow sun of the same day. This new airplane industry has also given jobs to hundreds of thousands of people all over the world. Each day new improvements are being made. I read in Life magazine that in 1975, the United States is going to have the Boeing SST which will go up to a speed of 1,000 miles or so an hour making the time between places even shorter. Besides the jet advancements, there's the automobile. This vecle is the one most often used for transportation. It has advanced from a so called horseless carriage to a gas engine moving veicle. In today's world this machine is no longer a luxury but a necessity. People now depend on it for going to work as well as for pleasure rides in the country. Because the world is moving so rapidly, these machines are working for man in an important way.

Although these machines have helped man, machines used today are also killing him. The automobile is one of the greatest killers. The National Safety Council reports that 56,400 deaths resulted in car accidents in 1970. I watched one example first-hand. One afternoon last December a small boy on a new red bike rode carefully across 217th Street in Queens as he normally does every afternoon. Only this time a sports car zoomed around the corner at a high speed. The boy not expecting this went right through the windshield with a crash of broken glass. I had to close my eyes when I heard the boy scream. He died the next day. This is just one of the accidents that occur each year. Automobiles don't only kill man by accidents; but also poison him by polluting the air. The New York Times Almanac shows how much of today's pollution is caused by the great number of automobiles in use, and how pollution causes a number of deaths for people with lung diseases and for old age people.

Machines may have their bad side, but the good they do is of greater quantity. What would we do without these machines like the automobile? How could we advance in medicine, transportation and manufacturing? What would our lives be like?

Although I personally find the single narrative event a much more exciting type of written assignment, the student has worked reasonably well with the paragraph that uses more than one instance to support a position. The design of the essay itself as a simple comparison-contrast employs substantial details of the sort the students work with all semester long. And the form shows some mastery: the proposal is stated at the end of the first paragraph; each body paragraph makes a clear statement of intent in the first sentence; the transition between paragraph two and three is effective; and the conclusion does attempt—albeit unsurely—to conclude.

The stress on writing from experience has many advantages, but one of the most important is that such a stress allows the student to come to terms with his own existence. By sifting through his singular confrontations with life and time and employing these in a written composition, the writer develops a sense of his own responses, a way of thinking about his motivations and impressions. This sense is often blinded in the rigorous attention to the abstract essay that forms the basis of most freshman writing, so I frequently assign theme topics that insist upon the experiential event and its exposition through sensory language. To me the narrative is not a form alien to expository writing nor excluded from its ranks. And the coming to terms with his own life that narration frequently demands is the indispensible service for the student that the good composition program performs. In no other college classrooms (except perhaps in creative writing electives) is the student the subject matter of the course; for that reason I am a staunch proponent still of required writing in the freshman's plan of study. Those who urge its demise have missed the extraordinary opportunity to act as guide for intellectual and emotional growth, to provide a comfortable and impartial setting for the exploration of motive and behavior, of response and action, of feeling and thought. To the string of benefits properly enumerated by a recent spokesman for required courses in communication skills—"mental discipline, increasing sensitivity to the subtleties of language, and basic writing skills"[7]—must certainly be added the advantage of self-exploration.

Putting one's own experiences in the framework of abstract concepts is a notable method of thinking and makes access to the community of ideas a much more concrete process.

---

[7]George L. Groman, "Freshman English at Rutgers-in-Newark," *The CEA Forum*, I (February, 1971), 8.

RICHARD J. BASGALL

On Teaching Relationships

WHILE TEACHING a course in freshman composition I had a class session that I think was particularly good in teaching the importance of relationships or seeing things in terms of other things. I want first to describe the events that occurred in that class and then draw some conclusions about the benefits that I think can be derived from assignments and classes similar to this one.

The course required the students to write a short essay on an assignment for each class. I read each essay and then selected one for class discussion. The particular assignment we were working on was the following: "Describe a visit to a city about which you had some preconceptions. What new things did you learn by visiting it? What preconceptions did you revise and how did you do it? As you were doing this, what was happening to the city itself?"

To start the class discussion, I selected the following sentence from one student's paper: "I began changing the thoughts and images in my mind of the city as compared to what I saw standing before me." I selected the phrase "standing before me" and asked one student what he saw standing before him in the city he had visited. He answered "palm trees." I asked him to elaborate on that a little and it turned out that he had been to Long Beach, California, and had been

particularly impressed by the rows of palm trees there. I asked him to explain further what had impressed him, and he said that the trees were all in a row and were so tall and beautiful and close together.

I then drew some "palm trees" on the board:

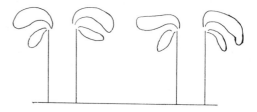

When I asked him whether that was the way they looked, he answered, "No, they were closer together." So I measured the distance between my "trees" on the board and exclaimed in mock surprise: "You mean they were closer than six inches apart?"

After the laughter died down, the boy insisted they weren't closer than six inches apart but that they still were "closer together" than mine were. This, of course, brought up the question: Why would he say his trees were "closer together" than mine when mine were only six inches apart? What does "closer together" mean here and how does one determine it?

We didn't answer these questions right away but instead went on to other problems of seeing and judging. We talked about the height and width of my trees and the student insisted that his trees

Richard J. Basgall is a free-lance writer who is working toward a Ph.D. from Kansas University. He is also teaching at Dodge City Community College.

Reprinted from *College English*, Vol. 36, No. 5, January 1975.

were taller and thinner. Again the same question came up: What do "tall" and "thin" mean and how does one come to these judgements?

After some discussion of these problems, I added a little man to my drawing:

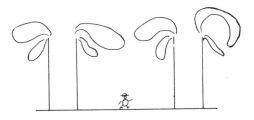

I asked whether that was as tall as the real trees were, and the boy said that he thought it was. So then I asked whether the trees had changed and everyone agreed that they had not. The question of "tallness" then came up, and, after much discussion, most of the students saw that one's impressions of tallness, shortness, thickness, thinness, and practically all other "qualities" that we tend to *attribute to a thing* in writing and speaking are not attributes of that thing at all but are simply relationships that *we make between things* and which we then, unfortunately, attribute to the things themselves.

From this we went back to the matter of preconceptions, and I asked the student what kind of preconceptions he had formed and where they had come from. He said he had a cousin who had been stationed in Long Beach while in the Navy who had told him about the city. I asked what his impression of the city had been from this discussion with his cousin, and he said he had thought of Long Beach as nothing but docks, ships, oil wells, bars, and smelly fish. Then I asked him if that was the way he now felt about Long Beach and he said "no, he had gone there with that impression

but had left with a sense of the beauty of the place . . .": the "tall" palm trees and white beaches and the large, well-kept homes and lawns in the northern residential section of town. I then asked him whether his cousin had thought of the city as a nice place and he said "no, his cousin didn't but he did." When I asked him who was "right," he said "both, I guess—it depends on how you look at it." When I asked him if he really believed that, he thought a moment and then said "no—I think I'm right," which is what I had really expected. Most of my students give lip service to this idea of "it depends on how you look at it" but very few actually believe it or understand what it means to believe it. Rather, they tend to hold on to the idea that a thing is a thing with certain distinctive qualities and attributes inherent in it to be defined permanently in the dictionary or in their heads by a name or a "label."

This assignment, however, made it clear to some of the students that it is ordinarily misleading to say something like the "city itself" because there is no such thing. There is only the city as seen by someone through an individual, chosen perspective. We can only talk or think about a thing in terms of some system of thought or relationships, such as sociology, economics, politics, physics, chemistry, religion, psychology, etc., and even within these systems of thought we have a wide variety of perspectives to choose from. But whatever perspective we choose, it is still a perspective or a way of looking at a thing. The *thing itself* always eludes us.

The importance of developing this awareness in a freshman college student is twofold. First is the fact that most beginning college students come from cultural backgrounds where they are

taught to think in terms of absolutes—
or, worse, in terms of clichés, regional
folklore, myth, rumor, and *expected*
trains of thought which are customarily
taken as absolutes. Consequently, their
essays are filled with either borrowed
ideas that have not been thought through
and made their own or they reflect attitudes and thinking habits that are rigid
and unreceptive to new and possibly
more useful ways of seeing the world
and responding to it. It seems to me that
one of the goals of freshman composition
is to free the student from these restrictive habits of thinking early in his college career and thereby open him up,

so to speak, to the new perspectives that
he will encounter in various disciplines
along the way, while at the same time
bringing him to realize that these are but
systematized perspectives, some of which
are more fruitful and useful than others,
but none of which are final absolutes.
This freedom, of course, will be somewhat frightening at first, and there will
be a tendency for the student to withdraw into the safe and comfortable
world of his childhood and adolescent
patterns of thought, but until he learns
to take this step towards intellectual
freedom, very little learning, critical
thinking, maturity of behavior, or creative expression will occur.

Secondly, our language itself is so
structured (and taught) that we habitually think about the world of things
around us in terms of the structure of
the language that we use to describe it.
A tree *is* a tree and that's it. An eraser *is*
an eraser, although at present it may be
serving as a doorstop, a paperweight, or
a missile. In other words, the student
tends to become bound by the sense of
identity that our language structure sets
up between words and things, and he
finds it difficult to break away from this
customary, established identity and call
things by new names, as he must do if
he is to progress in his thinking, and
especially if he is to be creative in his
own personal expression.

KEN MACRORIE

The Circle of Implication

EVERYTHING WE WRITE JUDGES. No matter how objective we try to be. If we describe clinically the corolla of the blue monkey flower at the edge of the pond and keep our opinion and ourselves out of the paragraph, we still judge, because we confer on the monkey flower the tribute of our attention. Whatever we write draws a circle of implication around the objects or persons we write of. It says "This flower is valuable," or "This institution is inhumane," or "This man is wrong." We judge with integrity only if we place also within that circle our own flowers, our own institutions, ourselves.

The best judges sit high on a bench but see themselves walking on the courtroom floor to the witness stand. They judge all men as judges and all judges as men. "You did wrong, and I point to the experience in law books to show why that wrong injures others as well as yourself. But I might have done the same wrong had I been in your place."

A great judge remembers how hard it is to be good. Senator John L. McClellan forgot this as Chairman of the Senate Select Committee on Improper Activities in the Labor or Management Field and as chairman of the Senate Permanent Subcommittee on Investigations (the titles read like names from George Orwell's novel *1984*). He became obsessed with locating evil and exulting in it, like a censor who loves to read dirty books. In his book *Crime Without Punishment*

Mr. Macrorie is Professor of English at Western Michigan University and is the author of numerous articles on writing and the teaching of writing. "The Circle of Implication" is reprinted by permission of response, Western Michigan University, (c) 1966.

(Popular Library, 1963) he wrote:

Vito Genovese was a top-ranking hoodlum when he appeared; he still is, even though he is behind prison bars. He looked the part, and even his smoked glasses could not conceal the hard, cold eyes. His studied arrogance and deliberate malevolence seemed to have more effect upon committee members and staff than most of these criminals could produce . . . (p. 119)

Senator McClellan himself practices a deliberate and malevolent violence on the sanctity of the private person. His questions speak a sadism as destructive of men's selves as the brainwashing of alleged foreign spies by Chinese or Soviet Communists. At hearings he has said:

1

Senator McClellan to Vito Genovese: Do you operate on that . . . basis of killing everything that gets in your way?

Genovese: I respectfully decline . . . (citing the Fifth Amendment)

Senator: Can you give an answer to any question at all without incriminating yourself?

Genovese: I will have to hear the question first.

Senator: All right, I will ask you. Did you ever do any decent thing in your life? (p. 120)

2

Senator McClellan to Joey Glimco: Would you employ a known criminal, a known burglar to write and publish such articles as that?

Glimco: I respectfully decline to answer . . .

Senator: Don't you think anyone who would do such a thing and then refuse to acknowledge it is a moral coward? (p. 153)

3

Senator McClellan to George Barker: When you can hide behind the privilege, you are perfectly willing to be a witness against others. Isn't that correct?

Barker: I assert my privilege . . .

Senator: When you do that don't you think that you are kind of a moral coward, when you go out and publish a statement like that and not have the guts to walk in like a man and admit it and say why you did it? (p. 153)

Like all Grand Inquisitors, the Senator conducts his Inquisition from a position of immunity. He cannot be sued or held liable for what he says as chairman of a Senatorial committee. Yet in his lifetime, Senator McClellan has demonstrated courage. During the Army-McCarthy hearings he refused to let Senator McCarthy ride without opposition and he often spoke with humor and compassion. But he grows ever more righteous about corruption. It is "insidiously gnawing." He has looked "into the faces of thousands of witnesses, many of them criminals and listened to their voices: many of them arrogant, sullen, mendacious, boastful, unrepentant, and unremorseful." He found James Hoffa to be a "chunky man" with "powerful, lumpy face" and "thick forearms and heavy, blunt hands." Writing of his beloved subject, crime, he speaks of "twining tentacles," "sneaking corruption," "slackening morality," "insidious ways," "malignancy."

I am not asking the Senator to quit judging men but to judge himself while he judges others, to put himself in the same circle. For then what he sees will change. It may remain evil, but it will have been tested against human standards. A look in the mirror should tell Mr. McClellan his mouth is hard, tight, pinching. I grant him that mouth without blame. I have a large nose and an overworried forehead; I hope they will not count against me on Judgment Day.

In *Crime and Punishment*, Dostoyevsky shows us Raskolnikov living a punishment by conscience outside the law. Anyone who reads that book for ten pages knows that Dostoyevsky must have injured others and committed outrages against humanity and himself or he would not have understood Raskolnikov so well. Dostoyevsky always wrote within the circle, as did Chaucer, Shakespeare, and Chekhov.

A thin line wavers between Senator McClellan's judging and the judging of critics like William Hazlitt or Edmund Wilson, but it is a crucial line. In *The Spirit of the Age*, Hazlitt excoriates his contemporaries yet he also praises them. Mr. McClellan could learn much from Hazlitt's observations on Lord Eldon's physiognomy:

Lord Eldon has one of the best-natured faces in the world; it is pleasant to meet him in the street, plodding along with an umbrella under his arm, without one trace of pride, of spleen, or discontent. . . . There has been no stretch of power attempted in his time that he has not seconded: no existing abuse so odious or so absurd, that he has not sanctioned it. . . . When the heavy artillery of interest, power, and prejudice is brought into the field, the paper pellets of the brain go for nothing: his labyrinth of nice, lady-like doubts explodes like a mine of gunpowder.

This is not Mr. Hazlitt's exclusive perverseness or overactive imagination: Lord Eldon struck Mr. Shelley similarly (in "The Mask of Anarchy"):

Next came Fraud, and he had on,
Like Eldon, an ermined gown;
His big tears, for he wept well,
Turned to millstones as they fell.

And the little children, who
Round his feet played to and fro,
Thinking every tear a gem,
Had their brains knocked out by them.

Mr. Hazlitt raged against hypocrisy, pretension, cruelty, and stupidity in men who governed and who wrote but he allowed them their humanity, their frailty.

Any good writer must feel strongly, think deeply, and not fear to praise or blame. And he must remember to place himself in the circle of his own implications. Bernard Shaw despised the artificiality of the leading actor of his day, Sir Henry Irving, but he saluted the skill with which Irving commanded his own style. In our day, Edmund Wilson has been solidly fair to writers. When Ernest Hemingway's short stories first appeared, Mr. Wilson wrote:

His bull-fight sketches have the dry sharpness and elegance of the bull-fight lithographs of Goya. And, like Goya, he is concerned first of all with making a fine picture. Too proud an artist to simplify in the interests of conventional pretenses, he is showing you what life is like. . . .

Yet Mr. Wilson was not carried away. He held Hemingway to the highest standards:

It is only in the paleness, the thinness of some of his effects that Mr. Hemingway sometimes fails. I am thinking especially of the story called *Up in Michigan*, which should have been a masterpiece, but has the curious defect of dealing with rude and primitive people yet leaving them rather shadowy.

These critics are trying to use all their powers for finding the truth in the world out there and in themselves. Often the two truths intersect for them. Mr. Wilson had to ask: "What do I really believe about this new writer Hemingway? Am I trying to throw him in the face of the conservative readers of America and in so doing overestimating him?"

Ralph Emerson was hard on all of us. He spoke of how small we scale our lives. Yet he drew himself inside the circle of implication so that when he came upon a man who had done something Emerson knew he couldn't do himself, he let loose his joy and said to him at once:

I greet you at the beginning of a great career.

He was right to say this to Walt Whitman. The largest men first recognize large men.

I think of a ridiculous and instructive failure to implicate oneself in the circle. Asked to write in a college course an essay growing out of her experience, a young woman produced a paper in which she spoke against liars. She thought them unforgivable, she despised liars. It was an incredible paper, as self-righteous and empty as Senator McClellan generalizing on the immorality of American criminals.

"Why did you write that?" I said to the girl.

"Well, because I feel very strongly about liars," she said after a moment of silent shock.

"Why did you write it? What led you to write that paper and read it to us?" I asked.

A light broke in her eye and she began to think about the question.

"I guess," she said, "I guess because this last weekend I was lied to in a way I will never forget."

There lay her story. She had not told it. She had been cut deeply by one man's lie. She had jumped to an attack on all liars and ended up putting no liar at all in her circle. So far she had to go before she could write that paper. First she had to put that young man in her story, in her circle, and herself and her reaction, and then—in a move that had not even crossed her mind—she had to think of herself as a liar, at many moments, large and small. Only then could she put the lie down for what it was to her, not simply as an injured, disappointed lover but as a member of the human race.

In the same writing class, a forty-five-year-old woman who had already sold an article to a magazine for $400, wrote down her supposedly honest feeling about the act of writing. She said writing was pure agony for her. She couldn't sleep. Up and turn on the light to rewrite at two in the morning. She got headaches until she had completed the work. As a writer she said she stewed in a pot of indecision and self-recrimination. That was what writing was. "Don't kid yourself," she said to the four young students in her critique group, "It's hell."

I said, "I don't believe you. You're not being honest. At times you must like writing. You must get fierce joy from doing a good job and being complimented." The next day I received an angrily crossed-out and marked-up letter from her saying I had failed her as a teacher. She thought I had some sensibility and now knew she had been mistaken. I had insulted her, failed to sense her purposes. I knew she was hurt. I had thought she could stand that much truth in front of four classmates or I wouldn't have been so direct. Just barely she got by that experience and recovered to write better than before. But I had apparently miscalculated how she would feel in the circle; I had forgotten to put myself in the circle and see that as a professional writer I—like her—would have been unready for a public exposure of my professional blunders. I should have talked to her alone.

Drawing the magic circle of implication around oneself as well as around others protects one from making a fool of oneself. And once that circle is drawn, everything and everyone in it is illuminated like a baseball diamond at night.

ELAINE CHAIKA

Who Can Be Taught?

ELICITING VERBIAGE and refining style are the principal concerns of the English comp teacher. In fact, J. Ross Winterowd specifically disclaims the English teacher's responsibility for more basic problems.[1] Certainly, being able to explain thoughts fully and in an effective fashion aren't trivial, concerns, but they are second order problems for the truly non-proficient writer, the one who habitually produces deviant sentences [See (1)-(6) below], or who can't say what he means [See (7)+(8) below].

Group composing as espoused by John McNamara in "Teaching the Process of Writing" may seem to be a viable method for teaching the very unskilled.[2] However, it violates one important principle of language acquisition, and learning to write is, to a great extent, a language learning problem. This is readily seen when advice such as Lou Kelley's, to "talk on paper," is examined.[3] What are the actual ramifications of such advice, which is also rather commonly given in the form "Just write it the way you'd say it"?

Students of mine who have been told this frequently complain to me that it is very aggravating advice. No matter how they try, the written sentence doesn't come out like talking. And no wonder. Talking and writing are separate skills actually governed by different networks in the brain. Studies with aphasics have shown that damage to one skill does not necessarily imply damage to the other. Furthermore, telling students to "talk on paper" misleads them. It falsely implies that writing is as easy and natural as talking, and, patently, it is not. Moreover, if the student is led to believe that he should be able to write just because he can talk, and he fails, he can feel pretty stupid. It is far better if, at the outset, he is made aware of the nature of the task before him. In my experience, students are grateful to know what it is they have to learn: a new skill. Furthermore, they are stimulated to try to learn when they realize that their failure to write doesn't imply lack of intelligence, merely lack of a skill.

All the information imparted by tone, stress, tempo, intonation, clarity of enunciation, and a variety of other phonological gambits is, obviously, missing from writing. Instead, there is increased complexity of lexical choice and sentence structure. Indeed, it may well be that certain combinations of structures belong entirely to the written language. At any rate, even the most non-proficient students have no diffi-

Elaine Chaika earned her PhD in Linguistics at Brown University. She is currently an assistant professor of Linguistics at Providence College, Providence, R. I.

[1] W. Ross Winterowd, "'Topics' and Levels in the Composing Process," *College English,* Feb. 1973, pp. 701-09.

[2] John McNamara, "Teaching the Process of Writing," *College English,* Feb. 1973, pp. 661-65.

[3] Lou Kelley, "Toward Competence and Creativity in an Open Class," *College English,* Feb. 1973, pp. 644-60.

Reprinted from *College English,* Vol. 35, No. 5, February 1974.

culty bringing in samples of written English not likely to be spoken, such as:

> By that I mean to suggest that the selection of a location formulation requires of a speaker (and will exhibit for a hearer) an analysis of his own location and the location of his co-conversationalist(s), and of the objects whose location is being formulated (if that object is not one of the co-conversationalists).[4]

> While the economy rule does not preclude the use of combinations of membership categories for single population Members, its presence does mean that the task of being socialized to doing adequate reference does not involve having to learn combinatorial possibilities for each pair, triplicate, etc. of categories as a prerequisite to doing adequate references.[5]

Regardless of how one judges such selections, it is incontrovertible that they represent one style of written language, but not of spoken.

The following are examples of non-proficient writers' attempts to explain either their thoughts or their knowledge:

(1) The need to find out who he is, is something every freshman wishes he could make.

(2) The basic question is not the color of the prisoners to determine the government's action but to put down the rebellion.

(3) He will see how convenience and gain are no substitute for a true love of the way one uses his life for real accomplishment according to an earlier period of human spirit.

(4) Even though they make their money

[4] Emanuel Schegloff, "Notes on a Conversational Practice: Formulating Place," in *Studies in Social Interaction*, ed. David Sudnow (New York: The Free Press, 1972), p. 83.

[5] Harvey Sacks, "An Initial Investigation of the Usability of Conversational Data for Doing Sociology," in *Studies in Social Interaction*, ed. David Sudnow (New York: The Free Press, 1972), p. 35.

this way, newspapers print scare headlines.

(5) As opposed to standard English speech where the 's is used to show possessive, the non-standard dialect use a formation of words in a sentence to show it.

(6) The use of plurals also shows up a great deal in non-standard Negro English.

These last two sentences appeared on an essay exam. Later conference with the student revealed that he certainly was aware that standard English uses "a formation of words" to indicate possession, and that using plurals "a great deal" is a feature of all English dialects. He meant, and said spontaneously, that black English, omitting the redundant genitive marker, often relies on placing nouns next to each other to show possession, and that black English does not always mark plurals as standard English does.

Sentences (1)-(4) above were picked at random from my voluminous file of deviant sentences produced by freshman comp students in classrooms as free, friendly, and open as I could possibly create. All of the creators of these sentences speak normally, or at least not recognizably oddly. They just write strangely. Asking such students to "[restate] sentences that are not clear" (Kelley, 1973:653) or seeing that "he adds some concrete details or visual images. . . ." (Kelley, p. 653) is almost beside the point at this state of their art. For, many of the students who fail to achieve proficiency in English comp actually do not know the syntax of the written language. Perhaps it is more accurate to say that they have gaps in their knowledge. The implication of this is that learning to write is a language learning task, much as learning French is. It is not just a problem of developing style.

What, then, can be done with (or should it be *to* or *for*?) such students? First, there is the very real question of whether they can be taught at all. Winterowd says:

> If the student . . . is incapable of generating these core sentences [George kisses Mary—Mary is kissed by George] there is obviously some dysfunction that is beyond the reach of pedagogy. (p. 707)

Actually, I have never come across any adolescent who could not create a passive sentence with the verb *kiss*, or, for that matter, *make, cook,* or *cut*, to mention a few common verbs. But consider:

(7) —pollution loses lives.
(8) Since American support is gradually depleting—

The errors evinced here are akin to not being able to passivize correctly. That is, in many sentences, more than one noun may be a subject. If an object is chosen to be subject, then a passive sentence results. In (7) the deviance was caused by incorrectly making *pollution* the subject. This should read:

(7a) —lives are lost because of pollution.

Does this writer have a "dysfunction beyond the reach of pedagogy"? Or is he aware of alternations like:

(9a) Cowardliness loses wars.
(9b) Wars are lost because of cowardliness.

Thus, he might assume that *lose* allows a noun denoting cause to be subject when, at this stage of English syntax, it does so only if the noun derives from an adjective plus the suffix *-ness*, or if a noun denoting Beneficiary is stated as in the informal:[6]

7b) Pollution loses them their lives.

Such intricate and, yes, arbitrary restrictions on the positions a noun may take relative to a verb are extremely important in English syntax. [See (10)-(16) below for further explanation.] Sentence (8) is another example. This should have been:

(8a) Since American support is being gradually depleted—

Here, the passive should have been used. Does such an error, comparable to saying "Mary kissed George" if George was the agent, indicate some sort of pathology? Or, did the author of (8) know that *diminish* does not require the passive:

(8b) American support is gradually diminishing—

Since *diminish* and *deplete* share semantic features, the unwary might well assume that they appear in the same relationship to nouns in sentences. As it happens, *deplete* requires an overt object in a sentence. This can be signalled either by using the passive, as in (8a), or by placing a noun in direct object position. *Diminish* does not require an object. The errors in (7) and (8) do result in a failure to generate core sentences correctly. Winterowd seems to reflect the attitude of the profession accurately when he assumes that teaching such basic sentence relations is not the function of the English teacher. If this is true, then the function of the English teacher is merely to refine style. This is, to be sure, the basic assumption behind every article in the February 1973 issue of *College English*, an issue devoted to composition, as well as, I might add,

---

[6] Speakers do not seem to categorize in this fashion on a conscious level. That speakers use rules and categories is well-known, but precisely how these are used is not.

behind virtually every rhetoric text on the market. Even the Christensen and Mellon works which Winterowd justifiably praises are addressed to complex sentence formation, not core or kernel relations (p. 707). If, indeed, the inability to produce simple sentences were necessarily pathological, then English teachers could say, "Whew! get rid of those kids. They're not college material, and English 101 is not for them." However, it is apparent that errors in simple sentences, like those in complex sentences, may result from not knowing a rule or from applying it incorrectly. Neither of these conditions necessarily derives from a "dysfunction beyond the reach of pedagogy." By rules, of course, I don't mean shibboleths like when to use *like*, or other inventions of 19th century grammarians. Rather, I refer to the rules which produce sentences accepted as non-anomalous English by educated readers.

If no pathological condition is the cause of sentences (1)-(8), what is? Earlier in this article, I pointed out that learning to write is a language learning problem. It takes a child years and years of constantly using language and listen ing to it to get the rules down pat. If anywhere near a proportionate amount of time were spent on learning writing there would be far fewer proficiency problems. As it now stands, however, many schoolchildren do not get a regular chance to write entire sentences, much less compositions. Instead, they underline correct answers in workbook fill in the blanks, or circle the right number. Even if they are occasionally asked to write an essay it is frequently not corrected thoroughly, or, if it is, all too often the teacher has done so using the handbook numbers game. The pupil dutifully looks up the numbers and

finds that he can't make any connection between his sentence and whatever the handbook is describing. Analysis and comparison of syntax is a sophisticated skill well beyond the ability of the uninitiated, especially if the sample sentence in the handbook bears no surface resemblance to the sentence in the essay which the writer has to correct, a rather common occurrence. It is now well known to linguists, at least, that children learn to speak by checking their utterances against those they hear. Thus they extrapolate rules of language which they constantly refine until they speak in an adult fashion. They might likewise learn to write if they were urged to write and if their writing were restructured for them, but few teachers have the will or the time or the whatever to do this.

It can now be seen why McNamara's group composing fails as an effective teaching device for the non-proficient. It gives too little opportunity for every student to create entire sentences which express what he wishes. In any event, the consequence of inexperience in writing is the number of college freshmen who are grossly deficient in writing. At Providence College, for instance, this number is approximately two hundred, usually about one-fourth of the entering class.

Experimenting with seven classes of these freshmen, I have found that the teaching of core sentences which Winterowd so summarily dismisses is actually a highly effective, many-pronged tool. The very fact that one can start with relations that even the most frightened and defeated students can recognize and discuss is of great importance. The simplicity of the early exercises shows them that they need not be afraid to notice and to make judgments. Since their attention is first focused on structures they can understand, their curiosity about language and its manipulation is stimulated. Thus, they become increasingly sensitive to written language, noticing more and more about their own and their classmates' as the semester progresses. This, of course, is essential for continuing progress in writing. If awareness can be aroused, the student will continue to develop after leaving freshman comp.

But sensitivity is not enough. One must be able to play with sentences, and to evaluate the effect of rearranging words in the sentence. Consideration of the basic relations of the nouns to the verb, as in sentences (10)-(16) gives ample opportunity for developing both skills. Furthermore, it is impossible to ignore matters of discourse when dealing with such sentences, for which noun in a sentence may become subject is as much a matter of focus, style, or context as it is of syntax.

Finally, and crucially, presentation of core sentences quickly convinces students that language is rule governed behavior; thus one's being able to understand a sentence is no guarantee that it is not deviant. Then when the teacher corrects their sentences, students don't feel that he or she is capricious or merely trying to impose his or her own preferences (assuming, of course, that teachers confine themselves to correcting deviance and style, not the message!). And, of course, students can then better understand what is at stake in learning to write, what sorts of things they must pay attention to and learn.

Best of all, these lessons are not learned by lectures. They are learned from the students' own analyses. For instance, sentences such as these are presented to the class:

(10) Max planted corn in the garden.
(11) Tony gave Dave a sock in the nose
(12) Gwen poured Fred a cup of coffee.
(13) Irate citizens swamped the post office with mail.
(14) Max cut the meat with a cleaver.
(15) The flag fluttered in the breeze.
(16) The breeze ripped the flag.

First students are asked to change the positions of the nouns in (10) or whatever sentence I start with. They readily come up with:

(10a) Corn was planted in the garden by Max.
(10b) The garden was planted with corn by Max.
(10c) Max planted the garden with corn.

Two lines of discussion are opened by these. First, that (10b) and (10c) imply that the entire garden was planted with corn, whereas (10) and (10a) are ambiguous in this respect. These may be used whether or not other items were planted. Although implication governs whether or not *garden* will be placed so that it may appear without its preposition, other considerations govern whether or not the agent, Max, is to be subject. This brings us to another discussion. Although students consistently and readily supply the [by + agent] at the end of a passive, they just as readily agree it sounds funny. I tell them to substitute: "the tall, dirty freckle-faced kid with blue overalls" (or a similarly lengthy noun phrase) for "Max." The consensus, predictably, is that the heavily modified agent phrase seems more natural in a passive sentence than in an active, and conversely that the single word agent is better in an active. The principle that lengthy phrases and clauses tend to be zapped to the end of an English sentence is thus established.

Someone usually manages to comment

that "by Max" need not be mentioned at all, whereupon I point out that avoiding mention of "who done it" is a common reason for using the passive. This leads to the subject of using the passive as a device for getting rid of a superabundance of *I*. Several *I* sentences can be thrown at the class so that it may passivize them for practice. Keeping a collection from old themes helps in such an exercise.

Next we discuss when it would be permissible to use "by Max." The very fact that it is not usual makes it what linguists call a marked construction. Therefore it is used if special focus is to be made on Max. Often I ask the class to write contexts for the sentences under discussion. For instance, for (10a) someone might produce:

(10d) The garden was planted with corn by Max, not Alec.
(10e) Although you'd never believe it, the garden was planted with corn by Max.

At the very start, when they first paraphrase (10), many students express surprise that they automatically supplied certain prepositions; if not, I ask them "Where did the *with* (or *by*) come from? How did you know which to use?" This starts our discussion of syntactic rules, deep structures, and transformations. So one sentence like (10) introduces several important rhetorical principles: rules of syntax, implications, criteria for naturalness, markedness, focus, context. If (10e) or the like is elicited, then presupposition can be added to the list at this time, for students readily note that this can be used only if Max was not likely to plant corn. As far as possible I allow ideas like presupposition to arise naturally from the class discussion. Somehow before the semester

is over, most conceivable facets of writing do get mentioned, either in the grammar lessons or while discussing themes. For homework the class is given sets of sentences to paraphrase and/or to write contexts for.

A similar format is used for the other sentences. A brief rundown on lessons to be drawn from (11)-(16) might explain further, especially for those unversed in current linguistics. Note, however, that a teacher need not be a linguist to use this method. It is not necessary to use the jargon of transformational or case grammar, to use labels like *agent, range, dative*, or to draw complex trees. In fact, insisting that students learn labels or snowing them with jargon puts a damper on the whole discovery process. It is vital, if students are to learn, that they do the discussing and the analyzing, and that they make the points. The teacher can prod, can ask questions, can suggest activities, but, except for occasional rescue work, should refrain from lecturing. With this digression aside, on to (11)-(16).

Both (11) and (12) reinforce the principle that long phrases normally find their way to the end of a sentence. Substituting *money* for *sock in the nose*, and *beer* for *cup of coffee*, allows *to Dave* and *for Fred* to appear at the ends of their respective sentences with no special focus. Similarly, substituting *the obnoxious kid with the broken hand* for *Dave* or *Fred* forces their removal from indirect object position. Another point easily raised by sentences like (11) and (12) is that the positions which can be filled in a sentence, such as indirect object, are highly dependent on the particular verb. Although they can be readily understood, (17) and (18) are rejected by most students:

(17) *Wash Mary the dishes.
(18) *Drift John the log.

That even direct object position cannot always be filled even if the meaning of the verb doesn't prevent it is shown by:

(19) *The magician disappeared the rabbit.

The periphrasis "made the rabbit disappear" must be used. Knowing the raw meaning, so to speak, of a word is not enough. One must also learn its permissible contexts. Both (13) and (14) contain instrument phrases [*with* or *by* + noun]. When asked to make *post office* or *meat* subject, students rapidly supply the passive, but when asked to make *mail* or *a cleaver* subject they are stopped short. Of course, they get

(13a) Mail swamped the post office.
(14a) The cleaver cut the meat.

But what happened to *irate citizens* and *Max?* Again, the arbitrary nature of syntax is revealed. If the instrument is subject, the agent can't be mentioned in the same simple sentence. Using the instrument as subject is, then, another way of avoiding mention of who did the action. Also, (14), but not I think (13), allows a paraphrase of the type "use something to do something," as in:

(14b) Max used the cleaver to cut the meat.

Whether or not this type is freely interchangeable with that represented in (14), "do something with something," can bring on a debate. The implications of intentional versus nonintentional action may govern which is used. That is, the class usually agrees that (14b) is marked to mean deliberate action, whereas (14) is not. A similar marking can be achieved with the alternation of *by* and *with* as in:

(19a) The building was hit with a rock.
(19b) The building was hit by a rock.

Sentences (15) and (16) again point up the primacy of the verb as sentence shaper, for although *flag* can be subject in (16), *breeze* cannot be in (15), at least for the majority of my students. Some, however, do insist that

(15a) The breeze fluttered the flag,

is fine and some, not necessarily the same, that

(16a) The flag ripped in the breeze,

is not. Those that reject (16a), however, accept

(16b) The flag ripped because of the breeze.

After all this discussion of the rule-governed nature of language, the uninitiated might be chagrined by this business of "some accept" and "some reject," but this is a natural result of the fact that people learn language by extrapolating rules from what they hear about them. Everyone doesn't learn all the rules the same. Regional and social dialect differences exist; so do differences between generations, and even between individuals. Language is always changing, always in the process of becoming, and English teachers must be alert to this. Fortunately most structures elicit wide agreement. For those which don't, a discussion of the variations in rules can be fruitful. Also, whether a certain form is permissible in informal but not formal speech may be a pertinent question. Sometimes, when a student insists upon the correctness of something which sounds un-English to most of the rest of the class, he can be asked to see if he can find it in print somewhere. The students and I have all been given a few jolts from such assignments.[7] The important thing, however, is that the controversial sentence really makes students notice. It sends them delving into print. It makes them argue about language and think about what they do with it. That everything isn't laid out one hundred percent sure and proper is what makes language interesting.

Of course only a tiny sampling of a semester's work can be described here. A partial list will give an idea of the rest:

A. Causatives (for which (15) and (16) may also be used!: *make* + verb; *have* + verb; *because, from,* of — noun, etc.).

B. Pronominalization (what does *his* mean in "His creditors bankrupted John" and "His brothers hate each of Mary's sons," etc.).

C. Verb tense and aspect (Forget the old saws. This cries for new solutions. For instance, "I have taught in junior high, but never again" versus "I taught in junior high, but no more").

D. Co-ordination (So why can't you say "John made the bed and the coffee")?

E. Sentence embedding (Not just combining, but "I hate loud singing" vs. "I hate singing loudly." What is the subject of *singing* in each?).

Even those who have never had a course in modern syntax can find paradigms and other data to present in class by leafing through linguistic journals. I'm not advocating that anyone actually read the articles on syntax. Most are far removed from the concerns of English teachers, but the sentences and other paradigms used as proofs of vari-

ous theories can be given to classes to chew on. I find Robin Lakoff's and Sandra Babcock's presentations very useful for such purposes, for instance. There is no reason why grammar classes can't be discovery times for teachers as well as students. Of course student themes are a great source of grammar material, and, as often as possible, should be used to illustrate points. As I correct themes, I always keep file cards handy. Sometimes figuring out what went wrong can be a real teaser for everyone. Amazingly, however, as the semester rolls along, the students always seem to come up with reasonable solutions. The important thing is that they learn to recognize and correct deviant or odd phrasing.

Needless to say, grammar lessons are only an adjunct to the main business: writing and correcting writing. Each class selects its own weekly topic, often a controversial one. Then, usually, they debate the issues in class. I rarely ask students to read what a professional has written, as emulation of the artist, reporter, or scholar is far beyond their capacity. It takes a good deal of linguistic sophistication to pull off that feat. It's enough at the start to get them to say what they want so others can understand it and not be offended by it.

Basing an English teaching method on the latest psycholinguistic and syntactic theory usually assures its efficacy, but many a good theory has a funny thing happen to it on the way to the classroom. Not this one! The students themselves, on anonymous questionnaires, affirm that the grammar lessons helped teach them to write, gave them insights into language, and, wonder of wonders, were interesting. Some even complained that there wasn't enough grammar. Less than ten percent overall found the gram-

---

[7]As linguists have long known, people are not always aware of how they really talk, e.g., what structures they use, much less what others use.

(Continued on page 204)

PHYLLIS BROOKS

Mimesis:
Grammar and the Echoing Voice

IF ENGLISH TEACHERS at the university level are supposed to be adding some new element, some sophistication, some elegance to the prose of their students, and not just making up for real or imagined deficiencies in teaching in high schools, they must continually seek new methods and resurrect into a more glorious life some old ones. Teachers at the "remedial" level are all too frequently inclined to regard such an effort as icing on the cake, as a luxury that can be indulged in only at the lofty level of "regular" freshman composition courses, or even in advanced courses in creative writing or stylistics. The remedial course, tacked onto the bottom of the English department or otherwise shunted into some sub-academic campus position, is the place for tire-patching and bringing the truth about the dangling modifier to an unbelieving mass of ignoramuses. The idea that the student in a "remedial" course may be there through no fault of his own and that he may be as intelligent, or even more intelligent than his brother who has escaped the indignity of such a course has only recently been challenged, by Sabina Thorne Johnson in her article "Remedial English: the Anglocentric Albatross" (*College English*, 33 [1972], 670-685). Once we accept this premise we must

necessarily go on to the further idea that he may not only be able to write as correctly as any other student but may even be able to write as stylishly.

Style is a vague concept, but some writers do have an individual style, or an effective style, or a curious style that sets them apart from all other writers. It is an indefinable quality that everyone can recognize. I do not want to get into a deep discussion of the nature of style, but would rather concentrate on a few technical details that can contribute to something recognizable as "good" style, and how these can be encouraged and nurtured in a course that has as its first purpose the correcting of grammatical and organizational errors. In fact, I should like to claim that the conscious encouragement of variety, elegance, and individual voice in writing may prove to be a useful tool in impressing students with the value of precision and accuracy in syntax and word choice—major aims of the remedial course as well as of the regular freshman composition course.

One way to encourage the variety and elegance lacking in the prose of freshman students is the archaic technique of paraphrase, but a form of paraphrase revived and reconsidered with specific purposes in mind. During the past few years the members of the Subject A departments at the University of California at Berkeley have been teaching droves of students ranging from the children of Chinese-

Phyllis Brooks is Lecturer and Supervisor of the Subject A Department, University of California, Berkeley. She is working on a study of Tevfik Fikret, 20th century Turkish poet.

Reprinted from *College English*, Vol. 35, No. 2, November 1973.

American households where English is a shallowly acquired *lingua franca* to the Chicano from the pachuco-speaking barrio of Los Angeles to the dialect-wielding black from the East Oakland ghetto to the middle-class white who has conned his way through his high school English classes but really has no notion of how to make a statement, or how important it is to be able to make that statement. We have adopted the somewhat unorthodox techniques described by Mrs. Johnson in her article: give the student something to say, make him aware of an audience that he must try to reach, and demand that it be his voice that comes through the writing, not some depersonalized characterless spirit. It is true that the urgent desire to get his opinion across and to make his point of view on a question very clear will drive the student to refine his grammar and vocabulary, especially with a certain amount of peer criticism to egg him on. But the student seeking to express his own personal voice needs further help beyond the correction of his errors and the encouragement to speak for himself.

Successful writers, whether sincerely or not, often make the statement that they learned to write by copying other writers. I still have to wrestle mightily with the effects of an early infatuation with Carlyle combined with translation, sentence by sentence, of large chunks of Cicero. All influence from writers of the past is not necessarily good. But how are we to get our students to imitate desirable models? Are we simply to hand them a piece of prose by a famous writer with the instruction that they are to prepare a paraphrase? If students have heard of paraphrasing at all, they are likely to have seen it only in the form of what we prefer to call the "translation" paraphrase: "Take this sonnet by Shakespeare and rewrite it, showing what he really meant."

Shakespeare knew very well what he meant, and the average high school or university student is well aware of the presumption and futility involved in trying to turn the sonnet into modern English prose. Sometimes, more profitably, the material presented for paraphrase is in prose and so more amenable to translation into an idiom readily understandable to the common reader. The translation paraphrase tests the student's ability to read, and to write an acceptable form of standard English, but it does not *add* anything to his repertoire of skills.

On the other hand, carefully selected *persona* paraphrases can help the student towards an awareness of the variety of expression possible in the language and can add to his stock of usable sentence structures. In fact, I firmly believe that the *persona* paraphrase can be used to good effect in teaching everything from the use of the verb "to be" to the selection of the apposite structure to suit a particular pattern of thought. I hope that the following selections may bolster my argument and encourage others to try more daring and possibly more fruitful paraphrase exercises.

In planning and assigning a *persona* paraphrase the instructor hopes to get from his students a valuable imitation of the voice and sentence patterns of a particular writer. The novice writer is unsure of himself. He doubts his own abilities, especially in dealing with a sentence including such complications as apposition, parallel structure, or parenthetical expressions. If we give a certain number of workbook exercises in detecting errors in parallel structures and correcting them, we still have no assurance that the student will actually go out and try to use the structure he has been laboring over. In fact, he may come away from his workbook more overawed than ever by the complexities that lurk in the depths of such sentences. If, however, he is handed a passage from a writer whose name he may recognize, and is then told to imitate her sentence structures, there is a chance that by building up his own sentences on this model he will gain the confidence to experiment further with the arcane skill he has proved he can handle.

We have found that students are easily discouraged by this kind of assignment; they have to be led into it. Rather than demand that the students "write a paragraph in Norman Mailer's style" after having read a passage by Mailer, we present them with a more carefully composed exercise. We select a specific passage, illustrating a particular kind of structure, and require that the student copy its structure, phrase by phrase, sentence by sentence, but substitute a completely different subject matter. Each instructor who has used this particular tool approaches it in a slightly different way, but in general we proceed as follows: The students are given a paragraph—rarely more than twenty typewritten lines—double spaced on a sheet of paper. The instructor reads the passage, emphasizing the pattern of the passage, the natural breaks in sentences, the switches in tone. The class is then guided into some discussion of how the passage works. What are the main features of the prose and where does the writer reach his point? Are there any confusing syntactical structures? Any particular little tricks that make the passage effective? From there on the student is on his own. We tell him to try out several possible topics, writing in pencil above the actual words on the page, until he finds one that is amenable to expression within the structure there on the page in front of him. But an example can show the method

much more clearly than can further discussion.

Parenthetical expression

When a student starts to modify his statements, he is inclined first of all to adopt a Christensenian style and tack all modification onto the end of his sentences. The next step is to put some of the modification at the beginning of the sentence. It is the rare brave soul who tries to add a parenthetical modification in some position other than those two. James Baldwin is a writer who, on almost every page, provides beautifully articulated examples of parenthetical modification. Here is a complex model for parenthetical style, from Baldwin's *Notes of a Native Son*:

> When I was around nine or ten I wrote a play which was directed by a young, white schoolteacher, *a woman*, who then took an interest in me, and gave me books to read, and, *in order to corroborate my theatrical bent*, decided to take me to see what she somewhat tactlessly referred to as "real" plays. Theatergoing was forbidden in our house, but, *with the really cruel intuitiveness of a child*, I suspected that the color of this woman's skin would carry the day for me. When, *at school*, she suggested taking me to the theater, I did not, *as I might have done if she had been a Negro*, find a way of discouraging her, but agreed that she could pick me up at my house one evening. I then, *very cleverly*, left all the rest to my mother, who suggested to my father, *as I knew she would*, that it would not be very nice to let such a kind woman make the trip for nothing. Also, since it was a schoolteacher, I imagine that my mother countered the idea of sin with the idea of "education" which word, *even with my father*, carried a kind of bitter weight.

Instructions to the student included the following specific pointers, good for all *persona* paraphrases:

Start by substituting words and building a new atmosphere in the passage; you may find that you have to move to whole phrases, replacing, for instance, "with cruel intuitiveness" by "in a scarlet rage," in order to make your new version of the paragraph understandable. Play around with the words and phrases, but try to keep them in the same order, and the paragraph in the same shape.

But not only does the student have the structural model of Baldwin's sentences before him; he also has to select a subject matter that fits the structure, another set of "emotions recalled in tranquillity," as one of our colleagues described the content of this passage. He has to try, and reject, several possibilities before he reaches one that will not be distorted by the structure he is bound by. Any old thought pattern cannot be imposed on a paragraph. The student comes to realize very rapidly that the *shape* of an idea is necessary, not whimsical, that there is some purpose to our criticisms of the way he expresses himself.

What kind of thoughts can a freshman student pour into the Baldwin mold? The variety is amazing. Here is an amusing example:

When I was approaching the age of forty I got married to a young girl who was still in her teens and although I was twenty years her elder, she was quite infatuated with me, thinking that I made a great substitute for her father. The marriage would not have met with my father's approval, but, with an astuteness that had come with age, I suspected that my wife's small fortune of three million dollars would meet with everyone's approval. When, during our first week together, she suggested that we move out of my parents' house, I did not, as I might have done if she had been my mistress, find a way of discouraging her, but agreed that we should talk to Mother and Father about it. I then, very cleverly, left the details to my Grandpa Joe, who suggested to his children, my father and mother, that I was a grown boy with a wife and that the only fair thing to do would be to let me move out. Also, since I was about to turn forty, it would be a nice idea to celebrate at my new residence my birthday, which word, even with my father, hit a soft spot in his heart.

—Kevin Axelrad

The structure of the paraphrase, rather than limiting student imagination, provides the crutch that makes it possible for him to give his imagination free rein, without the worry about how to finish a sentence he has once started. The paraphrase, since it is such a close copy structurally of a polished original, rarely shows any mechanical errors. The student used to getting back an essay covered with markings often looks at his first *persona* paraphrase with an expression of complete disbelief. He has produced a piece of writing he can be proud of. And it is his. Although he had a skeleton to build on, the flesh is all his own. Almost inevitably the next formal essay he writes will contain some turn of phrase, some sentence structure that he has "learned" from his model. An unsolicited student criticism of one teacher's course as a whole provided this comment on paraphrasing: "The topics which allowed for the most creativity and imagination produced the best results. The paraphrases were exceptionally good because they let us write on a variety of ideas. I honestly liked writing the paraphrases for they allowed me to express ideas of mine in styles which were pleasing to read."

Apposition and Modification

There need be no consistency of style among the models chosen. To give students a notion of the possible complexities of apposition, the restatement or amplification of an idea without the use of subordination or coordination, I have used with great success a highly mannered passage by Rose Macaulay, a richly textured description of the city of Istanbul that ends:

> Once the capital of imperial Rome; later the greatest city in Christendom, the richest city in the world, the spiritual head of the eastern Church, the treasure house of culture and art; then the opulent capital of Islam; this sprawl of mosques, domes, minarets, ruined palaces, and crumbling walls, rising so superbly above three seas, looking towards Europe, Asia, and ocean, oriental, occidental, brooding on past magnificence, ancient rivalries and feuds, modern cultures and the spoils of the modern world, Constantinople has ruin in her soul, the ruin of a deep division; to look on her shining domes and teeming streets is to see a glittering, ruinous, façade, girdled by great, broken, expugnable walls.
>
> —*The Pleasure of Ruins*

Instead of wondering that anyone would have the temerity to offer such a sentence to a freshman for imitation, look at some of the results. The students were told to replace Istanbul with any city they were familiar with that had a layering of different historical periods. Particular stress was placed on the care with which Rose Macaulay selected her words—all the adjectives work hard in her description. There is no vagueness, despite the final generalization, because of the concrete quality of the images—streets, façade and walls.

> [Bodie, California] First an assemblage of mining claims; later the largest gold camp in the north, the social hub of all the miners, the place where that shining vein of gold rose up to the earth's surface, the gathering of men in search of fortunes; next the prosperous community, the spread of general stores, town halls, homes that are vacant and drooping fences, sitting so quietly among tall mountains, gazing upon wilderness, nature, and undisturbed lands; silent, solemn, holding past memories within its decayed walls, gold discoveries and finds, the absence of new inventions and the industry of a modern world, Bodie has death in her future, the death of a useless land; to view her boarded windows and dusty streets is to visualize her glowing past, broken by long, uninterrupted, deplorable solitude.
>
> —Leslie Froisland

Obviously the appositions work, despite the complexity of the model.

Parallelism plus Reference

Parallel structure is one of the trickiest ideas to explain and to teach. Errors in coordination, errors in apposition often have their roots in some misunderstanding of the *balance* of a sentence. Students can laugh at sentences like "He went to the White House in trepidation and a tuxedo" (semantic parallelism abused) and can see dimly that something is wrong with "He likes swimming and to row small boats" (structural parallelism abused), but go on producing comparable bastards in their own prose. As a result, any kind of balanced period of the John Henry Newman type—"The true gentleman is never mean or little in his disputes, never takes unfair advantage, never mistakes personalities or sharp sayings for arguments, or insinuates evil which he dare not say out"—is a very rare bird in a freshman paper. Yet with a little conscious effort the student can prove to himself that complex parallelisms are possible and usable.

A paraphrase that has proved useful in demonstrating balanced sentences governed by careful parallelism of structure and ideas is the following passage from Mark Twain, a description of the Sphinx.

At the same time it is a valuable exercise in controlling the reference of pronouns (thus the surprising bracketing of these two items in the subhead). The passage is generously sprinkled with *its*. As the student begins to construct his picture within the Twain frame, he has to consider the reference of each pronoun in turn. There are no structural *its* in the paragraph; each *it* functions as a true pronoun:

> After years of waiting, it was before me at last. The great face was so sad, so earnest, so longing, so patient. There was a dignity not of earth in its mien, and in its countenance a benignity such as never anything human wore. It was stone, but it seemed sentient. If ever image of stone thought, it was thinking. It was looking toward the verge of the landscape, yet looking at nothing—nothing but distance and vacancy. It was looking over and beyond everything of the present, and far into the past. It was gazing out over the ocean of Time—over lines of century-waves which, further and further receding, closed nearer and nearer together, and blended at last into one unbroken tide, away toward the horizon of remote antiquity. It was thinking of the wars of departed ages; of the empires it had seen created and destroyed; of the nations whose birth it had witnessed, whose progress it had watched, whose annihilation it had noted; of the joy and sorrow, the life and death, the grandeur and decay, of five thousand slow revolving years. It was the type of an attribute of man—of a faculty of his heart and brain. It was *memory—retrospection*—wrought into visible, tangible form. All who knew what pathos there is in memories of days that are accomplished and faces that have vanished—albeit only a trifling score of years gone by—will have some appreciation of the pathos that dwells in these grave eyes that look so steadfastly back upon the things they knew before History was born.
>
> —*The Innocents Abroad*

In this paraphrase, as in most others, students found themselves earnestly considering the structure of the passage and the progression of thought. From a concrete image Twain moves farther and farther into realms of abstraction—the thoughts suggested by the material object and its meaning for the observer. Only by trying to construct a new paragraph on Twain's model can the beginning student of language become completely aware of and involved in this process. Here is a student's effort:

> [A College Dorm] After a lifetime of anticipation, it loomed before me. The tall structure was so cold, so bleak, so lonesome, so much without any personality or character of its own. There was nothing unique in it at all, and inside on the tile floor were heel marks of all the students who had been there before. The building wasn't human, but it wanted to speak. If the appearance of a building was ever trying to give a warning, then it was this building that was philosophizing. It was talking to me, yet also to others—others who would soon enter its halls. It was thinking of all that it had seen from the present to the past. It was fascinated by the movie of its memories—of all the single frames and incidents which, one by one, quickly add up till they produce a moving image. It was thinking of all the people who had come in wanting to make the world better; of all the idealism and romanticism that had once flourished; of the individuals with such questioning minds, whose regression it had watched, whose decay was observed; of the beginning and the end, hope and death, the illusions and reality, of all the people who had ended up as they did not originally want to. It was a lesson to Man—of the meaning of hypocrisy. It was MEMORY—KNOWLEDGE—brought into reality. All those who have a conception of life—who can easily realize what message is being conveyed—will realize what the warning is—for experience has told this college dorm that people who enter with young and optimistic

ideas leave with old and rational realizations.

—Craig Weintraub

Statement and Predication

Any teacher must be prepared to tackle both semantic (conceptual) and structural (grammatical) errors in statement and predication as well as in parallel structure. This double analysis of errors in the building of a sentence (semantic and structural) is useful when trying to convince a student that he needs to overcome sloppiness or inaccuracy in expression as well as outright grammatical errors. Students do not revolt at being reminded that the structure of English is such that plural nouns are followed by the word "are" while singular nouns are followed by "is." Grammar has rules. But conceptual errors are harder to pinpoint and explain; the reader sometimes has to patiently extricate the fundamental core of the sentence from a mass of distracting verbiage in order to point out semantic errors in predication and statement. Statement errors, errors in which there is a serious dislocation of meaning between subject and verb, or verb and object, are rife in student papers, especially those treating abstract subjects. At its most obvious, the fault is the familiar mixed metaphor: we have all seen "spirals of inflation" that two lines further on manage somehow "to slam the door in the face of prosperity." More subtle are misstatements like "Expressions were said differently by different classes." It is hard to convince a student that one says a word but uses an expression.

Any written exercise must be marked with a constant watch for the fitting together of subject and verb, verb and object. When the verb involved is the verb "to be," or any of the verbs that pattern like "to be," the dislocation (an error in a predication) can be examined closely through *persona* paraphrase exercises devoted to that structure specifically. Here poetry can be used as a rich source for materials.

Since poetry is metaphor, the most radical violation of the rules of predication, students can learn from looking at it why the logic of prose, if it is to explain rather than transform, must conform to a rather rigid system of etiquette. The poems of Emily Dickinson, in their blunt wrenching of the conventions normally governing the union of subject and object, are splendid places to confront students with outrageous comparison, and to instruct them in the absolute equality, the identifying nature of the verb "to be." For example, the lyric "Hope is the Thing with Feathers" says exactly that— Hope *is* the thing. We all know that hope, while it may be an emotion, an abstraction, a commendable virtue, is certainly *not* a thing, especially a thing with' feathers. But then, of course, it is after all, for the thing "that perches in the soul" is the bird that traditionally symbolizes the longing for God. So, by yoking with a stark *is* that which both is and is not at the same time, the poet has pushed us to the point of contradiction which is the illumination of poetry.

Students can be invited to imitate her audacity by being asked to write four or eight lines of "Despair is the thing that . . ." and encouraged to shock the reader by breaking the rule as hard as they can. The instructor can at the same time cite examples of such misbehavior from their own essays, with the comment that while such violations may be the beginnings of fine poems, they cannot function as conveyers of logical thought since they negate the process of reason. Here is one of the results that delighted the students:

Despair is the iron window,
The lock slung closed,
Receding footsteps hollow, slow,
The chilly absence of repose.

Conclusion

These exercises are only a few of the paraphrases that we have used with great success over the past two or three years. Admittedly I have selected some of those that worked best—a paraphrase is a deceptive creature: those that you have high hopes for sometimes misfire, while others that you present with great misgivings (like the Rose Macaulay extract) catch the students' imagination and lead to glittering results. But I must stress that this is only a small sampling of the paraphrases we have found useful.

The same process of selection went on in the choosing of student samples to accompany each paraphrase. I did choose those that caught my eye for some particular spark of ingenuity or originality, but even after setting high standards I was forced to put aside with regret many that were equally as good. Even the least successful student paraphrases almost inevitably have good sentences; I have never had to hand back a paraphrase without at least one positive comment.

We intend to continue to use *persona* paraphrasing as a crucial tool in the developing of variety in student style, and we hope to refine further its use in the teaching of specific grammatical points. All we need now is the patience to comb piles of writing for suitable texts, and the luck to find what we need.[1]

---

[1] The members of the Subject A Department have contributed greatly to the writing of this article. Ruth Nybakken tried out specific paraphrases in her class, while Frank Cebulski and Nell Altizer made large and invaluable contributions to the final form of some of the ideas expressed here.

Who Can Be Taught?

(Continued from page 196)

mar lessons not helpful in teaching writing or not interesting. Surely another measure of the success of the method outlined here is that the incidence of deviant sentences drops sharply as the semester progresses. If I wish data for my files, it must be collected in the first part of the semester.

MARY VAIANA TAYLOR

The Folklore of Usage

DESPITE THE NUMEROUS STUDIES which have appeared in the decades since the Leonard survey in 1932 and the courses in teacher training institutions which have attempted to deal with usage from a responsible point of view, the fact remains that little impact has been made on the teaching of usage in our schools. The reasons for the negligible effect are complex, but we might glance at what typically happens in teacher training courses as an indication of the nature of the problem. Prospective teachers are introduced to the studies and the surveys, lectured on the concept of "levels of usage," and advised of ways in which to treat usage in their classrooms. Unfortunately, the subsequent performance of these students as teachers clearly indicates that there has been no change in their basic attitudes toward language use. I suggest that our treatment of usage has been inadequate because it has been factual and unemotional, permitting the students to assume a passive role and, more crucially, implying that usage is not an emotional topic. Is there an alternative presentation of the facts about usage which would not permit passivity or ignore the emotional factor? I would like to describe briefly a method of presenting the usage issue to prospective secondary school teachers which has been successful in treating the central questions, demands the active involvement of the students, and by so doing, focuses on the nature and source of the emotional reactions to the usage controversy.

The chief component of this approach was a questionnaire, but I prefaced the actual examination of usage with a brief consideration of some basic principles of linguistic change, illustrated with examples from the history of English. Derivational processes (for example, the formation of verbs from nouns and adjectives as in *terrorize* and *finalize*), multiple developments in some changes (for example, which form is chosen in the collapse of the past participle and the preterit of strong verbs in Middle English), analogy (for example, the application of the regular past tense inflection *ed* to verbs originally belonging to the strong verb category as in OE *smēōcan*, preterit *smēac*, NE *smoke*, preterit *smoked*), and typological change (for example, our language's change from synthetic to analytic—that is, from a case language to one which relies on word order), received particular emphasis.[1]

I initiated the discussion of usage by distributing a questionnaire containing a

---

[1]In the classical generative framework, the traditional term "analogy" is subsumed under the term "generalization"—see Robert King, *Historical Linguistics and Generative Grammar* (New Jersey: Prentice-Hall, 1969), pp. 127-134. For our purposes, the distinction is irrelevant.

Mary Vaiana Taylor teaches English Language and Linguistics at the University of Utah. She recently did a year's research in Scotland on dialectology and sociolinguistics.

Reprinted from *College English*, Vol. 35, No. 7, April 1974.

number of the typical usage shibboleths: split infinitives, sentence-final prepositions, omitted relatives, *who* for *whom, can* for *may, will* for *shall, further-farther, between-among, proven-proved*, etc. The students were asked to judge the appropriateness of these usages (1) in writing of a formality equivalent to their own class assignments (2) in speech, also of the kind used in a classroom. Having made these judgments, they were asked to indicate whether they themselves used such constructions in written or oral assignments. The results of these questionnaires revealed a consistent discrepancy between what the students judged acceptable and what actually occurred in their work; this discrepancy was more striking in the oral category.

The initial reaction of the majority of students to this discrepancy is best described as guilt. These prospective teachers felt that their language skills were inadequate or sloppy, and most admitted to a long-standing sense of apprehension about the imperfection of their linguistic performance, especially since, as English teachers, they would be expected to speak and write perfect English. Some students indicated that, although they knew what the handbooks prescribed, they felt that certain constructions sounded too formal, especially in speech. These reactions invited discussion of the difference between written and spoken standards and the historical sources of standards. The students were asked to look up the constructions in question in standard references such as the *Oxford English Dictionary*, Bryant's *Current American Usage*, and Jespersen's *Modern English Grammar* and to note the number and kinds of authors cited as using them. We also examined some of the items in the light of the principles of linguistic change which we had discussed: for example, the relationship of the case of a pronoun to its placement respectively before and after the main verb in sentences like "Who were you talking to?" and "It's me" and the way in which the relationship of a pronoun to the verb is interpreted in an analytic language. We read some of the material from the *Webster's Third* debate and compared the quasi-moral connotations of the language used by those lamenting the decline of usage standards to the students' own feelings of guilt about their grammatical "lapses."

Since the main concern in this process was simply to make the students conscious of the multiplicity of factors involved in judgments about usage, we covered these topics rather rapidly. The students were then asked to construct their own usage questionnaire, consisting of three parts.[2] The first section was to investigate sources of usage: where one might look up a disputed point of usage, what kinds of people spoke "good English," whether English teachers spoke "good English," and what a simple definition of "good English" might be. The second section was to contain fifteen to twenty items of disputed usage, to be drawn from any standard handbook, from the sample questionnaire in Postman and Weingartner's *Linguistics: A Revolution in Teaching* (New York: Dell, 1966), or from the Marckwardt and Walcott study *Facts About Current English Usage* (New York: Appleton-Century-Crofts, 1938). I suggested that the response to these items should be

---

[2]This use of a questionnaire was suggested to me by Diana Major, who has used the technique for several semesters with excellent results. I have discussed many of the ideas in this article with her and have profited in many ways from her experience. I am also grateful to Ken Eble and William Slager for many helpful suggestions.

acceptable or *not acceptable*, and that a distinction should be made between speech and writing. The third section was to examine the correlation between the responses given in the second section and the informants' actual linguistic performance and to determine what the informants felt were the best reasons for learning "good English." The questionnaires were to be given in written and/or oral form to at least ten people.

The actual questionnaires varied a good deal depending, of course, on the zeal and imagination of the individual students, but the following questionnaire is typical.

Usage Survey (reproduced with the permission of Fred Peterson)

I. Please indicate the degree of acceptability of each of the usages below by writing the appropriate letter in the space provided to the left of the sentence:
A = always acceptable B = acceptable formal usage C = acceptable informal usage D = questionable usage E = not acceptable
If a usage is not always acceptable, please write an acceptable version in the space provided below the sentence.

_____ 1. Your viewpoint is different than his.
_____ 2. Bill went to bed without scrubbing his teeth.
_____ 3. Bryce Canyon is quite unique.
_____ 4. It's like that, you know.
_____ 5. I am older than him.
_____ 6. She says I am, but I ain't.
_____ 7. Houses are built to live in, not to look at.
_____ 8. Max decided to really try hard.
_____ 9. Who did you see yesterday?
_____ 10. This throng of people was gathered to pay their tribute to the heroes.
_____ 11. It's me.
_____ 12. Someone forgot to wash their hands.
_____ 13. Neither you nor she is tall.
_____ 14. Let's keep this between you and I.
_____ 15. Winstons taste good like a cigarette should.
_____ 16. Each of these students are going on the field trip.
_____ 17. You don't have no claims on me.
_____ 18. I haven't got any.

Please indicate those usages which appear in your writing and/or conversation (whether acceptable or not) by placing a circle around the number of the corresponding sentence above. Example—not acceptable, but used anyway:

__E__ (25.) She invited John and myself.

       She invited John and me.

II. Please answer the following questions.
 1. What is good grammar (or good English)?
 2. Who uses good grammar?
 3. Where do you look, or whom do you ask, to find out which usage is correct?
 4. Do you use correct grammar?
 5. What usage errors do you consider to be the most objectionable?
 6. What reasons are there for using good grammar?
 7. Should teachers always use correct grammar?

8. If you could improve your grammar, would you? Why?
9. Do English teachers, or other teachers in the humanities, need to be more careful of their grammar than do science, technical, or P.E. teachers?
10. Where, when, and in what way did you first learn grammar?
11. Should different usages be employed to suit different purposes or audiences, or is it better to use correct standard English in all situations?
12. Should a teacher employ the same usages as his students?
13. Should use of informal English be encouraged in the classroom? In written assignments?
14. What should a teacher do when students use bad grammar?
15. How should acceptable usage be taught?

About fifty percent of the questionnaires were distributed to university students, but other groups, including factory workers, secretaries, secondary school students, university professors, and elementary school teachers were also investigated. The twenty-seven students in my class administered 222 questionnaires.

On the day scheduled for discussion of the questionnaires, the students were excited about their individual findings and even more impressed by the degree to which the general findings of the class coincided. The observations which resulted from discussion and comparison fall into seven major categories.

1. There is wide-spread discrepancy on almost every educational level between what people claim is acceptable or unacceptable usage and what they admit they actually use.

2. Most informants were very concerned about answering the questionnaire the way the questioner wanted. Typical student remarks were: "Most people were more concerned about what I would think if they did not answer questions 'correctly' than whether or not the questions were actually correct. Therefore, some of their responses were not totally honest." "The most striking response to this survey was, in my opinion, the anxiety that people displayed as they completed the questionnaire."

3. Students who were able to administer some questionnaires orally remarked on the difference between the results of the oral and the written questionnaires, and noted that those who responded orally were far less anxious about the correctness of their answers.

4. On the basis of sociolinguistic studies such as that of William Labov in New York City, we would predict that social bias would play an important role in linguistic judgment; responses to the question "Who uses good grammar?" consistently betrayed such a bias.[3] Typical anwers were that "educated" or "upper class" persons spoke good English while "uneducated" or "lower class" persons spoke poor English. This equation of education and high social rank is also reflected in the observation made by several students that informants with less formal education seemed far *more* apprehensive about completing the questionnaire and far *less* lenient in their judgments of acceptability. Sometimes answers to this question reflected cultural bias— thus "the British" or "not Texans" use good English.

5. This correlation of linguistic and social judgments was apparent in the reasons given for speaking or studying "good English." Typical answers were "to seem educated," "to improve myself," "to get a better job." Significantly, "to get a better job," the only clearly pragmatic reason, was least mentioned.

6. Informants almost unanimously chose the dictionary or a grammar book as the ultimate source of authority in matters of disputed usage. English teachers were less frequently cited. (I will have more to say about these authorities in Section II.)

---

[3]William Labov, *The Social Stratification of English in New York City* (Washington: Center for Applied Linguistics, 1966).

7. Despite a variety of judgments about the acceptability of any given usage item, the list of "most objectionable usage errors" was surprisingly small and surprisingly consistent. Since only a small set of pronunciation differences from a non-prestige dialect are socially stigmatized by the members of the speech community, we might expect the same kind of selective marking to be characteristic of grammatical differences.[4] In the class list of most objectionable errors, *ain't* led by a wide margin; one student remarked that for her informants, it apparently epitomized "bad grammar." Double negatives, the improper case for pronouns (including *who* and *whom*), the improper preterit or participle for irregular verbs, split infinitives, and sentence-final prepositions all received frequent mention. Particular items of usage cited were *different than, everyone-their, finalize,* and *between-among.* No other constructions or particular items received more than an isolated citation although several informants found "swear words" or "huh" very objectionable.

How significant are these results? The students who administered the questionnaires were not trained field-workers, and their questionnaires are not the questionnaires of professionals. Their informants were sometimes friends, sometimes complete strangers. Informants were asked to use labels such as "acceptable" or "good." Clearly, such labels are quite vague, and even if a student defined these terms for each of his informants, there is no guarantee that his definition would be consistent with the definitions used by the rest of the students in the class. Nevertheless, the results are a valid indication of the basic connotations which a large number of people of various levels of education attach to the concepts "good English" and "bad grammar." They are also a very informative sampling of the kinds of "errors" which, in the minds of many people, mark language as belonging to the latter category. Therefore, as long as the inherent limitations of the data are kept clearly in mind, we may examine here, as I did in subsequent class discussion with my students, the implications of these results.

Every English teacher who has admitted his occupation to a traveling companion has witnessed a manifestation of Questionnaire Neurosis. The inevitable reaction to "I'm an English teacher" is some variation of "Oh . . . I'd better watch my grammar." While the predictability of this response can be a momentary source of amusement, it should also be a cause for serious reflection. There is no way to escape the conclusion that we, as teachers, have done an extremely effective job of conditioning human beings to respond with feelings of inadequacy to a situation which, in their opinion, demands that they be discriminating in their selection of linguistic forms.

What are the steps in our conditioning program? First, we separate judgments of acceptability from actual usage; second, we emphasize that usage never changes standards, which are, by definition, absolute; third, we reinforce the sense of the divine and unchanging nature of standards by our methods of teaching and correcting. The success of this conditioning program is amply attested by the high percentage of responses in which an informant marked a usage as "acceptable" but said he never used it, or marked it as "unacceptable" but said he did use it. We ask students to "fill in the blank with the correct form" without providing a linguistic or social context in which the choice is to be made, thereby implying that there is

---

[4]For example, r-lessness is highly marked as a non-prestige item in the New York City speech community. See Labov, especially pp. 63-89.

one correct form which is *always* correct. Since every student knows by the time he is seven that "Whom did you see" may be correct on his English quiz but will get him into trouble on the playground, he quickly draws the conclusion that there is no inherent relationship between the nature of the language being examined on that quiz and the nature of the language by which he survives. It is logical, therefore, that these languages be judged by different criteria. The standards of the former are absolute, and are identified and protected by teachers; the standards of the latter are relative and are identified and protected by the immediate favorable or unfavorable social response. Every student practices constantly with the language of survival; his experience with classroom language is more limited, less personal, and generally less successful. Small wonder that, student or traveling companion, confronted with the absolute standard in the form of a written assignment or an English teacher, assumes that his performance will be inadequate.

The reactions of my students and of their informants to the oral-written distinction also support the hypothesis that the standards for the language of the classroom have been established as absolute and inflexible. The informants to whom the questionnaire was given orally did not display acute Questionnaire Neurosis and were willing to give their opinions about the appropriateness of various usages; they were also far less prescriptive in their judgments. It is apparent that spoken language was not, in the view of these informants, subject to classroom standards; therefore, an oral questionnaire was not cause for terror. Even more striking was the surprise my students expressed at the discrepancy between the oral and written results. This surprise suggests that these students certainly did not recognize that oral and written standards of usage should vary; if they had been exposed to the distinction at some time in their formal education, they had no confirmed commitment to it. Clearly, the distinction would never have been made subsequently in their own classrooms.

Chemistry teachers are not loath to add another element to their charts, and physics teachers do not resent acknowledging an alternative theory about the structure of matter. What is it about a changing language and changing tastes in language that English teachers generally find so threatening? I suggest that English teachers establish and protect absolute standards for linguistic performance because in so doing they are establishing and protecting their own prestige, and they feel it is necessary to establish and protect it because they are themselves linguistically insecure.

There is evidence to support this claim. The relevance of the conditioning process described above is obvious. We should also note the clear social bias in linguistic judgment displayed not only by our students' informants, but also by informants in controlled sociolinguistic investigations such as the New York City study (Labov, pp. 405-504). The absence of the stigmatized items—whether pronunciations or usages—was always associated with the "educated" or "upper class"; the presence of the items was associated with the "uneducated" or "lower class." The fact that the traditional role of the English teacher in the United States has been to identify and dispense standards of linguistic performance would, in itself, be sufficient motive for teachers, as a body, to resist the pressure for change exerted by "common speech"—pressure which is also, therefore, a challenge to their social rank associated with "correct English."[5] However, there is the additional factor that all speakers tend to be unaware of their own actual performance, attributing to themselves instead the forms which are for them the prestige forms. There is ample documentation of this tendency in the Labov study (Labov, pp. 455 ff.). Although Labov's study was a phonological one, there is no reason to believe that the patterns of lexical usage would differ in any significant way. One portion of Labov's discussion is particularly relevant. Having noted that all classes in the New York sample manifest the tendency toward linguistic insecurity, Labov states that the middle class, especially the lower middle class, is the most profoundly affected.

> The hypercorrect tendency of the lower middle class seems to be rooted in a profound linguistic insecurity. This insecurity is perhaps an inevitable accompaniment of social mobility and the development of upward social aspirations in terms of the socio-economic hierarchy. . . . The tendency to spelling pronunciations such as [ɔftɪn] for *often*, or [pɑlm] for *palm* is another expression of the same process [of hypercorrection]. The development of linguistic insecurity has accompanied the development of the doctrine of correctness. . . . social mobility . . . created a need for a doctrine of correctness, and led to the elevation of the schoolmaster and the dictionary as authorities for speech in both England and America. (p. 475)

Labov also observes that "on every count, women show much greater linguistic insecurity than men" (p. 495).

It is unnecessary to stress that a very large percentage of elementary and secondary school teachers in this country come from a middle class background and are female; it should also be unnecessary to stress that my concern in making this point is *merely* to suggest that the majority of public school teachers, by virtue of their class, sex, occupation, and two hundred and fifty years of a particular pattern of social forces, are likely to be prescriptive about linguistic standards and attribute these standards to their own linguistic performance even though this performance may not in fact reflect these standards.[6] It is this situation which I mean to describe by asserting that English teachers are linguistically insecure.

To summarize the hypotheses about the characteristic linguistic environment in our schools:

1. There is no functional distinction made between oral and written standards.
2. The standards of the classroom have no relationship to the language of survival and do not reflect the need for situational variation.
3. The standards of the classroom do not constitute a comprehensive approach to writing or speaking "good English"; instead the focus of attention is a small number of highly stigmatized items, reviewed year after year. As Gleason notes, this practice denies the systematic nature of language, and the continual repetition of a very

[5]H.A. Gleason, Jr., *Linguistics and English Grammar* (New York: Holt, Rinehart, and Winston, 1965), pp. 3-27 and Sterling Leonard, *The Doctrine of Correctness in English Usage, 1700-1800,* Univ. of Wisconsin Studies in Language and Literature, No. 25 (Madison: Univ. of Wisconsin Press, 1929.

[6]Two students noted in their summaries that in the course of the interview, their informants used constructions or items which they had earlier judged unacceptable and said they never used. These observations are indicative of the tendency described.

limited set of proscribed items aggravates the classroom situation by "adding boredom to vacuity."[7]

4. Perhaps most crucial of all, there is every reason to expect that the actual linguistic performance of the teacher in the classroom does not reflect the teacher's standards—certainly not consistently—although the teacher demands that the students consistently adhere to them. In this regard, I cannot improve on the observation of one of my students who commented that " 'Standard English' is non-existent, but psychologically real."

What did we accomplish in the three weeks we spent gathering and interpreting data and examining our own linguistic motives and the possible motives of former teachers and future colleagues?

We did not find definite answers to the classic usage questions: Should usage be taught? How does one teach usage? What should be the standards for oral work? Should English teachers require higher standards of linguistic performance than teachers of other subjects? How much influence should the language of survival have on "Standard English"? In fact, it is probably accurate to say that there was more immediate confusion about these points after the usage unit than there was before we began it. I suggest that this is a desirable result; confusion about complex issues is infinitely preferable to the confidence of ignorance.

There are a number of areas, however, in which the students undeniably benefited from this unit.

1. The principles of linguistic change with which we had begun our discussion were now viewed from an entirely different perspective. From Old English times, analogy has worked to remove verbs from the strong class and add them to the weak or "regular" class. This is a *fact* about the history of English, and a particular example of the operation of a very general principle of natural languages. However, the results of this natural linguistic process are often held in the greatest contempt by persons who know little about the nature of languages, and unfortunately, many of these persons are teachers of English. I think it is likely that my students will now attempt to temper linguistic judgment with linguistic knowledge.

2. The students have a *specific* idea about the complex nature and sources of potential emotional reactions to linguistic variation of every kind. Therefore, they are equipped to deal with the manifestations of these reactions in their students. Some of my students had already observed Questionnaire Neurosis in the reactions of secondary school students to written assignments; the reactions were most acute in the case of minority students.[8] The clear establishment of different standards for oral and written work, the deliniation of a sliding scale of standards for different audiences and situations, the use of tape recorders and journals not subject to "grading," and many other techniques were discussed and evaluated in terms of their appropriateness for coping with what can only be accurately described as linguistic fear. None of these techniques is revolutionary; what will make them particularly effective is that they will be used in the context of a broad understanding of what the problem really is.

---

[7]*Linguistics and English Grammar* p. 15. Labov describes the same kind of selective teaching emphasis with regard to pronunciation (Labov, p. 493).

[8]Minority students at Indiana University, enrolled in a summer program to improve their language skills, repeatedly stated that they knew their language "had always been bad"; one student said he only spoke "slang." For these students, committing language to paper was a significant threat.

3. Corollary to this understanding is the strong sense these students have of the necessity of specifically teaching the facts of variation and encouraging a tolerant attitude towards them. Acknowledgment and appreciation of a broad spectrum of written and spoken styles is, of course, requisite both for attentive reading of literature and for confident self-expression. But acknowledgment of geographical and social variation is even more crucial since social judgments based on these variations deeply affect personal relations in the classroom and, subsequently, in jobs and in the communty. The study of some of the major non-standard dialects and the linguistic acceptance of the groups who speak them is an important aspect of this acknowledgment.

In my own class, I originally treated geographical dialects after situational and social dialects, but geographical variation is probably the most promising starting point for an examination of linguistic variation. The concept of "a different kind of language in a different place" seems to be a more readily acceptable form of linguistic variation for most speakers than the often threatening concept of "a different kind of language in the place where *I* live." A number of questionnaires designed for classroom study of geographical dialects are available.[9] The discussion of variation across space leads quite naturally to the consideration of variation across class and, subsequently, across situations. Thus a unit on dialect geography becomes not merely a pleasant change of pace in the secondary classroom but a viable introduction to the multi-faceted study of the interaction of language and culture.

4. Surely the most important thing my students learned from this particular treatment of usage is the absolute necessity of their being linguistically secure individuals before they attempt to be teachers. Being linguistically secure does not mean pretending to have answers to all, or even some, of the questions raised here. Nor does it mean never making a social judgment on the basis of linguistic performance. It does mean, however, having sufficient knowledge of the way in which language and social interaction change, to confront a variety of standards and performances without feeling threatened. It does mean immediately tempering social judgment with awareness of the sociolinguistic forces from which no one, not even a professional linguist, is exempt. The comments of one of my students exemplify the kind of awareness which I feel has value far beyond the narrow issue of whether one should write *who* or *whom*. In class discussion before the questionnaires were distributed, she stated that one of the minor crosses in her life was listening to a salesperson in a bakery talking about the "real fresh pies." After class examination of the questionnaire results had begun, she admitted privately in an office conference that she felt very guilty about her resentment of this usage and about her linguistic snobbery; however, she despaired of ever being able to prevent such a reaction. By the end of the unit, the student explained both of her previous states to her classmates with a good deal of humor, commenting that her hackles still rose at "real fresh," but that she saw her reaction simply as another example of the validity of the sociolinguistic principles which we had been discussing.

Students like this one are in a position to break the tradition of usage folklore in our schools.

A Lengthy Footnote Which Is Too Important To Be One

If I have given the impression in the preceding section that linguistic insecurity is found only in elementary and secondary school teachers, the following data should dispel it.

In the course of the analysis of the questionnaires, the class asked what the

[9]Hugh Agee, "The Analysis of Student Talk: Classroom Possibilities for Dialect Study," *English Journal* (Sept. 1972), pp. 878-881; Roger Shuy, *Discovering American Dialects* (NCTE, 1967).

attitudes of the Teaching Associates in the English Department were about usage. In order to answer the question, I devised a brief usage questionnaire. Informants were asked to designate whether a usage was acceptable or unacceptable (1) in written work in classes which they taught, (2) in oral work in classes which they taught, (3) in written work for classes in which they themselves were students, (4) in oral work for classes in which they themselves were students. The informants were to underline the offending item or items in sentences which they had judged unacceptable for any classification. The classes which the Teaching Associates regularly taught were Freshman Composition and a variety of introductory literature courses; I asked the informants to indicate the number of quarters in which they had taught these courses. The questionnaire was distributed in written form to eighty-five Teaching Associates; only twenty-one were returned.

The items on the questionnaire were drawn directly from the items listed in Marckwardt and Walcott's *Facts About Current English Usage*.[10] In their discussion, first published in 1938, Marckwardt and Walcott reviewed the earlier study *Current English Usage* by Sterling Leonard (Chicago: Inland Press, 1932), which sought to gather information about usage by securing the "consensus of expert opinion" from a group of 229 judges composed of linguists, editors, authors, businessmen, and teachers of English and speech.[11] Usages were labeled "established," "disputable," or "illiterate"; however, the "disputable" ranking meant only that the judges could not agree about the particular item. The Marckwardt and Walcott study examined the items in each of these categories, comparing the opinions of the Leonard judges with the linguistic testimony and citations available in the *Oxford English Dictionary* and its Supplement, *Webster's New International Dictionary* (second edition), Horwill's *Modern American Usage*, Hall's *English Usage*, and the grammars of Jespersen and Curme.

The questionnaire contained twelve items identified as "established" usage according to the Leonard Survey, and seven items identified as "disputable" usage. The comparison of the judgments of the twenty-one Teaching Associates with the judgments of dictionaries and grammar books is most interesting. In the following table, the item being examined is italicized. Figures represent the percentage of the informants who found the item unacceptable in the relevant category. When an informant found the sentence unacceptable, but circled an item other than the one being studied, his response was eliminated from the percentage; in a few cases, no answer was given for an item in a particular category, and these instances were also eliminated in figuring the percentages.

---

[10]There were minor changes in order to make some of the sentences more likely in a college classroom. The original sentences and their altered versions are, respectively: 1) This was the reason why he went home. This was the reason why he left the university. 2) We will try and get it. We will try and get the book as soon as possible. 3) We can expect the commission to at least protect our interests. We can expect the committee to at least protect our interests. 4) If it wasn't for football, school life would be dull. If it wasn't for examinations, school life would be more pleasant. 5) He stopped to price some flowers. Harold stopped to price some flowers. 6) Invite whoever you like to the party. Invite whoever you like to my wedding. 7) I wish I was wonderful. I wish I was intelligent.

[11]The actual division of the group of 229 judges was: thirty linguistic specialists, thirty editors, twenty-two authors, nineteen businessmen, and about 130 English teachers.

	Written work in classes which T.A.'s taught	Oral	Written work in T.A.'s own classes	Oral
CATEGORY I: "ESTABLISHED"				
This is a man . . . I used to know (omitted relative).	43%	5%	67%	20%
This is the chapter *whose* contents caused most discussion.	67%	26%	72%	53%
He did *not* do *as* well *as* we expected	9%	0%	24%	5%
This was the *reason why* he left the university.	70%	20%	84%	21%
We can expect the committee *to at least protect* our interests.	55%	15%	70%	40%
I don't know *if* I can.	20%	5%	37%	5%
If it *wasn't* for examinations, school life would be more pleasant.	81%	43%	95%	76%
Harold stopped to *price* some flowers.	20%	5%	33%	14%
You had to have property to vote, in the eighteenth century.	42%	0%	70%	5%
I felt I could walk no *further*.	29%	9%	43%	28%
I'd *like* to make a correction.	9%	0%	19%	0%
Galileo discovered that the earth *moved*.	45%	25%	50%	35%
CATEGORY II: "DISPUTABLE"				
None of them *are* here.	60%	32%	65%	50%
We will *try and get* the book as soon as possible.	86%	28%	90%	62%
We *only* had one left.	43%	9%	67%	19%
A treaty was concluded *between the four powers*.	70%	43%	85%	62%
Invite *whoever* you like to my wedding.	70%	10%	80%	26%
I wish I *was* intelligent.	62%	33%	90%	52%
My contention has been *proven* many times.	60%	30%	90%	37%

Obviously, the most important observation to be made about these data is that in fifteen out of nineteen instances, more than twenty-five percent of these graduate students find unacceptable in written work for introductory composition and literature classes usages which occur in the works of major figures of every kind of literature, sometimes from the beginnings of written English records. In the Marckwardt and Walcott study, *all* of these usages were placed in the *Literary English* category. The authors' definition of Literary English is: "If the expression was recorded without a limiting label in the collections of usage consulted, and if there was at least one citation from the nineteenth century, the expression was considered Literary English (p. 18). The authors note that even the *OED* found it necessary to limit the citations to one per century in many cases, and none of the items labeled Literary English relies on a single citation. The following citation is typical: I *had rather* go at once. The *OED* cites uses from 1450-1875. Jespersen cites Defoe, Thackeray, Shaw, Wells; Hall names thirty-two authors who use it. Put more bluntly, these students will later fill *PMLA* with scholarly articles on Austen, James, Hardy, and Meredith, but they find the language of these authors unacceptable from college freshmen.

Some other points should be briefly noted:

1. The comparison of the evidence from the dictionaries and grammar books with the judgments of these Teaching Associates clearly supports the earlier hypothesis that the shibboleths of usage are protected and propagated by oral tradition; certainly they are not based on the usage exemplified by literature of acknowledged value.

2. One might suggest that any individual may choose to be as prescriptive as he wishes about his own linguistic performance and, therefore, that the percentages of unacceptability relating to the graduate students' own work are irrelevant to this discussion. However, it should be noted that in every case, a high percentage of unacceptability for written graduate work corresponds to a high percentage for written introductory work; it often corresponds to a significant percentage for *oral* work as well. Unfortunately, there was no way to check these ratings against the actual written and oral usage of the graduate students although, on principle, one would be very suspicious of the high percentages, especially in the oral category.

3. The Leonard Survey suggests that a teacher "will certainly, in marking themes, accept from the average student any usage classed in this study as established or disputable . . ." (quoted in Marckwardt and Walcott, p. 15), and Marckwardt and Walcott remark in their discussion that the Leonard classifications were very conservative. Yet, in this survey, eight of the twelve items ranked as *established* usages in the Leonard Survey have a high unacceptability rating. In the *disputable* category, every one of the seven items has a high rating. It is interesting to note that all of the latter items except the last one received an "established" rating from the linguists in Leonard's panel and a "disputable" rating from the group as a whole (for the last item, the ratings were reversed). It is perhaps predictable, but unfortunate, that the judgment of at least this particular group of professional teachers of writing almost never coincides with the judgment of professional students of language.

4. The items which have extremely high percentages of unacceptability for both kinds of written work are, predictably: improper "case" for a pronoun, the lack of the subjunctive, the proper form of the participle, the *between-among* distinction, and certain bound phrases—*reason why, try and get*. These are the kinds of items which received frequent mention by my students' informants and which seem to constitute a lexical parallel to the small number of marked pronunciation features in a non-prestige dialect.

5. There was no correlation between the number of quarters a Teaching Associate had taught and the prescriptiveness of his linguistic judgment. It should be noted that one graduate student—but only one—remarked at the bottom of the question-

(Continued on page 219)

ENNO KLAMMER

Cassettes in the Classroom

WHAT STARTED AS AN EXPERIMENT several years ago has turned out to save time in correcting freshman composition themes. If I can believe my students, it has also helped them learn to write better. And that's what it's really all about. Briefly, the "experiment" consists of using cassette cartridges to correct freshman papers. The following is a sketch of the method with some comments about the results.

Each student in my composition sections is required to buy a cassette catridge in addition to the other required materials. If he buys it from our college audio-visual department, he may get a partial refund when he turns it in at the end of the quarter. What it amounts to, then, is that he is renting the cartridge for about ten cents per week. The audio-visual department has a number of cartridge playback machines available for student use in its listening room. This kind of machine is familiar to and popular with students. They have many available to them in the dormitories.

The student writes his assigned essay, places it into his folder, places the cassette in the folder, and hands in all three

Enno Klammer teaches English and Linguistics at Eastern Oregon College, La Grande, Oregon. He has in progress The Forms of Writing, a Freshman Composition text which uses T-G grammar to move from the concept of the organization of sentences to the organization of paragraphs and essays.

—theme, cassette, and folder—on the date due. I then put his cassette into my recording machine (supplied by the college) and read his theme, recording my comments as I go along. I first record the student's name and the date the paper was due. This is a safety measure, in case the paper and the cartridge get separated from each other. As I read the paper, I place numbers in the margin which correspond to the number of the comment I will be recording at the time. I still use a red pencil for the sake of visibility. After I have read the paper through and have assigned a grade, I return it with the cartridge, announcing a date for the rewritten version to be handed in.

Once the student gets his paper back, he goes to the library, checks out a tape player, and listens to my comments as he reads through his own paper. He may —indeed he is encouraged to—make whatever revisions or corrections he feels necessary. He may even rewrite the entire paper while he is listening to the tape. If there is a particular point which he has not understood, he can replay that part of the tape until he understands it.

The kinds of comments I make are varied as to type and importance. Some deal purely with grammatical or structural matters—for example, how to correct a sentence fragment by adding (usually) the verb or by attaching the fragment to another sentence. Some deal merely with the mechanics of writing— spelling, punctuation, manuscript form,

Reprinted from College English, Vol. 35, No. 2, November 1973.

and the like. The student might have to be reminded, for example, that he failed to double-space, and that the instructor is suffering from strained eyeballs as a result of his forgetfulness. I usually do not spell words for students; instead I send them to the dictionary by drawing attention to their errors. Often it seems best to try to give reasons for particular forms of punctuation rather than to merely list the correct mark: the student generally profits more from an explanation of *why* we use commas to set off nonrestrictive clauses and why we do *not* use them for restrictive clauses than he does from the simple comment, "You need commas here." Items that particularly benefit from being recorded have to do with such things as paragraph development and the organization of the whole essay.

From the instructor's point of view this method has advantages and disadvantages. To begin with, the very nature of the machinery makes the job cumbersome at times. The instructor has to carry a large box back and forth to class on those days when he is collecting or distributing papers and cartridges. Because the machine is necessary to carry out the project means that the work of correcting papers must be done in the office. A disadvantage which may occur when one is first trying out the method has to do with difficulty in dictating into a mike "on the run," so to speak, or in the presence of those colleagues who share the office. It also takes time to learn how to make an accurate and thorough critique during a once-through reading of a paper. Indeed, the whole method *is* time-consuming. There is no doubt about that. To correct a paper in this way takes at least half again as much time as the "old" method of writing a few cryptic comments and hieroglyphic symbols.

A final disadvantage lies in the matter of timing. When can one schedule the rewrite of a paper so that it will give the student enough time to hear the comments, correct the paper, and learn something in time to avoid making those same mistakes on the next paper he hands in? However, if one considers that writing skills are cumulative, it may not be as big a problem as it at first seems. One possible solution might be to require the student to buy two cartridges.

The advantages of the method, on the other hand, seem clearly to outweigh the disadvantages. The instructor can say much more and can say it more clearly. I estimate that a person can speak at least five times faster than he can write, which means that he can convey five times as much information in the same amount of time. The fact that the instructor can say so much more helps him to anticipate certain questions which any teacher of composition knows will be forthcoming from students who try to decipher the traditional hieroglyphics of the margin. This, in turn, may mean that the student no longer feels the need to corner his teacher for so many personal explanations of trivial matters, thereby saving everybody's time for more important things.

On the last full day of classes for the quarter my students were asked to write an unsigned, ungraded comment about their own reactions to the method. Forty-five of the forty-eight who survived responded. Only one was severely negative in his response. All the others liked the method and its results. The most common complaint concerned the difficulty of scheduling listening time in the library. In addition, the fact that the students had to go to the library to listen to the tapes was in itself an inconvenience for some.

Now, three years and some 450 students later, I am still using the method. During one quarter I abandoned it, but I came back to it quickly. I felt hamstrung by my inability to *write* as much as I wanted to *say* to help the struggling student. And the last of these 450 students still agree that the method is, if not exciting, at least interesting and helpful.

————————————

The Folklore of Usage

(*Continued from page 216*)

naire that "any of these could be acceptable or unacceptable depending on purpose and style of writing." It is not surprising that the percentages of unacceptability were very low on this questionnaire.

Twenty-one individuals is a small number on which to base any firm conclusions, and these results are presented as suggestive rather than definitive. But one wonders whether the small number of returned questionnaires is another manifestation of Questionnaire Neurosis. Would the returns have been equally small if I had asked about political affiliation or abortion laws? It may also be argued that the results have been distorted by a tendency on the part of the informants to mark an item unacceptable simply because it appeared on the questionnaire. If this is so, I would like to ask what it is about writing that does not occur between the covers of the latest Norton anthology that makes it eminently suspect. And might this tendency also apply to all usages which happen to appear in student writing? In either case, it seems that fear of seeming permissive in linguistic matters can only come from fear of seeming inadequate in linguistic matters.

I leave the last word to one of my students: "It's pathetic to think that our system of teaching language and our concern with rules can make a native speaker of English feel so inadequate about his own language."

Francine Hardaway

What Students Can Do to Take the Burden Off You

THERE HAS BEEN A LOT OF DISCUSSION about student-centered techniques lately, and research generally concludes that students learn at least as much from a "teacherless" class as from a traditional class, provided they write a great deal.[1] Student-centered techniques, then, would be perfect for beginning teachers. Such techniques are completely between student and teacher, require no radical revision of existing English programs, emphasize individual instruction, and make room for more actual writing practice. At the same time, they take some of the burden off the new teacher.

One obvious device to minimize the effect of a teacher's inexperience and maximize learning is peer group evaluation. Because this method lets students read other's papers, pointing out both errors in mechanics and problems of content and organization, it saves agonizing hours spent in correcting student themes by beginning teachers anxious to be fair and complete.

A new instructor who wished to use peer evaluation could spend class time at the beginning of the semester to arrive at some mutually acceptable standards for mechanical competence and good

organization. Perhaps some model essays from an anthology could be useful here, or even some student essays. From the discussions, a mimeographed form could be evolved. A copy of the form would be attached to every paper the student turns in (see appendix). On the form appear the criteria for acceptable papers, accompanied by several sentences of description. Below the criteria are four empty boxes in which four student readers will evaluate the attached theme according to the written criteria. Each student evaluator must assign a grade and justify it as a teacher would. He must sign his name to his evaluations, so the author may question him further if necessary. Mere mechanical errors need not be taken up in the boxes provided for evaluation; they are indicated right on the paper.

Arriving at the criteria for a good paper would probably be useful for the beginning teacher as for his students; it would give him some time to think out what he wanted from his students, making it unnecessary for him to fall back on assignments that bored him and would catapult new generations to tedium.

After the student has had his paper evaluated by four members of the class in the light of the new criteria, he has another task: he must revise his paper in accordance with his classmates' criticisms. If he disagrees, he must call his critics together and discuss the paper with them—perhaps they have misun-

Francine Hardaway teaches English at Scottsdale College, Arizona and reviews film for The New Times. She is the author of a composition text to be published by Prentice-Hall.
[1]Terry Grabar, et al. "Measuring Writing Progress: An Experiment," College English, 35 (January 1974), 484-5.

derstood, or perhaps they can make clear orally what they couldn't tell him on the evaluation sheet. At this point the teacher can enter the discussion again, but still only as a resource—not as a fount of specious authority.

All the actual work, then, is done by the students. This division of labor is effective for many reasons. First, it removes from the new teacher the responsibility of handing down standards by fiat (and of possibly being wrong). Second, it involves the student in the evaluative process, which ceases to be a mystery looked on with hostility. Having to find the mistakes of others makes the student more conscious of his own errors, and it teaches him the notion of an audience. For once he isn't writing only for the teacher; he must engage the attention of his peers, who aren't being paid for their kindness. Third, it frees the teacher from dealing with the obvious errors that are made over and over by students unto eternity—and can be found by anyone reading a student theme. The teacher then presumably has time and energy to tackle more complicated writing problems such as logical fallacies, immature style, and sentence monotony, which often get pushed to the background by less esoteric and more prominent inconsistencies.

The principle behind the apparent disappearance of professional authority in the classroom is another irony: in teaching, sometimes less is more. The teacher seems to teach less, and be less involved, but more frequent writing assignments actually mean that the student learns *more*. And the teacher does have some "free" time for more sophisticated writing problems, which involve him in more than a superficial evaluation of a student's difficulties.

As a check or balance on peer-group instruction, individual conferences are a necessity. Held twice during the semester, they enable the instructor to meet with "low-profile" students to find out if they are actually doing any work. At the first conference a student must present all his written work to date, all the peer-evaluation sheets, and evidence that he has done some revision to meet his classmates' criticism. Once again the student bears the responsibility: he must keep all his written work and produce it on demand. Why should the teacher act as file clerk by keeping papers? And why should the student discard a paper someone has carefully read and annotated for him?

Fifteen minutes is ample time to read all of a student's work if it has already been read by the class. The majority of students require no further attention— a mere corroboration of the class's opinion satisfies them. They now have had five opinions. But if, when reading the papers, the instructor sees a special problem—anything from missing work to lack of revision to problems not pointed out by student evaluators—he can arrange another conference.

The first conference ought to be held before mid-semester, so it can help the student improve. At the final conference, held just before the semester's end, the teacher can give a last evaluation of the student's work, looking both for improvement and for ability. But most students can tell with great accuracy what grade they deserve, because they have had at least four times as much criticism as the teacher alone could have provided. Difficult cases require a final writing assignment.

Lest the busy instructor shy away from spending extra time on conferences, let me suggest that these meetings be held mostly during class time. I have found it beneficial to vary the classroom routine twice during the semester by calling off the full class for two week periods—once at midterm and once before finals. During this time, students come in groups of four or five a day for conferences. Those who don't have a conference that day are free to work at home on a writing assignment that is due when the class reconvenes as a whole. The four or five students scheduled for conferences come to the classroom. While waiting for their conferences, students can revise their own papers, evaluate papers for the other four students in the room, discuss differences of opinion about previous work, or begin prewriting the next assignment. This little "lab" is a welcome break around mid-semester, and it gives everyone a chance to catch up. After all, there is nothing sacred about having all of the people in the classroom all of the time; some people think the classroom is a lousy place to write.

But the last method I suggest involves the classroom directly in the writing process: it is the prewriting and editing session. In the prewriting session, students divide into groups to try out theses, help each other with outlines, and read opening paragraphs to one another. In the editing session, students write in class and then discuss their work in progress. The best way to accomplish this is informally. The instructor could ask a student to read his unfinished work aloud during an in-class writing session. Or the class could once again divide itself into small groups to discuss work in progress. In some cases it is effective to walk around the room and read over students' shoulders when they write. The object of editing sessions, no matter how they are held, is to deal with compositions *before* they are finished so that they may be improved before the evaluation sheets are affixed and the sometimes cruel eyes of the peer evaluators are cast on the fledgling efforts.

The great value of prewriting and editing is thus preventive. In addition, it focuses the attention of the class on writing. Writing is like exercise: talking about it doesn't produce the same results as doing it. Even the best lecturer can't teach writing if the students never write. And one of the biggest problems about freshman composition is the staggering number of themes freshmen have to write if they are going to learn anything at all about the process of composition. Most composition teachers have unwieldly classes and too many themes to grade. Prewriting, editing, and peer evaluation make it possible to teach a large class with reasonable efficiency, shortchanging no one.

So these methods have something else in common besides their ability to exist without major curriculum and philosophical changes: they generate a good deal of writing practice with very little homework on anybody's part. They use every minute of the available class time in writing, evaluating, or conferencing. No time is wasted on days when the instructor is unprepared, because the course is not purely the responsibility of the instructor. And no time-draining discussions of peripheral issues occur. Almost always the students' own writing becomes the course's text.

With these few readjustments in the direction of student-centered teaching, it ought to be possible for even the most inexperienced teacher to run a mutually profitable composition class. And for the junior college teacher who must deal with many composition sections, the assumption of some burdens by the student would certainly be a welcome relief.

APPENDIX

————————————————————NAME OF AUTHOR

"Criticizing a story in class is a way of publishing it; everybody reads it. . . . The writer gets a real contact with the real world, not his wife, not his girl friend, not his mother. The student learns what the problem of communication is. He may have expressed his deepest feelings, but if people haven't gotten them, he has missed." Herbert Gold in *Writer's Digest* (9-20-72, p. 30)

Consider the following items when assessing each paper:
Thesis stated clearly or identifiably.
Subject matter clearly developed.
Respect for audience demonstrated by tone and consistent point of view.
Organization apparent in first paragraph; thesis and divisions
    developed in the middle paragraphs; transitions used;
    last paragraph concludes.
Sentence patterns made interesting through figurative language, examples, details.
Appropriate word choice.
Mechanics used for clear communication.

ACCEPTABLE GRADE: Mechanically competent, demonstrating original, creative, and clear use of language. Paper has a consistent tone and point of view. Thesis and organization are apparent. Subject matter within the scope of the assignment.

UNACCEPTABLE GRADE: Little detail, inconsistencies of tone and point of view, stylistically dull, poorly organized, more "telling" than "showing," problems of mechanics and word choice, poor transition, no thesis.

Name of Evaluator:	Name of Evaluator:
Strengths: Weaknesses: How to improve: Grade:	Strengths: Weaknesses: How to improve: Grade:
Name of Evaluator:	Name of Evaluator:
Strengths: Weaknesses: How to improve: Grade:	Strengths: Weaknesses: How to improve: Grade:

BARRETT JOHN MANDEL

Teaching Without Judging

AT THE MEETING of the National NCTE Ad Hoc Committee on Grading, Miss Jean Anderson of Burlingame High School in California turned to the group and asked, "How can one teach without evaluating or judging?" As a first-rate teacher, Jean could see, of course, how to judge gently and kindly, but she wondered whether in the teaching of literature it was possible to substitute for the judging of student work an entirely different pedagogical strategy.

Many college teachers of literature have recently been struggling with this problem. I would like to set forth a fairly detailed account of my own approach, not in the least as an example of Truth, potent for all professors at all institutions, but as one approach, which has borne results for me and which may provide helpful hints for some readers of *College English.*

My teaching uses no gimmicks and

Barrett John Mandel is author of Literature and the English Department. *He teaches at Douglass College (Rutgers) and is a Director of the College English Association.*

embodies no monolithic "Method." But it does work on the assumption that judgment in the form of grades and measurement (against "standards") does more to prevent education than to encourage it. This assumption is, fortunately, shared by a great many professors of literature today. But many of them have not found satisfying ways of translating their assumptions into classroom practice. My own practice may afford a few suggestions which others may find useful.

To Jean Anderson's question—Can one teach without judging?—I have come to feel that, for me at least, I cannot teach and judge as the same person. As a teacher I attempt to follow the following summarized rules of behavior, suggested to me not only by my own intuition and that of very talented colleagues, but also by my readings in third-force psychology, phenomenological psychology, and hermaneutics. However vague in listed form, these rules of thumb become powerfully practical for me in the literature class:

1. I listen until I hear.

2. I look until I see.
3. I psychologically support and encourage any signs of intellectual and emotional energy.
4. I encourage interaction among students.
5. I advise, but never force or require.
6. I try to be intellectually and emotionally honest and accessible.

Of course I *never* succeed at all of these at one time (though I occasionally fail at all of them), but they represent a goal which I keep before me constantly.

I will attempt to flesh out this skeleton now, but before I do, perhaps I should point out also in outline form, a few of the pedagogical devices I never use—for reasons which I hope will become clear below.

1. Never call on anybody who has not volunteered.
2. Never correct an interpretation.
3. Never berate students for lack of knowledge, understanding, or hard work.
4. Never use lecture as the dominant approach.
5. Never require specific projects at specific times.

For literature more than perhaps many others areas of human study a discussion format seems desirable. I am well aware that many lecturers and question-posers get high ratings in student evaluations of teachers and for good reasons, but I have come to believe that class discussion cannot be overdone—not if it is free and open. Many students and teachers have simply never participated in an open discussion in a classroom and define as "open," a rigidly controlled environment.

By "open discussion" I mean just that. The impetus, direction, style, depth, coverage, energy of the talk all are allowed to happen in the classroom as they would elsewhere, whether over coffee in a restaurant, or at a party, in an intense bull session, or in a work session among equals. The teacher has no lecture notes, no hidden agenda. Many teachers have commented to me that they hate giving (and preparing) lectures, that they find lecturing ego-building for themselves but not educationally valuable for students. Some of them have said that they do not want to direct Socratic discussions, but that if they give up this prerogative, they feel at a loss and do not know what their role should (or could) be.

A teacher in an "open discussion" has many ways of behaving. I mention some of them only to demonstrate practical steps a teacher who wishes to encourage open discussion can follow. It is reasonable and not inconsistent with the aims of open discussion to assume that the teacher will make sure that there is something to discuss—a focal point of attention—though this assumption by no means implies that he or she has to determine *what* the focal point should be. The teacher may conceive of his or her role as making sure that students meet in workshops early in the term for the purpose of designing a syllabus or developing a set of issues. For some courses, students arrive with very fixed ideas about what works they would like to study. At such times, the teacher can act essentially as a secretary, making sure that the books are in print, available, etc. A class is certainly off to a dazzling start when a sizeable number of students know what they have come to learn about. Much more commonly, naturally, students have very few ideas about the possible readings for a course, and the teacher may have to provide the appropriate titles. In either or any case, the "open discussion" format (for me, at least) implies that there will always be something to discuss, but that the discussion itself will not be controlled or directed. A rootless course with no fixed expectations would make me very tense and would drive me, because of my sense of the void, into the worst kind of pontification. Pure, undirected rap. (obviously valuable in its own right and occasionally what occurs in my classes) flourishes most positively when it is spontaneous. A class is not spontaneous. In my classes I choose to establish a context in which a work of literature is always the potential focus of attention. If my students choose on occasion to pursue their education by talking about something other than literature, it is not because there is no common reading to discuss.

The teacher has to do whatever can be done to make the classroom experience conducive to discussion and discovery. Superficial measures often help: having the class arranged so that everyone sits facing everyone else, as in life; allowing the discussion to take whatever shape it wants to on the assumption that what is meaningless for one person (perhaps the teacher) may be educative for another, that no one lecture or series of questions is likely to be as valuable for individual students as the questions and points they make in a natural, free-associational discussion about the play, poem, or issue at hand, if that sort of discussion can be generated.

Each class day—we often meet at my home or a student apartment or on the campus lawn—one student, each of whom volunteers for arbitrary dates on the first day of the term, acts as the discussion starter. This student does nothing more or less than that: he or she starts. It is not a report and it is not a project. The student gets no "credit" at all, beyond whatever pleasure there may be in triggering a lively discussion. He or she

may ask some questions, providing they are genuine questions, or may express an opinion as to the meaning or value of the work of literature at hand or may simply confess confusion about the literature. I have found that the "starter" nearly always takes this responsibility seriously. Never reminded after the first class day, the starter always shows up, always starts, and almost always learns from the experience. "Today I was the starter for *Stop-time*," writes one freshman woman in her journal. "Our class was very exciting. I learned the greatest amount from this class. . . ."

Often, especially at the very beginning of a term, if I find that the class is inhibited, I run some fast freeing-up exercises. There can be no open discussion, I find, when the potential participants are up-tight, full of self-doubt, suspicious, or bored. Often I do not need "freeing" exercises, but when I do, they always take the form of short answers (three or four sentences), written anonymously, to questions I pose concerning the students' inner reactions to what has been happening in the class. I might ask, "List one response—doubt, question, disagreement, confusion—you had to the starter's opinion." Or, "If *you* had started what what would you have said?" Or— simply: "What are you waiting *for*?" Naturally students who think that they are thinking "nothing," discover that they are "not thinking nothing," but that, as Duchess Alice says in Witkiewicz's *The Water Hen*, "Apparently you had to forget everything else." I collect the anonymous responses, shuffle them, and read them in a warm and supportive way. (I would only do such an exercise if I was *feeling* warm and supportive, aware of the students' fears and self-doubts. I pause after each one and ask for comments. Such an exercise seldom fails to trigger a lively discussion, and, more important, a pattern of lively discussion. The written statements are almost always psychologically validating for most of the students. Each one finds that her or his own confusion and self-doubt are reflected darkly behind the bland masks all around the room. This term I asked a freshman class the question, "What are you waiting *for*?" Twenty-one of twenty-two students wrote some variety of "I have no ideas of my own; I am waiting for somebody else to stimulate my ideas." Just hearing how insecure all of the others were freed many students immediately for their first genuine participation in an open discussion.

Whether or not written exercises are used, the class often stumbles along painfully at first, tentatively groping for a direction. What is the teacher's role during all of this apparent aimlessness? Again, I speak only about my own teaching which I offer as one way of defining one's responsibilities.

During this initial groping and seeming chaos, I do not under any circumstances take over the class and start "teaching." Having been greatly influenced by the writings of Carl Rogers, I basically run a student-centered class. This has been parodied as the "uh-hmm!" school of pedagogy, in which the student says (as one recently did), "What hit me the most about *The Quare Fellow* was the idea that everyone at the prison was equally responsible for the injustice and inhumanity which took place there," and the teacher says, "Uh-hmm!" That's a parody, but like all good parody it strikes close to the truth.

When a student makes a tentative comment during the early moments of a class, instead of my thought falling into the pattern which exclusively characterized my early teaching, that the remark was "good" or "bad" (that is, near to or far from my perception—or Robert Brustein's—of the truth), I now think something like the following: "From her point of view that's the way the things looks." Or: "For reasons of her own, she has chosen to present herself in that light." Now if no other student responds or there is reason to assume that I should respond myself, I can say, "Uh-hmm," or "Would you say, also, that there are no morally upright characters in the play?" or "I never thought of it from that point of view; can you think of some specific examples?" The particular palaver is not nearly so important as the teacher's frame of mind. The student is an adult with an opinion which he or she has a right to expect will be taken seriously. More often than not, the teacher does not have to say anything because some other student may catch fire from what has been said and add a new dimension or deepen the perception. As Rogers has discovered in clinical therapy, I have found in teaching that the more a student feels that the environment is safe for personal thinking and feeling, the less tentative become the contributions, the more accelerated the momentum, the profounder the insights and self-satisfaction. This uh-hmming approach is very hard on a teacher, molded, as I was, into an authoritarian. One must work hard against mind raping, against saying, however subtly, "You are wrong, my dear. Now listen to the truth." Teachers who have "tried this approach" and have found the students closing up like provincial post offices at lunchtime have, I fear, never fully convinced their students that *this* class is a really safe place. From my own experience I know that there is much a teacher can do to drain off the unproductive anxiety and occasional peer aggression.

I do this uh-hmming or whatever psychologically supportive activity I can (though I *never* start to "teach") until the natural rhythms of the session are established. In other words, when the majority of the students have begun to sound and look confident, I feel free to participate fully in three ways: 1) If I have an idea I have never had before and which occurs to me as a result of the class discussion, I tell it (if I can get a word in edgewise); 2) If I have a real question—one for which I do not have a secret answer tucked away—I ask it; 3) If a student asks for factual information about history, biography, bibliography, literary conventions, genres, and the like, I provide what I call a mini-lecture, which may take from twenty seconds to fifteen minutes, but which, hopefully, seldom goes beyond what the student apparently wishes to know. I try never to cut a student off, to take sides in an argument, or to dominate discussion. But most importantly, I try never to judge negatively and am even stingy with positive judgments. When I hear something I like, I occasionally say so, usually admitting only to the indisputable fact that I like it and less often to the more dubious assertion that it is "right" or "good." More often than not, I say something like, "If I understand you, you are saying that thus-and-such is the case." I always trust the class to make their own value judgments on ideas and interpretations.

As I understand the teacher's function, it is to listen until he hears. When students sense that they have not truly been heard (that is to say, understood), they —like their teachers or any other people —either harden into a strident dogmatism or shrink insecurely away from the fire: I mean they cease to learn. But when stu-dents feel that they have been under-stood, really heard, they intuit at once that there is litle reason to repeat or de-fend or flee in fear from what has now been heard and accepted. They para-doxically find themselves ready to form new thoughts because they are there and safe with the one they've got. They are in a mental posture of openness and willingness to move on to new ideas. The same holds true for all of us. If these words I am writing conform to your own thoughts, thereby helping to legiti-mize yours, you will feel relatively hap-py, open, and eager to share thoughts. If, though, from your point of view I am dishing out hogwash and am not thereby helping to legitimize your views, you will probably feel yourself hardening against me, tensing for a fight to defend your view.

If what I have been saying about hear-ing as a way of stimulating intellectual openness sounds like overly tender treat-ment of fragile student psyches, it may suggest how far we have allowed our-selves, in our roles as defenders of the Sacred Flame and molders of youth, to stray from reasonable human interaction with the men and women who are largely forced through sociological pressure to put up with us. I do not like to be molly-coddled, and I do not like to treat others patronizingly. Really what this descrip-tion of non-judgmental teaching calls for is nothing more or less than polite, re-spectful dealings with human beings who are made free by God or Nature to think what they want to think, even about literature. And though we may presently have the power to require certain obei-sances from them, I do not think we should honor the wielding of it by call-ing it education. None of what I have been saying is meant to suggest that I think any real learning can take place without discipline. But I favor self-discipline in myself and abhor its absence when I am lazy. I likewise favor allowing others their own discipline and their own guilt. As I see it, it is their business, not mine. Mine is to meet them where, when, and how they are ready to learn. I am, of course, speaking here of emotional time and space, "lived time" in Minkowski's useful phrase. I tolerate student laziness because I know too well my own; I "don't see" evasiveness and many forms of student dishonesty because I remember too vividly myself as a student. I know that behind the laziness is energy, behind the lassitude, interest, behind the evasion, commitment. A student of mine who sees herself as phoney, shallow, and lazy recently wrote, "I'm not doing what I deeply want to do! I'm not at all satisfied with my life because I am so fake! I'm unreal! I am a different character for each different group of people. I give most adults the answers they want to hear, not the answers I truly feel." Now, of course, she is fake and dishonest. Who doesn't accept her judgment as valid? What point would there be in calling this statement of hers a lie and self-deception, but to validate her own self-judgment? But, at the same time, who could fail to "hear" in this energetic self-depreciation a desire to build, grow, achieve, and learn? As a teacher, especially of literature, I feel that it is our business to tell students, through our support and emotional availability, that we "hear" them. It does not make me a psychoanalyst (that tired attack) or less of a professor of literature if I free a student to grapple with Donne by saying, in one way or another, "Sure you're lazy! Who isn't lazy? I'm lazy. Donne was lazy too! Now let's talk about what else we are—energetic, creative, and educable."

Much of what I have been saying applies to class discussion and conference interaction, but it applies just as well to the written work students may do for a course. I have found that since I have stopped grading the written work of my students, the papers I have received are more interesting to read than before, more personally worth my while, more informed with the kind of human presence I can respond to.

I am not going to argue here against the validity of grades as a psychologically valid pedagogical device. The mountain of psychological and sociological evidence on the subject and the various commission reports speak for themselves. The point of this essay is to share pedagogical experience of the kind that helps to make possible teaching without judging. Grades are fixed judgments. So naturally I do what I can, in an institution dreadfully out of date on this issue and repressive to teachers who monkey around with the grading system, to satisfy the Registrar's demand for grades without sacrificing what I hope are my sense of human decency and my knowledge of the ways in which people learn. My present grading compromise—I have hitherto tried and rejected blanket A's, student self-grading, various "in-put grading" procedures (a combined grade based on student self-evaluation, teacher evaluation, outside, objective judgment) —is to grade entirely, though flexibly, on a quantitative basis, rather than a qualitative one. Specifically, if students attend the class reasonably often and do one project, they get at least a "C"; if they do a "C"-level and a "B"-level project, they get a "B"; if they wish an "A" in the course, they hand in a "C", "B", and an "A" level project. The "C" level project often involves group participation: a prepared scene from a play, a presentation of seventeenth century music or art, or the like. Each person in the group receives a "C" for participating, no matter how little or much she or he does. The "B" and "A" level projects can each be selected from lists which I provide. Here are the options for a "B" in my present Modern Drama course; the student need only do one of these for a "B" in the course:

- —an intellectual journal covering the course readings and the class itself. Due twice: mid-term and end of the term.
- —"customized" exam (in-school? take-home? oral? on what? when?) Due any time after the second-third of the term.
- —paper on the influence of Artaud or Brecht on contemporary theatre. Due any time.
- —original play in the style of one modern playwright: Due any time.
- —close analysis of one play (if the analysis differs from that which evolves in class discussion). Due any time.
- —non-verbal project. Due by last *class* day of term.
- —one of your own, but must be cleared with the instructor.

The student who wishes to receive an "A" in the course would work on a "C"-level project, hand in one of the above "B"-level projects, and would add *one* of the following "A"-level contracts:

- —research paper on one of the authors discussed this term. Due any time.
- —take-home exam on the complete theatrical works of one of the authors discussed this term. Due any time.
- —objective exam on all introductory material in all the texts. Due any time.
- —detailed summary and review of two books on the background reading list. Due any time.
- —research paper on the existential background of modern drama. Due any time.
- —paper on the relationship of modern drama to the "modern" phase of the

subject of your own major studies. (In what way is the modernity of recent drama comparable to the modernity of recent sociology or home economics or chemistry or music?) Due any time.
- —one of your own, but must be cleared with the instructor.

An "A" student in my Modern Drama class may, then, have fulfilled the following, typical "contracts": reasonable attendance; participation in a presentation of a scene from *A Doll's House;* a paper on the influence of Artaud and Brecht on contemporary drama; a summary and review of Brustein's *The Theater of Revolt* and Blau's *The Impossible Theatre.*

The point is that the student gets the grade the moment he or she hands in the project, regardless of its quality.* Now, contract grading calls for an act—even a leap—of faith in students. For me this faith comes easy. For others, it may be difficult or impossible. I will, theoretically, *accept* trash submitted for an "A". But I *believe* that in a non-judgmental, unpunitive, encouraging context, students will want to work toward achieving self-styled and often very challenging goals. While nothing in the format of the course coerces a student to do anything which reason, energetic teaching, and the student's native curiosity do not inspire, I, needless to say, constantly encourage self-discipline and self-respecting work.

No human system is perfect. Of course I occasionally receive rushed or careless junk. But my approach to teaching is geared to those who can and want to learn, no to those who, for reasons they are entitled to, cannot avail themselves

---

*Hostile pressure from the Douglass Deanery has been so relentless that I have been forced to modify this grading approach. I do not have the guts to martyr myself for this cause.

of the opportunities to learn. I strongly feel that if my goal is to liberate minds through the liberal arts, I can only do it as a liberal role model and in a liberal environment. I remember too vividly the student journal published in the first issue of *Change* magazine in which the student, Kate, lambasted her left-wing professors for shooting off their mouths about liberal, human values, and teaching in an atmosphere of stuffy, conservative self-deception. Her stance was: put up, or shut up. Don't espouse one life style and live another. Don't speak of the liberation of the subjugated and then lower my grade because I hand in a paper late.

I believe that students want to learn and are willing to work *hard*. But they have a right to know what a teacher expects. Some teachers say that they expect a fifteen page research paper, with twenty footnotes. And they mean it. I say that I expect self-respecting, personally designed work. And I mean it. In both cases a teacher can *help* the student achieve the desired ends.

I may report that the work which I receive is enormously superior to the work I used to receive. It is better, really, by most criteria one could use: it is more imaginative, better written or organized, and often longer; it reflects a caring sensibility and is therefore interesting; it is more courageous in what it attempts. At the same time, without fear of a low grade, a student can learn from an unfinished project ("work in progress") or from one which fails to fulfill itself. Some of the most productive educational insights in my classes have been the result of a student's discovery of boundaries, limitations—the results of projects too heavy to float. I would want my students to learn as much from failure as from success. Naturally the grade is the same in either case.

In a non-judgmental context, a great many of our old pedagogical approaches find renewed vigor. For example, if a student knows that he will receive the grade he wants in a course and that no particular responses to exam questions or no failure of paragraph development in an essay will affect the grade he has contracted for, he begins to see that he may be able to take an exam or two, or write a paper, or give a report in a frame of mind conducive to intellectual growth. I give customized exams for those who want them. The students may choose the areas or material in which they wish to be examined. They may request in-school exams, oral or written, or take-home exams. They are free to ask to be examined even on bite-sized amounts of reading, but they almost always choose the whole term's reading or large swatches of it—this in the spirit of "I may as well see how I do with everything since I can't get shot' down if I bomb." Of course, having prepared for an exam they have designed so personally, very few students bomb at all. I don't know how many times I have heard students say after handing in an exam or paper, "Not having to worry about the grade really freed me to develop my thoughts during that exam. I really learned a lot."

As teachers we always say that an exam is or should be primarily a learning experience. In reality, though, how often does the exam experience teach the student anything beyond: I must have said the right things (or wrong) because I got a good grade (or bad)? Too many students learn from exam taking only how to take an exam. That was certainly true for me in college. What real learning I did occurred quite regularly out of the school or course context.

Since the grade I give to written work does not reflect the worth or value of the project in relation to peer group or professional or absolute "standards," it communicates nothing to me (beyond the fact that the student did a certain project) when I look up my records for letters of recommendation. What I do is very simple: I keep a folder with carbon copies of all my comments on student work. When I read the paper on Artaud that Charlene Brown has submitted, I slip a piece of legal-pad paper and carbon paper behind the last page, and as I record for her my responses to her work (about which responses I will have more to say), I make for my own records a copy of the response. On the top of the legal-pad sheet, I write:

Brown, Charlene
"Artaud's influence on Modern Drama"
7 pp.—original.

And then, after the carbon copy of my comment to Charlene, I may add certain observations for my own future reference about the growth and development of her literary sensibility, the difference between what I expected and what I received, some observations on her classroom performance, etc.—whatever striks me as likely to be valuable if I expect to have her in another class or if I think I will be called upon—*outside of the educational context* (i.e., after the term)— to *judge* the student in a letter of recommendation. If I cannot recommend a student, I tell him or her so.

Perhaps I should devote a few remarks to the way I approach the written work of my students. As with hearing in the classroom, I try to look at the written work until I see. I guess we all know how nearly pointless it is to tell a student, for example, that the sentence he or she has written is unclear. If it is clear to the writer, he will not be able to understand the teacher when the teacher writes "unclear" in the margin. From the student's point of view, it is the teacher who is unclear. But if the teacher struggles to see what the student means and then, say, comments on the passage by restating and perhaps agreeing with it, the student will be likely to become, in Cleaver's term, permeable to a new idea. If I write in the margin the judgment "weak" or "awkward" very little of educational value is communicated to the student. The student will have no way of knowing why the passage is weak or awkward and will either think I am arbitrary and mean or somehow privy to secret knowledge unattainable to the uninitiated.

In contrast, let's suppose the teacher writes in the margin, "If I understand you, you are implying that Josie's maternal love of Tyrone is productive and fulfilling. I had never thought that that was a possible reading, though now it leads me to suspect. . ." Such a comment begins by admitting that the student has befuddled you somewhat and that it may be partly your fault. It then restates the student's proposition in an alternate syntax which may strike the student as an improvement. The teacher goes on to take the idea seriously, thus signalling that it may be worth the writer's effort if it gains such warm support. The teacher concludes by adding to the proposition and further legitimizing the student's effort.

In the teaching of writing as in all other teaching, I feel we must play to the strengths of the students. The style is the man; to attack the writing is to attack the writer. To give a "C" to a paper is too often to say to the student, "You are a mediocre person." And that I believe is just about the cruellest judgment one can make. Few things inhibit affective and intellectual growth more. I certainly "correct" psychologically neutral mistakes in spelling, puncuation, and factual information. But I believe what we probably all believe—that syntax and metaphor reflect a writer's world view in powerful, however unconscious, ways. If we lay claim to such belief, we must be careful where we tread. To say that one's writing is bad is to say that one's world is wrong or false. Who wouldn't become resistant or defensive in such a painful plight?

I hope it is clear that I am not describing a phoney and empty power of positive thinking, but a genuine and always honest interaction with students in terms that will be of benefit to them without falsifying one's own sense of how open and decent human beings sharing an experience should relate to each other.

Some will say they have tried this way of teaching and found that it didn't work or that "students weren't motivated" or that "some force is necessary or 'they' won't learn." My suspicion is that many of these people never overcame some central obstacles. For example, I have heard this lament from teachers who spoke of trust but kept secret grades. Nothing violates the spirit of sharing and good faith faster than a teacher's reluctance to share the judgment he or she has made of the students. Other teachers have removed grades altogether, but have pressured the students into "covering," as we say, certain points, instead of trusting the students to discuss what is of interest to them. One approach is not "better" than another; different students will respond to different methods. But all students need psychological consistency and clarity. Some teachers who theoretically believe in the new, "open" discussion for the teaching of

literature still lack the faith that it requires and continue to manipulate in rather gross ways. If teachers remove the grade pressure, encourage interaction, try to deal humanly with students and, instead of learning, they go away in great numbers (and I don't know a teacher who hasn't had this awe-inspiring experience), it would seem to suggest not merely that the students are unmotivated—a classification too absolute in its implications to mean much, however often we use it—but also perhaps that the reading is meaningless to them or that the teacher is somehow inadequate for this group: listless, unprepared, dull, silly, defensive, ignorant, pompous, vague or any of the other blights that can afflict a teacher along with the rest of humanity, including the assumption that what is important to him or her is IMPORTANT.

This teaching approach is radically different from my earlier, graduate-school notion of the way teaching and learning take place. And some readers of *College English* would no doubt find it difficult. If it sounds like hard work— it is. I am forever conferring with students, making up customized exams, reading papers of different types which come in throughout the whole term, responding to journals which occasionally run to 140 pages. But on the other hand, I never make up a lecture or "prepare" teacher's "notes" for a Socratic discussion. I need seldom be bored by reading twenty or seventy exams on one subject at one time. Since I can send final grades to the Registrar *before* I read the papers carefully, I can take my time with the work, reading at leisure and in the right frame of mind; I can *take the time* to think of educative comments, and personalized comments, so that my energy and time will not be totally in vain. My colleagues rush in a frenzy to mark final exams, putting minimal and admittedly rather pointless comments on the bluebooks, in order to get grades in to the Registrar before the end of the term. I ask my students to hand in, with their final submissions, stamped, self-addressed envelopes. In my own good time—and it takes good time to read and respond to a 140-page journal! —I send the work back to the students, hopefully with the kind of feedback which they will really find useful.

Students and teachers must live together. If it is true that not every student is destined for great intellectual achievements, it is also true that not every teacher will be first-rate (though, of course, we can all do a better job than we have been). Perhaps the best idea would be to let students and teachers seek each other out as need dictates, so that only those who can work well together would agree to pursue a joint educational enterprise. But if such a Utopia is not to be expected soon, let us at least create an environment in which our students will be able to learn what they can without being the only ones penalized for what surely is as much our failures as theirs.